Brian Inglis was born in Dublin
served in World War II as a pil
with the rank of squadron leader.
writer and eventually parliament
He joined *The Spectator* in 1954 an
also worked in television as writer/presenter for *What the Papers Say*
and *All Our Yesterdays*.

Among his recent books are *The Diseases of Civilisation*, *The Paranormal:
An Encyclopedia of Psychic Phenomena*, *The Unknown Guest* and *The Power
of Dreams*.

He was elected a Fellow of the Royal Society of Literature in 1974.
He is a trustee of the Koestler Foundation and a member of the
Society for Psychical Research.

BRIAN INGLIS

Trance

A Natural History of Altered States of Mind

**PALADIN
GRAFTON BOOKS**
A Division of the Collins Publishing Group

LONDON GLASGOW
TORONTO SYDNEY AUCKLAND

Paladin
Grafton Books
A Division of the Collins Publishing Group
8 Grafton Street, London W1X 3LA

Published in Paladin Books 1990

First published in Great Britain by
Grafton Books 1989

ISBN 0-586-08933-0

Printed and bound in Great Britain by
Collins, Glasgow

Set in Baskerville

CONTENTS

Man cannot persist long in a conscious state;
he must throw himself back into the unconscious,
for his root lives there.

GOETHE

1
SETTING THE SCENE

What is trance?

When Charles Tart was doing the research for his *States of Consciousness* in the 1960s, he hunted for a definition of trance; but 'for every definite characteristic mentioned by one authority,' he found, 'another would be the opposite.' As a Professor of Psychology at the University of California, Tart was exploring the academic literature; I assumed that works aimed at the general public might be of more help. Not so; as if frightened off by the divisions in psychology, many of them have simply avoided the subject. Trance does not have an entry either in *Chambers's Encyclopaedia* (1971) or in the 1974 edition of the *Encyclopaedia Britannica*. The aim of the formidable-looking *Oxford Companion to the Mind* (1987), according to its Introduction, is to deal with as many aspects of mind as possible in ways which are 'interesting, useful and understandable not only to experts but to anybody interested in normal or abnormal behaviour'. Anybody interested in trance who turns to the *Oxford Companion* will be in for a disappointment; it does not qualify for an entry, and the occasional references to trance conditions are sparse and superficial.

The contrast with attitudes at the beginning of the century is striking, as that fine old standby, the 1911 edition of the *Encyclopaedia Britannica*, reveals. The entry was written by William McDougall, philosopher, anthropologist and psychologist, whose influential *Body and Mind* was published that year, and who throughout his life maintained an interest in trance conditions. He was far from sure exactly what conditions should qualify for inclusion; but among those he referred to as possibles were catalepsy, comas, sleep, somnambulism, mystical ecstasies, hallucinations, hypnosis, mediumship and dual personality. To judge from his other writings he would have added hysteria, closely linked historically to trance states; but it was dealt with separately by Sir John Tuke, President of the Neurological Society of the United Kingdom, who described it as 'a secondary subconscious mental state' in which appeared 'the dual personality which is typically exemplified in somnambulism and the hypnotic state'.

McDougall was uncertain whether sleep ought to be included; the common impression today is that it should not. I discovered this because in the absence of academic guidance I have fallen back on button-holing people at parties and other gatherings to ask them what 'trance' brings into their minds. The common reaction might almost *be* a trance; few people have an immediate and clear mind's-eye picture. The one which emerges most often is of somebody out of this world, rapt, with unseeing or staring eyes. But soon, other forms begin to come to mind, particularly when there is a group to throw ideas around. They tend to be much the same as McDougall's, and they will be mine – though with a few additions. I must, for example, put in a word for sleep.

Sleep should be included not merely because dreams, apart from providing the most familiar of hallucinatory experiences, can often be tapped for useful information. Sleep is a state of *mind*; it can work for us – clearing up problems for us overnight, as that redoubtable Irish bluestocking Frances Power Cobbe pointed out in an essay in 1872; 'setting to rights' for sleepers in much the same way as a parlour maid in those days was setting to rights, while they slept, their dining-rooms and drawing-rooms. There was also, she noted, 'the ordinary but most mysterious faculty possessed by most persons, of setting overnight a mental alarm-clock, and awaking at will at any unaccustomed hour out of dreamless sleep'.

Another familiar form of trance today, though McDougall would have been unlikely to encounter it in 1911, is an everyday experience for some drivers. Deep in conversation, absorbed in a radio programme, or racked by some worry, they reach their destination – or sometimes pass it – with no recollection of their journey. What has amounted almost to a conspiracy of silence about the subject has been broken only recently, when in the summer of 1988 a managing director, Harold Miller, pleaded not guilty in a Bristol court to a charge of reckless driving. Miller had 'dropped into a trancelike state,' a research scientist, Dr Ivan Brown – an adviser to the Department of Transport, and assistant director of the Medical Research Council's applied psychology unit – explained to the court, in which 'steering the vehicle becomes subconscious', a condition which he described as 'highway hypnosis', analogous to sleepwalking. The judge appeared sufficiently impressed to accept the plea; Miller was fined and banned from driving for three years, but escaped the prison sentence which he might have been given, as he had two previous convictions for speeding, and his recklessness on this occasion had led to an accident in which two young women had been killed.

Is highway hypnosis of this kind really a trance condition? Many people, I have found, regard trance as a form of abstraction so complete that driving a car would be an impossibility. There are such trances, but scores of experiments with hypnosis have shown that they can occur side-by-side with ordinary consciousness. In a light trance, a hypnotized subject may be fully aware of his surroundings and only realize he has been hypnotized when he finds he cannot move his hands until instructed by the hypnotist to move them.

Colloquially, trance has a range of meanings, particularly in connection with sport. It is commonly used about somebody who is in full possession of his faculties, but in a frame of mind which makes him oblivious to his surroundings – P. G. Wodehouse's Bingo Little, for example, was 'one of those fellows who once their fingers close over the handle of a tennis racket, fall into a sort of trance in which nothing outside the radius of the lawn exists for him'. But it has also often been employed to describe a condition in which the player feels taken over, almost possessed, by a force which seems to play through him, and for him, better than he could hope to play himself.

Accounts of such experiences were collected by Michael Murphy, founder and guiding hand of the Esalen Institute, and Rhea White, a librarian, and published in *The Psychic Side of Sports* (1978). Recalling his inspired form for Brazil in the final of the World Cup in 1955, Pele believed that 'he played that whole game in a kind of trance'. When Roger Bannister broke four minutes for the mile, he recalled that from the half-way stage he had a feeling of 'complete *detachment*'. Groping for an explanation of his world record in the 400 metres hurdles, which he won by the widest margin in Olympic Games' history, David Hemery said that he had no need to force his legs to work; it was as if his mind was in control of them. There was 'something spiritual, almost spectral', about certain rounds of golf, Arnold Palmer claimed. 'I'd liken it to a sense of reverie – not a dreamlike state, but the somehow insulated state of a great musician in a great performance'; the musician is aware of what he is doing, on such occasions, but his playing is dictated 'with an internal sense of *rightness* – it is not merely mechanical, it is not only spiritual; it is something of both, on a different plane and a more remote one.'

Yet another type of trance can be observed any day, in any supermarket. At the Market Research Society's annual conference in Brighton in 1988, two investigators described how they had investigated 'shopper's trance' using hypnosis; when hypnotized, the shoppers had a much better recall of the supermarket's brand information than they had when they were questioned in the standard clipboard interview – which goes some way to explain why people's expressed preferences, captured on clipboards, have so often been found to be misleading.

Anyway, I propose at the start not to be too selective about what trance is, and to concentrate upon what it has done, and can do, for us; and this means that one common misconception needs correction. Trances, particularly when they come unexpectedly, out of the blue, are widely feared. Hallucinations – 'seeing things', 'hearing voices' – are thought to be pathological symptoms, as indeed they often are; they can be an indication of schizophrenia, or of epilepsy, or of poisoning by a variety of drugs. Yet even in this capacity they should be regarded as useful warning signals, which need to be listened to and, wherever possible, interpreted. Unluckily 'dissociation', the clinical term, is all too often regarded as something that needs to be cured. Psychiatrists tend not to realize its extraordinary range. Professor Liam Hudson has noted in his *Night Life* (1986), and its influence on our memory and our personalities; they do not appreciate its relationship with our dreams, waking fantasies and 'imaginatively conceived actions'.

And with much else, besides! Hallucinations have been the inspiration for some of the most revered figures in history: the Buddha, Saint Paul, Muhammad, Joan of Arc. The voice of Socrates' 'daemon' had guided him wisely, he claimed at his trial, all his life; and he would enter trance to listen to it. Engrossed with a weighty subject, according to Alcibiades, he once became entranced for a whole day and night, as he was apt to do when his mind was preoccupied with problems; 'he then never interrupts his meditation, and forgets to eat and drink and sleep – everything, in short, until his inquiry has reached its termination or, at least, until he has seen some light in it.'

Hypnosis, too, tends to be feared; but this is mainly because it is so callously exploited commercially by professional entertainers, who use it to make fools of volunteer subjects. It has nevertheless provided us with a remarkable range of benefits, from pain-free dentistry and childbirth to improved performances on the track or the golf course. For all the suspect image that spiritualist mediums tend to have in the public mind, they too, from time to time, have demonstrated powers which cannot lightly be rationalized away. As for those fortunates who have enjoyed mystical ecstasy, they usually regard it as the crowning experience of their lives.

The search for the unconscious

Why, then, has trance fallen so far from serious consideration by psychologists that the editors of encyclopaedias feel they can safely leave it out?

To understand what has happened it is necessary to look back to the period, a century ago, when research into trance was psychologists' primary concern. They were trying to establish psychology as a new academic discipline, liberated from the dead hand of philosophy, to find a new home in science. But this was difficult. Descartes' model – 'I think, therefore I am' – was proving unsatisfactory. Thought, it was coming to be realized, is only one aspect of existence, and critics were pointing out that there are forces at work which appear to be doing the thinking for us, as it were: prompting, guiding, interrupting. And in his *Philosophy of the Unconscious* (1869), Eduard von Hartmann put forward the case for accepting that the other 'thinker' resides in our unconscious minds.

We may delude ourselves, Hartmann argued, when we are in conversation, that we are consciously choosing our words. But a moment's reflection shows that 'only what is *already* selected emerges from the night of the unconscious.' The necessary information is ready for us even though, a moment before, we had been unaware we would need it. And if it is *not* ready for us, we cannot always summon it. If we forget a name, we know that it is wise not to try to remember it but to take the conscious mind off the subject and wait until 'the unknown one', as Hartmann called it, is ready to deliver it.

The impact of *The Philosophy of the Unconscious* was all the more remarkable in that Hartmann was only 26 when it was published, and until four years before he had been serving as an artillery officer in the Prussian army. It was savagely critical, too, of the prevailing materialist dogmas. But as Lancelot Law Whyte pointed out in *The Unconscious Before Freud*, 'Hartmann had struck at a favourable moment; the unconscious was in the air.' The book went through numerous editions, expanding in the process, so that by the time it was translated and published in English in 1882 it was in three volumes, totalling over 1000 pages. By this time it had dated, and was far from easy reading; it is not surprising, Whyte observed, that its influence has been underrated. Nevertheless it opened the door for research into mind of a type which had been done before, by the mesmerists, but discounted because orthodox science had no place for trance, except as a form of insanity.

As soon as the existence of the unconscious was conceded, it became possible to investigate it through the medium of hypnosis – the modified version of the induced mesmeric trance which achieved a measure of scientific acceptance in the early 1880s. From then until the turn of the century the leading psychologists concentrated mainly on research into the unconscious, through the medium of trance – spontaneous, as in hysteria, or induced, as in hypnosis. I will be dealing in detail with this research later; for the present, it will be sufficient to single out the work of the two men, William James and Frederic Myers, who did most to build on Hartmann's foundations – though, ironically, neither of them was disposed to give him the credit he deserved.

The subliminal self

William James's initial reaction was contemptuous, because Hartmann had avowed himself a disciple of Schopenhauer. Hartmann was an evangelist of despair, James complained; one of those 'aristocratic misanthropes, dyspeptic pleasure-seekers and unappreciated geniuses who exist in every country but are not taken seriously' – except in Germany, where *The Philosophy of the Unconscious* had proved to be 'one of the greatest literary successes of the time'. But this was written in 1875 when James, still in his early thirties, was lecturing on physiology at Harvard. As it happened, it was the year in which he made the transition to philosophy and psychology – possible in those days, before the academic demarcation lines had been drawn; and this was eventually to take his own views closer than he realized to Hartmann's.

They appeared to be more apart than they actually were because

James was wary of 'the unconscious'; it was an excuse, he feared, for 'believing what one likes in psychology'. Psychology, he insisted, must work from what is *known*. 'The first and foremost concrete fact, which everyone will affirm belongs to his inner experience,' he pointed out in his *Principles of Psychology* in 1890, 'is the fact that *consciousness of some kind goes on*. "States of mind" succeed each other.' Only what reaches consciousness and becomes a state of mind, could profitably be studied.

Nevertheless, James had to admit that some states of mind point to the existence of a peculiar gap in consciousness, 'and no mere gap. It is a gap that is intensely active.' Like Hartmann, James cited what happens when we try to recall a forgotten name. 'A sort of wraith of the name', he observed, appeared in the gap, 'beckoning us in a given direction, making us at moments tingle with the sense of our closeness, and then letting us sink back without the longed-for term.' *Wanting* the name does not help. Consciousness, wanting the name, can reject a wrong one; it cannot, unassisted, summon the right one. 'If we could say in English "it thinks", in the same way as we say "it rains",' he suggested, 'we should be stating the fact most simply.'

James declined to speculate further about what might be happening in 'the gap'; but he was so fascinated by the ways in which the material arising from it reached the 'stream of consciousness' that most of his research was devoted to trance conditions, through investigations of hallucination, hypnosis and mediumship. He realized, though, that these were still exploratory, and consequently dealt only briefly with them in his *Principles*, designed as it was to cover the whole widening field of psychology.

For Myers, trance conditions were important precisely because they provided clues to what was happening in 'the gap'; clues, he decided, which revealed a reasonably clear picture of the workings of the subliminal mind – the mind that lies below consciousness's threshold.

'Subliminal' is a useful term, because the alternatives have been a source of endless confusion. In colloquial English, for a start, 'unconscious' is ordinarily used to convey the condition of somebody who has been knocked out in a road accident or the boxing ring. 'Conscious', too, is rarely used in quite the sense James used 'stream of consciousness'; the tendency is to think of the stream as welling up unbidden from the *sub*conscious mind. 'Subconscious' has been a useful enough standby, but is disliked by psychologists as vague; and 'unconscious', which many of them prefer, is used in some different and even contradictory senses.

Freud, for example, though he picked up the term from Hartmann, used it in another sense. He thought of it, according to his biographer Ernest Jones, as 'a chaos, a cauldron of seething excitement', with abundant energy but 'no organization and no unified will, only an impulsion to obtain satisfaction of the instinctual needs'. This was also far removed from Myers's theory. Although Myers was one of the earliest to recognize the importance of Freud's contribution, the subliminal for him was a goldmine as well as a rubbish tip; and although he shared James's dislike of Hartmann's book, which he dismissed as 'a loose and extravagant parody of important truth', his conception of the subliminal was close to Hartmann's unconscious.

So, too, was Myers's most important contribution. His theory of the existence of a subliminal *self* was a logical development from Hartmann's 'unknown one', who produces spontaneous witticisms from us which we have not prepared; and it was close to James's 'it thinks'. But whereas James left it at that, Myers was chiefly concerned to track down the 'it' who thinks for us, providing the forgotten name we are groping for, or, if we are lucky, the appropriate witticism. The subliminal self, in his view, is endlessly seeking to put across information to us, but keeps finding itself blocked by consciousness. Trance is one of the devices by which it forces its way through: in dreams and daydreams, under hypnosis, and in hallucinatory or hysterical states, such as possession. The material which actually reaches our stream of consciousness may be confused, as it is in dreams; but for Myers it was always meaningful, if it could only be interpreted – often as a warning, in the sense Freud was to use it, of disturbances in the subliminal mind; but occasionally as a flash of intuition, or inspiration, of the kind that led Archimedes to shout 'Eureka!' and has given us some of the most treasured of works of literature and art.

In the period Myers was working on his theory of the subliminal self, and surveying the trance conditions through which it can manifest itself – the last quarter of the nineteenth century – he was only one of many leading psychologists and neurologists in Europe and the United States who were fascinated by the discoveries which were being made in connection with hysteria and hypnosis. As the records of international conferences reveal, trance states were psychology's most debated issue; and as Freud's version of the unconscious did not take its shape until later, Myers's theory of the subliminal mind appeared to have a chance of acceptance. But by the time he died, in 1901, the materialist tide was so strong that it was sweeping psychologists along with it, compelling them to concentrate on research which could be claimed to be scientific, such as laboratory experiments with dogs. Animal behaviour, the theory was, could be objectively watched, reported on, quantified. And out of these trials developed behaviourism, which explained the behaviour of man, too, as a succession of conditioned reflexes. Such terms as 'mind' and 'consciousness', its protagonist John Broadus Watson claimed, were simply either fallacious interpretations of the observed facts, or 'metaphysical irrelevancies'.

The behaviourist case was to be put even more effectively by B. F. Skinner during and after the Second World War. For a while behaviourism became the dominant faith in university psychology departments in the United States; and although it failed to gain so firm a hold in Britain, its influence permeated even to those departments which would have rebutted the charge that they were preaching Skinnerism. 'Among present-day psychologists words like "consciousness", "mind" and so forth have become not merely unfashionable but even faintly heterodox,' Alan Gauld of Nottingham University noted in 1968. 'Many psychologists have not wittingly used them in their professional moments these twenty years.'

Inevitably, trance ceased to be an attractive proposition for academic researchers. A few continued to investigate hypnosis, but chiefly with the aim of removing it from the trance category, making it amenable to behaviourist preconceptions, so as to fit it for absorption into conventional psychology. Recently, however, the term 'subliminal' has sidled back into contention; conveniently, for my purpose, as the implications tend to confirm Myers's theory, though his name has rarely featured in the controversy that has surrounded its re-entry.

In the 1940s neurophysiologists needed a term to describe a phenomenon they had discovered in the course of their research: subjects were reacting to information when they were not aware that they were receiving it. If a word was flashed on a screen for too short a time for them consciously to register it, they might none-the-less show by changes of skin resistance, monitored on the lie-detector principle, that they must somehow have perceived it. They would react differently, for example, to 'love' and 'death'. This, the investigators argued, must indicate the existence of 'subliminal perception'.

'Hardly less interesting than the phenomenon of subliminal perception has been the resistance to accepting its validity,' Norman Dixon,

Professor of Psychology at London University and a leading researcher in this field, has recalled. It met with intense hostility, 'presumably because it seems to threaten notions of free will and autonomy.'

From my experience of psychologists, this is unlikely to have been their chief worry. Behaviourists, conditioned by Watson to reject 'mind' as a fallacious misinterpretation or a metaphysical abstraction, naturally did not care to admit its existence, let alone on a subliminal level. And even those psychologists who were waking up to the absurdities of behaviourism on the Skinner model must have been uneasily aware that the existence of subliminal perception threatened them with yet another 'hidden variable' to add to their growing problems in trying to keep their laboratory experiments scientific. The opposition became progressively more desperate as further tests overrode their objections, notably when researchers at Johns Hopkins University showed that if subjects were given a string of meaningless words and conditioned, like laboratory rats, to expect electric shocks whenever certain of them appeared, the subjects sometimes believed they had actually glimpsed one of the 'safe' words, but their skin resistance would react if it was in fact a 'shock' word. Evidently their subliminal perception had got it right.

Whatever psychologists might feel, the term itself caught the public's fancy after it was disclosed that *Playboy* magazine had been experimenting with subliminal representations of the word 'sex', printed in letters just too small to be seen, and that a commercial enterprise was claiming that subliminal 'Eat pop-corn' and 'Drink Coca-cola' advertisements had led to a fantastic increase in demand for them. So I propose to adopt 'subliminal mind' and 'subliminal self' in this search for a better understanding of trance.

Where, then, should the search begin? One of the rare occasions on which trance has actually featured as the title of an academic paper was in 1969, when Arnold M. Ludwig, then Director of Education at the Mendoba State Hospital in Madison, Wisconsin, asked the audience at the annual conference of the American Psychiatric Association to consider a question which, he thought, had not attracted sufficient attention. Psychiatrists might think of trance as a symptom of incipient or actual mental disorder; but surely, Ludwig argued, it must originally have had some evolutionary function, perhaps connected with survival in life-threatening situations? And was it not possible that it might still have its uses? On the evidence, he felt emboldened to speculate 'that many of man's higher mental functions, such as empathy, rapport, group identification, imagination, creativity, are either derived from or are intimately related to his capacity for trance'.

Although this Myers-based proposition failed to rouse psychiatrists, it is worth recalling for Ludwig's suggestion that trance and its relationship to the higher (as well as the lower) mental functions need to be examined from the evolutionary standpoint. How did trance arrive in the first place?

INSTINCT, HABIT AND IMPROVISATION

Two components are easy to trace through evolution: instinct and habit. James defined instinct as 'the faculty of acting in such a way as to produce certain ends without foresight of the ends, and without previous education in the performance'. A spider does not have to be taught how to weave a web; the ability is inherited. Habit 'simplifies our movements, makes them accurate, and diminishes fatigue'. In the process, too, 'it diminishes the conscious attention with which our acts are performed.' It takes over in much of our waking lives, getting dressed, eating breakfast, walking to the station, and so on, throughout the day, while we consciously concern ourselves with other matters. We are in this form of trance all the time, thanks to instinct and habit collaborating to provide us with automatism.

This robot element in us is also capable of remarkable feats, as the psychologist W. B. Carpenter emphasized in his description of 'unconscious cerebration', a term he had introduced in the 1840s to try to account for some of the phenomena which were later to be absorbed into the concept of the unconscious. The first of the great stage magicians, Robert Houdin, told Carpenter he had trained himself as a performer by practising as a juggler until he could keep up four balls in the air while reading a book.

Frances Power Cobbe, who was trying to persuade the scientific establishment (for which she had little respect) to take Carpenter's ideas seriously, provided an even more striking example. A pianist, she pointed out, seems to have 'not one slave but a dozen. Two different lines of hieroglyphics have to be read at once, and the right hand has to be guided to one of them, the left to another.' The individual fingers, too, have to perform their duties on the keys; and the two feet on the pedals. 'And all this time the performer, the *conscious* performer, is in a seventh heaven of artistic rapture at the results'; or perhaps, Cobbe mischievously added, she is 'lost in a flirtation with the individual who turns the leaves of the music-book, and is justly persuaded she is giving him the whole of her soul'.

Clearly the automatism provided by instinct and learned habit alone can provide remarkable trance skills. But at some stage they are reinforced by another component. A pianist may dispense with the music-book while she is playing. She does not even have to have practised what she plays. She may improvise, stringing together new combinations of notes, even inventing new melodies.

For Hartmann, improvisation was one of the key features of evolution. He could not accept natural selection in the blind step-by-step form Darwin had presented it. An experimental element is at work, he insisted, which can even be detected in plants; and he cited the results of some experiments which were being conducted at the time.

One of these entailed turning a vine leaf upside down so that the underside was exposed to the light. The vine promptly did its best to turn the leaf the right way up again; and thus far, the process could readily enough be accounted for in simple Darwinian terms. But when the initial effort failed, the vine actually shifted the leaf away from the window of the glass-house 'in order to approach the light in the opposite direction'. Other naturalists had subsequently repeated this experiment with similar results. One of them had observed that the movement 'is always executed *by the shortest course*, the leaf turning now up, now down, now right, now left'; leading the experimenter to say he was almost tempted to believe 'there dwells here a secret intelligence which chooses the most appropriate means for the attainment of the end.'

Heretical though Hartmann's theory was, and still is, there is a great deal of evidence for improvisation through the prompting of a 'secret intelligence'. Perhaps the most significant are the skills displayed by termites, as described by the South African naturalist Eugene Marais in *The Soul of the White Ant* (1937). The members of a termitary, although they are blind, collaborate to produce remarkably sophisticated structures, such as arches of a kind which man was not to learn how to build until quite late in civilization. It was difficult enough, Marais realized, to account for the actual building process, with its surprisingly sophisticated level of collaboration; but how to account for the architecture? As a Darwinian, he was uncomfortable with the term 'soul'; but 'group soul', he felt, came closest to conveying his impression that the ants must be under some form of remote control by a planner.

Although the discovery of pheromones helps to show how communication works between the members of species in communal tasks, nothing has transpired since Marais' time to account for the impression that an architect or designer, in some form, appears to be involved. An ant, as Lewis Thomas has pointed out in his essay 'On Societies and Organisms', consists of 'only a few neurons strung together by fibers'. It 'cannot be imagined to have a mind at all, much less a thought'. Yet ant colonies behave as if regulated *by* thought of some kind. This problem, Thomas notes, biologists have tended to evade, realizing that 'instinct' will not do. (They might just as well explain wind, Marais had complained, 'by saying it is *wind*'.)

The existence of a group mind has obvious, though as yet hardly recognized, implications for all of us. At the simplest level it can help to account for mass hysteria, in which people appear to be taken over by an emotional contagion which can largely submerge their individual identities. More than that, it offers a possible explanation for the astonishing evolutionary development of the human mind – far too rapid a process to be accounted for on conventional biological theories. How, for example, did the 'glory that was Greece', Athens in the classical era, emerge? For cultural evolution there is no precedent, as Niko Tinbergen, one of the founders – or revivers – of ethology, admitted: 'It is a totally new experiment of nature, and we are the guinea-pigs.'

As a group mind, in some form, must have been operating in termitaries, there is no reason to doubt that it is still influencing all living creatures, including ourselves. I propose to examine trance in its role as go-between, delivering to the stream of consciousness (whenever it can get through) messages, warnings, tips and a variety of information which the subliminal self has ready for us, taken not only from memory, but also from the vast resources of what, for the present, is best loosely described by Jung's 'collective unconscious'; beginning with the historical evidence, from earliest times until our own (when I shall revert to the first person singular, as I shall be in the role of participant and observer, rather than chronicler). I have pulled out two aspects of trance to treat separately: mystical experience, or 'ecstasies', hard to deal with as they are essentially ineffable; and certain phenomena long associated with trance which are embarrassingly mind-boggling.

Not that these are entirely missing from the historical section; I fear that some of the evidence will come up against many a 'boggle-threshold', to use Renée Haynes's engaging concept. But in all ages, in all communities, trance has been associated with mysterious happenings which conflict with commonsense notions of what *can* happen in everyday life; to ignore them would be like staging *Hamlet* without the ghost. The credibility of the accounts can only be gauged by assessments of the credibility of the people who have witnessed them – coupled, naturally, to the frequency with which they have been reported. Paradoxically, some of the hardest to accept – as no less a sceptic than David Hume realized – are among the best attested. I have thought it best to consider them separately before my summing-up.

2

DIVINE – OR DIABOLIC?

SHAMANISM

The function of trance in man

Granted that there is satisfactory evidence to account for the early evolution of trance, how did it eventually come into being in man? There is a gap in the evidence which paleontology can do little to fill; but it is reasonable to speculate on the basis of the anthropological evidence, particularly the accounts given in the reports of Portuguese and Spanish explorers, missionaries and traders who came upon tribes living a way of life which in all probability had remained little changed for millennia. Almost all of them, wherever they were encountered throughout the world, had a feature in common: a shaman, witch-doctor or medicine man – part seer, part magician. And the shaman was chosen, or in effect selected himself (it was not an exclusively male profession, but men predominated), because when his services were required he could enter into a trance condition in which he could communicate with the tribal spirits, to obtain their advice or warnings on behalf of the tribe.

The term 'shamanism' was originally applied to the quasi-religious practices of certain Siberian tribes. They relied on a 'technique of ecstasy', as Mircea Eliade, the world's leading authority on the subject until his death in 1987, described it, involving so close a relationship with the spirits that shamans in their trances were believed to have left their bodies and ascended to the spirit world. In this they differed from those medicine men or witch-doctors who might be described as consulting with the spirits on a rather more business-like basis, perhaps using aids to divination. Yet it was hard to maintain a clear-cut distinction. 'Shaman' and 'shamanism' have come to be loosely used (and loosely pronounced: 'sham-', 'sharm-' and 'shame-' still compete for supremacy) to describe any and all the techniques which involve the exploitation of trance for spirit communication on behalf of the tribe. Eliade vehemently opposed this dilution but, as Saki had observed, it 'is not in mortals to countermand success'; the impression made by Eliade's *Shamanism* (1951) only served further to establish the term in its more relaxed sense.

Accounts by witnesses of shaman trances showed some variations, but the basic assumption was consistent: that the shaman was taken over by a spirit. After a brief period of abstraction, he would go into convulsions in which he would be 'tossed and shaken in fever, pained and wrenched as though some living creature were tearing or twisting him within', as Edward Tylor put it in *Primitive Culture* (1971), the first attempt to survey the chaotic mass of anthropological and ethnological evidence, and try to give it some coherence. Sometimes the mysterious unseen power 'makes him leap upon the bystanders with a giant's strength', and impels him 'with distorted face and frantic gesture, and voice not his own nor seemingly even human, to pour forth with incoherent raving, or with thought and eloquence beyond his sober faculties to command, to counsel, to foretell'. Then, 'quitting the medium's spent and jaded body, the intruding spirit departs as it came.'

For missionaries, who were among the earliest investigators, the explanation was only too obvious. Convulsions, notoriously, were indications of diabolic possession. The devil must have seized the opportunity to gain control of the heathen, through shamanism. Nor were they surprised to find that the shaman often appeared to enjoy second sight, and other magical abilities. The devil would, of course, have provided them, to strengthen his hold on the tribe by instilling awe at the shaman's powers.

In the eighteenth century, when belief in the devil waned, observers were inclined to attribute the trances to epilepsy or mania. Shamans were clearly out of their wits – or, in so far as they seemed able to work magic, they must be clever tricksters. During the nineteenth century the term 'magic', originally applied to what were taken to be genuine feats, became equated with sleight of hand – as did 'conjuring', which originally meant the calling-up of spirits for consultation. 'Ventriloquism', too, formerly used about the spirit voices which emerged through the shaman – often, to the onlookers, apparently from a point a little distant from him – came to be interpreted as the shaman's way of 'throwing' his voice to delude the tribe into believing it really was spirit communication.

Tylor realized this explanation would not do. He was impressed by the fact that shamanism (though that term had not yet come into use) bore a striking resemblance to spiritualism, then very much in vogue; and, little liking though he had for spiritualism, he knew enough about mediums to realize that they could not all be dismissed simply as cheats. He was sufficiently impressed by some of the reports of the powers of shamans to admit that if research into mediums, which some well-known scientists were undertaking at the time, produced results, 'the savages on whom some ethnographers look as degenerate' would be able 'to turn on their accusers, and charge them with having fallen from their high level of savage knowledge'.

This, however, Tylor was reluctant to believe. Shamanism, he decided, was probably 'a sincere but fallacious system'. And in *The Golden Bough* (1890), James Frazer brushed all doubts aside. Shamanism, he asserted, was 'a spurious system of natural law as well as a fallacious guide of conduct; it is a false science as well as an abortive art.' Although much of Frazer's work was demolished by Andrew Lang at the time, and has since been more comprehensively discredited, it was Frazer's, rather than Tylor's, view which anthropologists in general adopted.

Instinct revived

This left unsolved the problem which worried Tylor. If, as he assumed, shamanism was an evolutionary development, it presumably must have offered tribes something which they needed. The faking might come later, if shamans lost their powers; but the weird phenomena could not have been introduced fraudulently all over the world. Surely there must have been some advantage from shamanism, even if beliefs which had attached themselves to it, such as in spirits, were fallacious?

This was a question which interested Henry Sigerist, when he gave up his chair at Johns Hopkins University to prepare his *History of Medicine*: a monumental undertaking which, had his death not interrupted it when he was still at work on the second volume, would have superseded all previous histories. In the first volume – published by coincidence in the same year, 1951, as Eliade's *Shamanism* – Sigerist speculated on how tribal medicine could have reached the remarkable level of effectiveness, even extending to a knowledge of drugs and their uses, which explorers had reported and anthropologists had since confirmed. The explanation, Sigerist decided, must lie in the exploitation of instinct.

It could safely be assumed, Sigerist argued, that man's instincts were 'the purer, the less developed his civilization was'. Anthropologists had in fact confirmed that under very different geographic conditions, it was the most primitive tribes which had 'invariably found a balanced diet, one best adapted to the environment'. In the less primitive tribes – primitive, that was, by civilization's standards – instinct about what to eat and what to avoid had been largely replaced by learned habits passed down from parents to children. When confronted by new problems, such as those which arise out of enforced or misguided changes of diet, or outbreaks of unusual disorders, instinct's loss could be worrying, and even dangerous.

How serious a problem loss of instinct could be was to be demonstrated by Eugene Marais in one of his experiments with animals. He hand-reared an otter and a baboon for three years before restoring them to their natural surroundings. The otter had never seen a river, but it plunged in and soon caught a fish. The baboon proved helpless either to feed itself or protect itself. Nature, Marais surmised, had settled for the loss of inherited race memory as the price to be paid for the emergence of greater individuality, in which learning would begin to play the decisive part.

There is little need to look further for an explanation of the development of shamanism. Any individual who could go into trances involuntarily might, with training, be able to enter them at will, and in them allow instinct to take over. It might not be a reliable source of information, but that would be up to the tribe to assess. He might also be able to advise on other matters of a kind which animal instinct had provided, such as where to find water in a drought, or when to prepare for an impending storm.

Gods and spirits

Sigerist's theory accounts well enough for the development of the trance component of shamanism, but not for the other feature which was everywhere found: the assumption that the shaman owed his powers to his ability to communicate with – and in cases of 'pure' shamanism, Eliade claimed, to control – the tribal spirits, for the tribe's benefit. Was spiritism a necessary component of shamanism, or simply a belief which happened to attach itself?

In *The Origin of Consciousness* (1977), Julian Jaynes of Princeton University presented an intriguing hypothesis to account for the belief in spirits. At a time when man was still an automaton – his life dictated by instincts and learned habit, but awaiting conscious reasoning power – evolutionary improvisation would be aiding and abetting the process as best it could. Although in the period immediately before consciousness developed, man must have been guided by instinct and learned habits, improvisation would also have been at work, feeding him with the information which consciousness would soon enable him to provide for himself. The closest parallel (though Jaynes did not use it) is with Marais' termites, collaborating as if obeying instructions of a more sophisticated kind than simple instinct and learned habit could account for. Evolution could surely have found a way to provide a still better service for mankind.

An obvious expedient would have been hallucination. Clearly an alarm signal of the kind which consciousness had tended to shut out could be effective if the information was passed to him in the form of, say, a voice calling 'look out!' Hallucinations of this type, though, coming from some apparently external but invisible source, would have given the impression that discarnate beings must be responsible, providing 'the most plausible hypothesis', Jaynes contended, 'for the origin of belief in gods'.

Jaynes cited Homer in support of his thesis. The characters in the *Iliad* do not think out what they should do; they act as if they were in a trance, leaving them open to dictation from the gods. Clearly they have 'no conscious minds such as we have, and certainly no introspections'; the gods provide their consciousness.

To lean too heavily on Homer would have left Jaynes open to derision; but he could, and did, provide corroborative evidence from other early civilizations, Egyptian, Babylonian and Assyrian. And, shrewdly, he provided a neurophysiological scenario derived from the research into the roles of the brain's two hemispheres. The voices of the gods, he suggested, must have emanated from the individual recipient's central nervous system exploiting the right hemisphere, leaving the left free for the emergence of consciousness; 'the language of men was involved with only one hemisphere in order to leave the other with the gods.'

Possession

But how, then, to account for 'the phenomenon known as *possession*'? The evidence suggested that possessed shamans were not simply relaying information they received from their central nervous systems in hallucinatory form; it might be coming 'directly from the prophet's vocal apparatus without any cognition on "his" part during the speech, or memory of it after'. If so it would represent 'not the loss of consciousness so much as its replacement by a new and different consciousness'; and this could be held to suggest that 'metaphysical essences', as he called spirits, might actually exist. There was no simple answer, Jaynes admitted; but any theory about the development of consciousness must face some obscurities.

Yet is the gap really so wide? If evolution, improvising, was capable of providing a form of central control in termitaries, and an early version of a hallucinatory Tannoy system for the Greeks and the Trojans, it was surely capable of providing a mechanism whereby its instructions could be transmitted through the individual whom the tribe relied upon as capable of tuning in to the correct wavelength; and even arranging that in the trance the voice should sound different, so as to ensure that what he was saying was recognized as inspired, rather than as the thoughts of the shaman.

The idea that evolution could be responsible for such developments might sound far-fetched; but as William McDougall had pointed out in his *Modern Materialism and Emergent Evolution* (1929), it has produced countless startling phenomena, such as mind itself. McDougall's research while he was Professor of Psychology at Harvard led him to adopt a modified Lamarckian theory, which gave mind a leading evolutionary role; it was purposive, he argued, creating evolutionary development as well as being created. This had become familiar to breeders of dogs and horses, using their skills to influence the shape, or speed, of later generations of their animals. That the process should have been at work before it was consciously adopted, however, proved too much for the Darwinians to swallow.

Jaynes was not prepared to swallow it, either. He cited Alfred Russel Wallace's assertion that man's conscious faculties 'could not have been developed by means of the same laws which have determined the progressive development of the organic world in general'. But Wallace became a spiritualist – a believer in 'metaphysical essences', which left him outside conventional science's boundaries. Worse, he accepted – as did McDougall – the possibility that some shamans in their trances enjoyed magical powers.

On this issue most ethnologists have since either been sceptics, or anxious not to become involved. But some of the most respected of them have believed that shamans can have powers which conventional science cannot account for. In her *Search for Security*, Margaret Field, who worked as ethnologist and psychiatrist in West Africa before and after the Second World War, made a shrewd appraisal of the evidence she had collected, pointing out that one feature of shamanism – in trances, individuals displayed powers they did not possess in their everyday lives – was beyond dispute.

In his trance, the shaman might spin like a top for minutes on end: 'great feats of strength or endurance may be performed under this excitement', and not only by the shaman himself. One of the ways in which individual members of a tribe who were not well could be treated was through trance, induced with the help of rhythm and dancing; 'I have seen grossly fat old women, who normally could hardly waddle about, whirl nimbly round the dance arena, leaping high in the air,' Field recalled. 'The strongly possessed novice, with the urge to run away into the bush, requires the united strength of all the most muscular young men of the village to restrain him and, if he does escape them, his turn of speed ensures that he will not be caught until the spirit has left him.'

Trance, in fact, could work 'like magic'. But was the magic real? From her own experience Field doubted whether trance possession did more than lend the possessed astonishing strength; and she had not heard any trance pronouncements which impressed her as coming from some external source. She was certain, however, that even if they rarely provided anything more than sensible advice, it was often much better than the shaman would have been capable of giving when he was in his everyday mind. The mind in trance, she believed – and in sleep, as she knew from her own experience – is capable of doing rather better than when it is fully conscious. She felt, too, that J. W. Dunne's account of his dreams in *An Experiment With Time* meant that it was 'not unreasonable to grant the dissociated mind an extended awareness similar to that of the dreaming mind'.

Eliade was prepared to go a step further. The shaman, he believed, 'foresees changes in the atmosphere, enjoys clairvoyance and vision at a distance', and has a close relationship, 'of a magico-religious nature, with animals', so that he can tell where game is to be found, or recover cattle which a member of the tribe has lost.

This would clearly have been unwelcome to Jaynes, who must have realized that his hypothesis would appear eccentric enough as it stood, without its giving any additional hostages to scepticism. He could be reasonably certain that few, if any, psychologists would be in a position to fault him about his knowledge of early civilizations; but if he were to stray too far into anthropology and ethnology he could be in trouble. He gave Sir James Frazer a casual disparaging reference, in passing; he made no mention of the work of the other leading ethnologists, from Tylor to Eliade, significant though it manifestly should be in any consideration of the evolution of consciousness.

The Old Testament

Another source of information about trance which both Jaynes and Field examined was the Bible, and in particular the Old Testament. As with the *Iliad*, Jaynes claimed, most of the books it comprises appear to have been stitched together from different and occasionally contradictory accounts, written at different times. But a few are believed to be exceptions; notably Amos, dating from the eighth century BC, and Ecclesiastes, from the second century. Jaynes invited his readers to judge for themselves that Amos is composed of speech heard in a trance by an illiterate herdsman, and dictated to a scribe. By contrast, the prophet of Ecclesiastes is his own man; he 'thinks, considers, is constantly comparing one thing and another, and making brilliant metaphors as he does so'. The interim period must have witnessed the transition from trance dictation to full consciousness; much as in Greece, the gods' trance dictation at the time of the Trojan war had given way to the full consciousness displayed in Plato and Aristotle.

In her *Angels and Ministers of Grace* (1971), Field was more concerned to relate the shaman component in the Old Testament to her own experience in West Africa, to see what light it could throw on many a familiar Bible story. Samson, for example, illustrated two of the cardinal elements in possession: 'firstly, that immense feats of strength may be performed when the spirit is in action and secondly, that anxiety can inhibit the process of dissociation, just as it can inhibit sleep.'

Saul was caught up in another manifestation of the dangers of a tribe relying too much on possession as an indication of suitability to become prophet, or shaman. When on occasion he became possessed, it astonished those who knew him. ('What is this that is come unto the son of Kish? Is Saul also among the prophets?') He had no proper shaman training, and eventually became so crazily unreliable that he had to be deposed in David's favour. The result was even more paranoia, with homicidal tendencies, which David was fortunate to survive.

David's career was to reveal yet another danger: the abuse of the power which possession, because it had elevated him to the leadership, had given him. Seeing Bath-sheba, wife of Uriah the Hittite, washing herself, and finding her beautiful, he arranged for Uriah to be sent into battle in the forefront, where he was most likely to be killed; as he duly was, enabling David to make Bath-sheba his wife.

In Elijah's case, the powers which possession gave were used in ways which had sinister implications for the future. He not only confounded the prophets of Baal by calling down fire from heaven, which they had been unable to do, and summoning rain; he slew them – the fate which has since befallen millions of men and women who have declined to conform to the dominant religion of their time.

For Field, the Old Testament reflected the decay of shamanism, and provided the reasons for its eventual collapse. Some, in retrospect, are obvious. One was that the more widely learned habits established themselves, the harder it became to find genuine prophets in the shaman tradition – a trend noted in the first book of Samuel. The prophet Eli was growing old, and his sons had taken up with prostitutes. He needed to find a successor; but 'the word of the Lord was precious in those days; there was no open vision' – no second sight. The infant Samuel had to be chosen merely because Eli found he could have aural hallucinations – the assumption being that he could hear the voice of the Lord.

At the same time, prophets were losing authority not only because, like David, they were tempted to exploit it for selfish purposes, but also because their commands could not be carried out if a ruling power, such as Egypt or Babylon, disapproved. This has also proved fatal for shaman possession in more recent colonial times. There are numerous cases where a shaman's words in trance have precipitated his trial, imprisonment and, in some cases, execution, when the colonial authorities have interpreted them as incitement to rebellion.

As Michael Gelfand observed from his experience as a doctor among the Shona in what was then Rhodesia, spirit possession also needed to be manifested in its natural environment. 'The more they adopt Western culture and education the more difficult it becomes for them to enter this state.' In tribal communities, ecstatic possession had served its evolutionary purpose, and the shamans who practised it were becoming rarer. Nowadays they are more likely to use devices to compensate for the loss of their predecessors' powers; they look for visions in a bowl of water, or scatter bones on the ground so that they can seek answers from the pattern in which they fall. Yet these, too, were initially trance-induced forms of divination, and often still appear to be. The shaman hopes to throw off consciousness sufficiently to allow intuition or second sight to break through. And the belief remains that spirits are responsible for the visions, and for the pattern into which the bones fall.

From shamanism to rationalism

Whether or not Jaynes's hypothesis is soundly based, at least it represents an attempt to come to terms with what remains the most mysterious and intriguing of all the problems associated with evolution: how did it come about that the trance-guided Greeks of the *Iliad* and the *Odyssey* metamorphosed with such astonishing rapidity (in the evolutionary perspective) into the Greeks of the Socratic era, whose intellectual pre-eminence remains unchallenged?

The available evidence about that transition was surveyed in meticulous detail by E. R. Dodds, Regius Professor of Greek at Oxford, in *The Greeks and the Irrational* (1951). He, too, had come to the conclusion that belief in the gods, displayed in the *Iliad*, arose through promptings which reached people, then as now, as if from an outside source – 'monitions', as he called them. 'The recognition, the insight, the memory, the perverse idea, have this in common, that they come suddenly into a man's head.' Man cannot call them 'his'; something has put them there; so he thinks of them as coming from a 'god' or 'daemon'. Sometimes the monitions take more positive hallucinatory forms, the gods being seen, heard and felt (as when Athena plucked

Achilles by the hair, warning him not to strike Agamemnon). Such trance manifestations, coupled with 'the sudden unaccountable feeling of power, of the sudden unaccountable loss of judgement', are the germ 'out of which the divine machinery developed'.

Dodds traced the course by which rationalism emerged in Greece, making the point that when scepticism began to be voiced about the gods and their power to influence man, sceptics were apt to assume that the accounts of the *experiences* of the believers, as well as the beliefs, must be rejected as untrustworthy – a tendency which could be misleading, considering that the beliefs presumably arose out of the experiences. The rationalism of the Socratic era did not, in fact, extend to rejection of trance as a way to obtain information of a kind beyond the reach of the conscious mind.

Shamanism was reinterpreted, but it was not thrown overboard, Dodds claimed. For Plato, 'the shaman's trance, his deliberate detachment of the occult self from the body, has become the practice of mental withdrawal and concentration which purifies the rational soul' – a practice which Plato claimed was traditional; 'the occult knowledge which the shaman acquires has become a vision of metaphysical truth.'

This, too, was the great age of oracles. The procedures at Delphi and other centres constituted a reversion to shamanism, though the Pythia were female. They appear to have been chosen because they could put themselves into trance through mental withdrawal, using some form of auto-suggestion. (The notion that they drugged themselves by inhaling vapours coming up from some underground sources, Dodds was able to show, was an invention; the myth had been revived by some nineteenth-century rationalist scholars, who had 'seized with relief on a nice solid materialist explanation'.) As the Pythia's pronouncements could be baffling, priests were employed to edit them and turn them, where necessary, into verse; but on the evidence, he felt, there could be no doubt that the trances and the information that came out of the possessed Pythia were genuine, even if the priests, in their own and their oracles' interest, sometimes indulged in obfuscation or falsification.

Obfuscation became necessary when, as must often have happened, the Pythia's pronouncements were unintelligible or misleading, but some answer was deemed necessary; the most celebrated example being the reply which, according to Herodotus, was given to King Croesus by the oracle at Delphi when he asked if he should launch an attack on Cyrus of Persia's forces. 'When Croesus has the Halys

crossed,' the reply was, 'A mighty empire will be lost.' He took the
word to mean that he should go ahead with his plan – and lost his
own.

Both obfuscation and falsification became even more essential when
the established order in Greece was overturned by conquerors who
needed to be placated; and eventually the oracles lost their authority.
For a time sybils, usually living hermit-like existences in remote
regions, carried on the shaman tradition, as the Cumaean sybil did in
Virgil's description of Aeneas' visit after the fall of Troy; at the onset
of her trance she went into convulsions, her body appearing to elongate,
before the god's voice broke through forecasting 'grim wars, and the
Tiber foaming with blood'. But by the time Virgil was writing, in the
first century BC, oracles and sybils alike were being gradually driven
out of business, not just by scepticism, Dodds contended, but also by
new forms of religion that were replacing the belief in the old gods.

FROM HIPPOCRATES TO SYDENHAM

Sacred and profane

A new attitude to trance emerges from the Hippocratic writings, dating
from the fourth century BC. 'I do not believe that the "sacred disease"
is any more divine or sacred than any other disease', one of the writers
– whether Hippocrates himself, or a follower – asserted. 'On the
contrary, it has specific characteristics and a definite cause.'

The specific characteristics which he named included choking,
foaming at the mouth, clenching of the teeth, convulsions, glazed eyes,
and trance – identical with those which had been attributed to spirit
possession. Divinity had been attributed to them, the writer complained, 'by the sort of people we now call witch-doctors, faith-healers,
quacks and charlatans'; by invoking the gods they had been able to
conceal their ignorance of the real nature of the disease, and to excuse
their failure to treat it successfully. It had nothing to do with the gods,
he insisted. It was a hereditary brain disease: epilepsy. As soon as a
better understanding could be reached of the role of the humours in
regulating health, physicians would be able to prescribe for, and cure,
the disease. Magic spells would be dispensed with.

The assumption that epilepsy was organic established itself with

physicians; but a problem remained. People often suffered from fits
who were clearly not epileptics. The fits resembled the effects of
frustration, irritation and silliness. Only women, Greek men assumed,
were susceptible. 'The Greek world of the classical age was a world of
the healthy and the sound,' Sigerist observed. 'Illness rendered man
inferior.' For a man to become convulsed with anger or grief was one
thing; to go into hysterics would have been humiliating. So fits which
were not epileptic, it came to be assumed, were a female disorder.
And in Greece in the fourth century BC, the physicians' desire to
extricate medicine from its shaman-oriented past led them to decide
that the fits, though not epileptic, must also be organic – the result of
disorders of the uterus. This in turn led to the diagnostic label
'hysteria', which has attached itself to them to this day.

Influential though physicians became in the classical era, they could
not wean the public away from belief in spirit possession; and when
men in epileptic fits, and women in hysterical fits, started to speak in
voices not their own, the assumption remained that the gods must be
responsible. As a result, trance in the shaman tradition came to be
divided into three categories, epilepsy, hysteria and possession. The
outcome was not simply intellectual and clinical confusion, but also
the growth of religious beliefs and superstitions which were to be
responsible for an appalling record of misery and cruelty in millennia
to come; a confusion from which we have still not succeeded in fully
extricating ourselves.

Possession

For a while, in the early Christian age, possession on the shaman
model continued to be regarded by the faithful as a mark of divine
grace. The gospels give many intimations of shamanism in Jesus's
career, his initiation in the wilderness; his second sight; his ability to
work magic – healing the sick, feeding the multitude, quelling the
storm. But Jesus's career, Jaynes suggested, can also be seen as
marking recognition of the need to revise the earlier Mosaic laws,
which had been designed to regulate behaviour by rules handed down
from what appeared to be divine dictation, to a greater degree of
flexibility in which the individual had more scope to decide what was,
and what was not, sinful.

After Jesus's crucifixion, Pentecost convinced the disciples that every one of them, and by extension those whom they enrolled, could be his own shaman; and Saint Paul left no doubt that the Church's aim, in his view, should be to revive the tradition – though in the new form; all Christians should be able to discover God's will through possession by the Holy Spirit. Such possession, he claimed in his first Epistle to the Corinthians, could bring a diversity of gifts: to one, wisdom or faith or healing powers; 'to another the working of miracles; to another, prophecy; to another, discerning of spirits; to another, divers kinds of tongues; to another, interpretation of tongues'. For the next century or so, Christians who could enter trances and speak 'in tongues' were highly regarded. But with the establishment of the Church in Rome as a centralized and increasingly autocratic bureau-cracy, trance-communicators became a source of worry. They were potential propagators of heresy, prompted by the devil and his demons – the rival spirits which, Saint Paul had promised, the gift of the Holy Spirit would enable the true Christian to discern, and unmask.

The Church's main worry was about the continuing Greek influence which, according to Dodds, had left a legacy in the form of Pythagorean asceticism, manifesting itself in 'a horror of the body and a revulsion against the life of the senses'. If, as Christians came to believe, self-indulgence on earth might lead to eternal torment in hell, they had a strong inducement to renounce the flesh; all the more so if, through its mortification, the spirit was liberated on earth with the chance of securing the gifts which Paul had forecast. The spread of Gnosticism, practised by those Christians who preferred to take their instructions from the Holy Spirit rather than from Rome, became a nagging problem for the Church.

The line the Church began to take was that the devil could imitate the Holy Spirit. No matter how divine the messages coming from the possessed might sound, they were not to be trusted. From the fourth century AD, Saint Augustine's view was accepted; the Holy Spirit had better, safer ways of communicating. Augustine's conversion from a life of lechery had been brought about, he believed, by divine providence arranging matters so that one day, when he happened to open the writings of Saint Paul at random, his eye lit upon the command, 'Put ye on the Lord Jesus Christ, and make not provision for the flesh, to fulfil the lusts thereof.' If the Holy Spirit could intervene in so subtly civilized a fashion, there was no further need for trance communication – which, for Augustine, was ordinarily a symptom either of insanity or of diabolic possession, depriving its victims of the use of their intelligence while 'an evil spirit, according to its will, makes use of their body and their soul.'

Possession by the Holy Spirit could not be ruled out entirely. Priests, monks and nuns often entered ecstatic trances in which the voices, when there were voices, made impeccably orthodox pronouncements; or in which the entranced individual appeared suitably rapt in contemplation at the time, and afterwards reported visions which could not be construed as diabolic. For the most part, however, episodes of this kind tended to be kept within a monastery's four walls, in case the individual concerned might fall into the sin of pride – a tradition established by Saint Francis.

'Great joy, even a miracle!' a lay brother who had known Francis wrote after his death. 'For a long while before his death, our Father and brother appeared crucified, bearing in his body the five wounds which are verily the Stigmata of the Christ.' In his lifetime Francis had refused to allow what had happened to be publicized; but when it became known after his death, the stigmata came to be considered a hallmark of divine favour. The Church learned to come down heavily on any establishment that tried to make its name and fortune out of exploiting any living inmate. After death, it was a different matter. The trances, the ecstatic pronouncements and the miracles were vigorously exploited to promote beatification and canonization, and to make the relics, real or spurious, the attraction for pilgrims.

The belief in the existence of diabolic possession was to have fearful consequences in the heresy hunts of the sixteenth and seventeenth centuries. Largely owing to the distortions of Michelet, Frazer and Margaret Murray, who allowed themselves to be deceived by the Church's propaganda, it has taken time for the realization to sink in that there was no basis for the belief in Satanic cults: they were an invention, designed to provide an excuse to wipe out Christian communities which continued to uphold the Gnostic tradition. In *Europe's Inner Demons* (1975), Professor Norman Cohn subjected Murray's influential *Witch-Cult in Western Europe* to a devastating critical scrutiny, demolishing both her pretensions to scholarship and her theory of a pre-Christian cult, surviving in covens.

Sects such as the Waldensians and the Cathars, Cohn showed, were savagely persecuted for heresy. The accusation of diabolic possession was thrown in merely as additional justification. Eventually, however, even the ruling classes in Europe were caught up in the confusion, accepting grotesque beliefs – derived originally from forgeries – that men and women who sold their souls to the devil gained the power, when possessed, to fly to sabbats, there to do him homage by kissing his anus, joining in his orgies, and enjoying his sexual favours, before returning home to put spells on their Christian neighbours.

Organized witch-hunting, Cohn argued, was the product of fantasy derived from forgery. Individual witch trials were a different matter; often they reflected 'impersonal fears and hatreds which occasionally still surface'. Doubtless there were always individuals who believed they had magical powers, or who used rituals and spells in the hope of obtaining them (the two categories being separated by some anthropologists into witchcraft and sorcery respectively; a distinction too blurred to be of much value). But there is no evidence, Cohn insisted, that such individuals were ever part of a cult; or that they operated in covens, which owe their initiation largely to Murray's unscrupulous distortions of the historical evidence to suit her now discredited thesis.

The belief in witchcraft, however, helped to keep alive a belief in diabolic possession, and in its ability to provide anybody who sold his, or her (usually her), soul with magical powers, such as second sight, and the ability to put a curse on those who offended her, as well as to materialize or de-materialize objects. The powers, the assumption was, could be activated with the help of rituals or drugs – usually salves, it was believed, applied to the skin – which facilitated possession. But the process left marks on the body, the 'devil's marks'.

The witch-finders believed they could identify a witch by pricking her in various parts of the body and noting if, and when, she did not howl. Unluckily for many innocent people, the fact that they howled at every pin-prick did not establish their innocence. But when there was some indication of insensibility to pain, it came to be regarded as a reliable method of detecting a witch. It was the devil's way of keeping tabs on his flock, even when they were not actually possessed. Torture would then be used to extract a confession; and tens of thousands of innocent men and women were hanged or burned as witches.

Mass hysteria

'What we have been examining,' Cohn noted in a postscript to *Europe's Inner Demons*, 'is above all a fantasy at work in history.' Initially the accusation of devil worship, and the structure built on it of the sabbat and its grotesque trimmings, had been adjuncts in support of heresy-hunting; 'in the great witch-hunt that fantasy became, as it were, an autonomous force.' Why? It must have arisen, Cohn thought, out of repressed hostility to the Church, unconscious hatred fuelling the fantasy. But beneath the terrain he had charted, he admitted, lay depths which could not be adequately explored by the techniques at his disposal.

'Why?' awaits further exploration; but the question *how* the fantasy operated can be most plausibly answered in terms of mass hysteria. The existence of occasional outbreaks of group contagion originally held an honoured place in Christianity, derived from the experience of the disciples at Pentecost. The Acts of the Apostles, Renée Haynes claimed in *The Hidden Springs* (1961), 'can be read as a chronicle of the new group-mind which had come into being' so that the collective, as well as the individual, powers of a group could be 'released, activated, and used by the Holy Spirit'. But collective possession met the same fate at the hands of the Church as individual possession. When it revived, towards the close of the Middle Ages, it was in the weird form of the Dancing Mania.

For the historical evidence about the outbreaks of hysteria we still have to rely too heavily for comfort on J. C. F. Hecker's survey in his *Epidemics of the Middle Ages*, written a century and a half ago. The contemporary accounts of the Dancing Mania, as he himself empha-sized, tended to be slanted according to the views of the writers. Dispassionate, trustworthy descriptions by reliable eye-witnesses were scarce.

Nevertheless the general nature of the symptoms, Hecker believed, could be extracted from contemporary sources without trepidation, because the accounts were reasonably consistent. A typical example was the outbreak in and around Aix-la-Chapelle in 1374, where men and women appeared to be suddenly 'united in one common delusion', losing control of themselves in wild gyrations. 'While dancing they neither saw nor heard, being insensible to external impressions through the senses, but were haunted by visions, their fancies conjuring up spirits.' The attacks usually began with what appeared to be fits, ending only when the dancers collapsed, exhausted. Sometimes voices appeared to speak through them, uttering prophecies. Although rogues and vagabonds soon began imitating the symptoms in the hope of receiving charity, observers were left in no doubt that some of the dancers were often genuinely possessed – by devils, it was assumed.

Sporadic epidemics of this kind were common in Europe in the fourteenth and fifteenth centuries. Subsequently they were less often reported, except in Italy, where they had come to be attributed to the bite of the tarantula spider – the 'tarantella' dance emerging into common therapeutic use because the victims were found to be susceptible to a form of control through music. Instead of behaving as if crazed, they would begin to dance in time with the music, often gracefully, until lassitude took over and they relaxed – so long as the music continued. If it stopped suddenly, the symptoms of disordered minds and bodies returned.

Paracelsus had suggested that the epidemics might be the consequence of overheated imaginations; Hecker was inclined to agree. He ruled out hysteria, but this was because he shared the still accepted assumption that it was a disease of the uterus, and there was ample evidence that men were susceptible. He also castigated those sceptics who had refused to credit that the symptoms of tarantism, as it had come to be known, were genuine – most physicians, he complained, 'in this controversy have shown the narrowness of their views and their utter ignorance of history'.

There was an element of imitation, Hecker admitted, but he felt sure there must also have been 'a loss of all power over the will' caused by what he described as 'sympathy', though he was careful to insist that this was an imperfect designation for what appeared to have been 'a common bond of union between human beings'. It was related, he felt sure, to the powerful waves of religious or political feeling which also sometimes deprived people of their will-power. To pursue this trail, however, would be to explore 'the profound secrets which lie hid in the inmost recesses of the soul'. His business, he felt, had been simply to relate how 'that morbid sympathy' developed, through which 'the dancing mania of the Middle Ages grew into a real epidemic.'

The mass hysteria reflected in the great witch-hunt of the sixteenth and seventeenth centuries was of a more subtle and sinister type. It afflicted the upper strata of society, and minds rather than bodies. But there were also sporadic outbreaks in which the contagion affected groups – hospitals, schools and convents – sending the inmates into convulsions, and apparently giving them unusual powers, as in the epidemic in an orphans' hospice in Amsterdam in 1566 when the children spoke in strange languages, and climbed like cats up walls and on to roofs. The French historian L. P. Calmeil described several of them in *De la folie* (1845), wherever reasonably reliable reports had been kept; the most serious was the epidemic at the Convent of the Little Ursulines at Loudun in the South of France, in the 1630s.

The Loudun case happens to be unusually well documented from the accounts of eye-witnesses and the lucid descriptions of their sufferings by some of the possessed. Because nuns were involved, it was assumed that they were the victims of witchcraft rather than themselves witches; it was the unlucky priest Urbain Grandier who was blamed and arrested, his screams when 'pricked' to the bone being audible to the crowd outside. The failure to find devil's marks did not save him from torture and the stake, so vividly described in Aldous Huxley's *The Devils of Loudun*.

His main accuser, Sister Jeanne des Anges, was more fortunate. She was permitted to behave diabolically – that is, in ways which her superiors, and the exorcists they despatched to Loudun, expected somebody to behave when possessed by devils. Her mind when she was possessed, she was to recall, was filled with blasphemies. 'I felt for God a continual aversion, and nothing inspired me with greater hatred than the spectacle of his goodness.' It so enraged her that she would tear off all her veils; 'I trampled them under foot, I chewed them, cursing the hour when I took the vows.' She suffered from fearful convulsions, the devils bending her over backwards; and her face contorted, taking on the different aspects of the devils who possessed her, each having his identity and his name.

T. K. Oesterreich's *Possession, Demoniacal and Other* (1921), still a standard work on the subject, quotes the moving letter written in 1639 by the ascetic and mystic Jean-Joseph Surin, describing how the devils he had come to exorcize turned their attention to him. 'In the exercise of my ministry the devil passes out of the body of the possessed woman and, entering into mine, assaults and confounds me, agitates and troubles me visibly, possessing me for several hours like a demoniac,' he wrote. He could not explain what happened, 'or how this spirit unites with mine without depriving me of either consciousness or of liberty of soul'; but the devil was able to 'make himself like me, as if I had two souls, one of which is dispossessed of its body and the use of its organs and stands aside, watching the actions of the other which had entered into them'. Surin could even feel 'a great peace under God's good pleasure' at the same time as he was feeling 'violent impulses to cut myself off from him and astonish the beholders'.

By the eighteenth century belief in possession by the devil or his demons was losing its hold on the public imagination; and in its most striking epidemic of mass hysteria, a century after Loudun, the contagion took almost a secular form in spite of the fact that it was triggered by the death of a revered Jansenist, François de Paris, and the manifestations took place by his tomb at the cemetery of St Médard. The *convulsionnaires*, as they came to be known, were not taken to be victims of witchcraft, even though they displayed familiar symptoms of possession, seeing visions, speaking in tongues, and performing a variety of physical feats of which they would not have been capable in their ordinary lives.

The symptoms of mass hysteria, it was gradually becoming clear, had basic similarities wherever and whenever they were encountered; but whatever beliefs were in vogue at the time would exercise a powerful influence, conditioning the hysterics to behave as they were expected to behave. Shortly after the St Médard epidemic, John Wesley was on the road in Britain and in Ireland in his capacity as an evangelist, seeking to bring people to the Lord; and his converts tended to react as he came to expect them to, going into fits which initially were alarming but which, he came to assume, were part of the conversion process. Preaching at Newgate in 1739, he noted that 'immediately one, and another, and another sunk to the earth; they dropped on every side as thunderstruck.' Even sceptics were impressed. A physician who came to one of the gatherings fearing to find imposture, instead found a woman he knew breaking out into 'strong cries and tears'; he observed every symptom, as 'great drops of sweat ran down her face, and all her bones shook.' At first he was baffled, realizing it was not fraud, but unable to think of any alternative diagnosis; 'but when both her soul and her body were healed in a moment', Wesley claimed, the physician 'acknowledged the finger of God'.

A Quaker nearby, who had also suspected fraud, had an even more startling experience. He was 'biting his lips and knitting his brows, when he dropped down as thunderstruck. The agony he was in was terrible to behold.' When he recovered, he, too, had to acknowledge that Wesley must be one of the Lord's prophets.

By the close of the eighteenth century, although evangelists were to continue from time to time to induce hysteria along Wesley's lines, the contagion was more often encountered in the new type of closed community which was being introduced by the industrial revolution. In 1787 the *Gentleman's Magazine* related that after a girl had gone into a fit at a cotton mill in Lancashire, other girls began to exhibit the same symptoms until the factory had temporarily to close. Girls in other nearby factories picked up the contagion, displaying 'anxiety, strangulation and very strong convulsions', lasting sometimes for twenty-four hours.

The common link appeared to be a fear that the raw material, cotton, was responsible; the doctor who was called in had the happy idea of giving the victims static electric shocks from one of the novel portable machines, reassuring them as soon as they were in a condition to listen to him that they had nothing to fear from the cotton. 'To dissociate their apprehensions still further, the best effects were obtained by causing them to take a cheerful glass, and join in a dance.' The next day, all but three were back at work.

By the end of the eighteenth century, the spread of rationalism was eroding belief in diabolic possession even among Catholics. That illness could be caused by demoniacal influences, Augustus Stohr insisted in his textbook on pastoral medicine in 1806, 'must be accepted by every Catholic believer as a fact beyond doubt', and where it occurred exorcism was the best authorized remedy; but similar symptoms, he warned, could be the consequence of a natural cause – hysteria.

Hysteria, new style

Hysteria, however, had itself undergone a transformation. The term was no longer applied only to trance symptoms resembling epileptic fits. Perceptive physicians were coming to realize that epilepsy was not the only disorder that could be mimicked.

The most bizarre form which the mimicry took was false pregnancy. Following her marriage to Philip of Spain in 1554, Queen Mary was pronounced pregnant, and bulletin after bulletin recorded her condition until eventually she went into labour and no infant emerged. It had been a case of dropsy, her embarrassed physicians claimed. The evidence suggests hysteria.

Case histories of the kind continued to appear, some commentators providing curious additional details, as William Harvey did in 1651 about a woman with whom he was 'very intimate', and who had experienced all the usual symptoms of pregnancy. 'After the fourteenth week, being healthy and sprightly, she felt the movements of the child within the uterus', and prepared a cradle, but nothing happened; 'as the abdomen had increased so it diminished.' Harvey had come across other examples which had deceived 'not only ignorant women, but experienced midwives, and even accurate physicians'.

A related form of hysterical mimicry was later to be given the name of couvade, adopted from the French, when anthropologists found that it was commonly encountered in tribal communities. 'There is an opinion abroad (whether idle or not I cannot say),' Francis Bacon wrote in 1627, 'that kind and loving husbands have a sense of their wives breeding children, by some accident, in their own body.' 'Having a sense of' was putting it mildly; husbands reported that they were feeling the pains of childbirth. 'That the man should sometimes suffer such pains, whilst the woman is well, and before she is in labour, is a problem I fear beyond all hopes of solution,' Robert Plot, Historiographer Royal and Secretary of the Royal Society, commented in 1677 on cases he had encountered in Oxford; but it had been reported to him by men of unquestionable veracity. One of them had assured him that the pains were unlike the griping of ordinary stomach-ache; they resembled those which his wife was to describe when she went into labour immediately afterwards – when his labour pains had disappeared. Plot would have thought this an absurd notion, he admitted, if he had simply heard it mentioned. But he had now been 'otherwise persuaded by sober men, who well knew how to distinguish between the manner of the pangs'.

It was left to Thomas Sydenham, generally honoured as the father of British medicine (though he would have been horrified at the mechanistic course it was soon to take), to point out in 1682 that hysteria did not confine itself to mimicry of epilepsy or pregnancy. 'Few of the maladies of miserable mortality are not imitated by it,' he claimed. It was far more common than had been recognized; 'of all chronic diseases, unless I err, the commonest'. So perfect could the imitation be that unless the physician was shrewd and skilled, he could easily be fooled into believing the patient was actually suffering from the disease itself, rather than from hysteria.

Sydenham was notorious among his fellow physicians for telling them what they did not want to hear. They were trained to make a correct diagnosis and to prescribe whatever was the accepted remedy. Hysteria could deceive them into making an incorrect diagnosis; and if they were not deceived, there was no accepted remedy. In any case, they felt, hysteria was obviously not a *real* disease. 'Physicians have bestowed the character of *nervous*', Robert Whytt, President of the Royal College of Physicians, noted in 1767, 'on all those disorders whose nature and causes they are ignorant of' – hysteria being a prime example. As there were 'no disorders so lucrative as those of the nervous kind', John Gregory, Professor of Medicine at the University of Aberdeen and Physician to King George III in Scotland, noted three years later, physicians would treat patients of assured social standing 'with the utmost care and sympathy'; but patients in general, he feared, could expect neither. On the contrary, it was not unusual to find doctors 'treating these complaints with the most barbarous neglect, or mortifying ridicule'.

For Sydenham, hysteria was a form of auto-hallucination, so powerful that the imagination imposed itself on the body. He did not believe that it was caused by a disordered uterus, nor that only women suffered from it; nor did he regard it as affecting only the weak-minded. What, then, was the explanation for the spread of this strange disorder?

One had, in fact, been tentatively provided by Robert Burton in *The Anatomy of Melancholy* (1621). He had noticed that women who were satisfied with their lives, or too busy to ask whether they were satisfied, rarely suffered from hysteria – 'the vapours', as it was known. It seized upon 'noble virgins, nice gentlewomen, such as are solitary and idle'. He had little sympathy for them if they were in a position to break out of their indolent habits. Nevertheless he recognized that in some cases it was the combination of powerful emotions with circumstances in which they could not find expression. At this point, Burton had checked the flow of his thoughts, in some embarrassment: 'Into what subject have I rushed? What have I to do with nuns, maids, virgins, widows?' As a bachelor who led a monastic life in college, he had to admit he was very unfit to pontificate on the subject. He could not, however, resist going on to denounce institutions which were permitted to impose vows of chastity on men and women – as distinct from permitting an individual, as in his own case, to embrace chastity voluntarily. Compulsion was contrary to the dictates of nature, of humanity, and even, he insisted, of religion.

For all his modesty, Burton had made a perceptive judgement. He had realized that the symptoms of hysteria may arise when strong-willed characters are confronted with barriers – social, educational, legal – which they cannot break down. Hysteria, too, was capable of producing a startling variety of symptoms relating to the beliefs held at different times, or in different places. What had all the appearances

44 *Trance*

of diabolic possession at Loudun might appear in Britain as couvade, or false pregnancy, or epilepsy, or – as Sydenham had realized – as any disorder.

In his *Table Talk* (1835), Coleridge suggested a name for this variety of hysteria, 'Mimosa', which was 'capable of counterfeiting many diseases, even death itself'. He clearly had in mind the form of trance which occasionally created a sensation, as it still does: coma.

Coma

Some sufferers from 'hysteric fits', the London physician John Purcell noted in *Treatise of Vapours* (1702), 'lie in trances for whole days, motionless, and senseless like dead bodies'. A few of them 'had the misfortune, as very credible authors assert, to have been buried alive in these fits'. He recommended in doubtful cases putting a feather or a looking glass to the mouth, or 'a glass brim-ful of water on the chest', so that the slightest breath would be noticed.

These precautions did not suffice to distinguish between coma and death in a case in which a retired army officer, Colonel Townsend, offered to demonstrate that he could put himself into a death-like trance. His offer was taken up by the celebrated Scots physician George Cheyne, and some colleagues. Cheyne reported that after the colonel had composed himself, his pulse gradually sank, 'till at last I could not feel any, by the most exact and nice touch'. Dr Baynard agreed: he could feel no motion of the breast 'nor Mr Skrine the least soil of breath on the bright mirror he held up to his mouth; then each of us by turns examined his arm, heart and breath, but could not by the nicest scrutiny discover the least symptom of life in him.' Eventually Cheyne feared he had actually died; but after half an hour he recovered sufficiently to transact business with his attorney – only to die in reality later that day.

Some of the coma stories related how individuals might have been buried alive but for the good fortune that they revived under autopsy. The Abbé Prévost was unlucky. In 1763, after producing scores of novels – and his one masterpiece, *Manon Lescaut* – he collapsed while out walking from what was thought to be apoplexy, and was taken to be dead. For some reason an autopsy was called for; the surgeon carried it out 'in such a thoroughgoing manner', George Saintsbury noted in his introduction to Helen Waddell's translation of *Manon*, 'that he at once ascertained that the patient was not dead – and killed him'.

The bizarre manner of the Abbé's death was not disclosed until twenty years later, and this understandably has raised suspicions. But as Saintsbury pointed out, the surgeon and others present would have been at risk from the law if the story had got around at the time. And periodically the possibility that people in comas may have been buried alive has been confirmed by episodes in which people have narrowly escaped that fate – as in a case narrated by Alexander Crichton in his *Inquiry into the Nature and Origin of Mental Derangement* (1798). Crichton, who among other jobs held the post of physician to Tsar Alexander I of Russia and head of the Russian civil medical department, was a careful observer, one of the first to try to apply psychological ideas to what had come to be known about mental illness. He had been deeply impressed by the account he had been given of a young woman who fell into a trance in which she was to all appearances dead, yet had been fully aware of what was being said and done around her. When she was put into a coffin, she tried desperately to indicate that she was still alive, but without success. Only when the lid of the coffin was about to be nailed on, 'the thought that she was about to be buried alive was the first one which gave activity to her mind, and caused it to operate on her corporeal frame.' Beads of perspiration began to appear; her hands and feet made small convulsive movements; and at last she opened her eyes, and uttered 'a most pitiable shriek'.

3

THE EXPLORERS

ANIMAL MAGNETISM

Exorcists and 'strokers'

In the course of the eighteenth century, as belief in diabolic possession waned, the medical profession turned to physical remedies such as esoteric drugs, virtually abandoning the attempt to deal with hysterical or nervous symptoms by any other means. Towards the end of the century, however, a theory was put forward which not only held out the prospect of a common quasi-physical source for both varieties of illness, but also offered a simple and inexpensive form of treatment. It had evolved from two sources, each originating in shamanism.

One was exorcism. As some disorders were assumed to be caused by witchcraft, the witch using his powers to call up spirits to do the damage, shamans treated the sufferers by inducing trances with the help of drums and dancing, the assumption being that the patients' convulsions indicated the successful banishment of the intruders. Jesus had adopted the same method, on occasion; but the beliefs attached to it had by his time been subtly altering. The convulsions were taken to be a sign the evil spirits were struggling to retain possession, wrestling with the divine force which was seeking to throw them out.

As described in the gospels, Jesus's method was simple. He conjured the spirits out of their victim partly by instilling him with faith, partly by enlisting divine authority to compel the spirits to realize they must find a new home. The Christian Church had settled for the same procedure; but, lacking Jesus's authority, the exorcists used rituals to impress the victim and, they hoped, the evil spirits. It was still thought that the convulsions would mean that the devils were taking their departure; all too frequently, to judge from accounts such as those of the Loudun outbreak, they simply signified effective resistance to, even mockery of, the exorcist's commands.

With confidence dwindling in the potency of exorcism, and with Protestants suspicious – Luther disapproved of it as paying too much attention to the devil; he advocated 'prayer and contempt' instead – another technique surfaced, practised by 'strokers'. This, too, was to be found in some tribal communities. It resembled massage, but the body was not, as a rule, touched; it was as if the stroker's hands, making 'passes', were drawing out the noxious substances which were in the patients' bodies, and dispelling them into the atmosphere – trance and convulsions indicating that the method was working satisfactorily.

In the seventeenth century, when magnetism was acquiring full recognition as a force of nature, and ceasing to be suspect as occult, the similarity of the way in which magnetism could be introduced into an iron bar by stroking it with a magnet impressed some of the practitioners. They began to use magnets in their treatment, with gratifying results. Most of them, however, preferred to avoid publicity, for fear of attracting the witch-hunters' attentions. Few reliable accounts of their methods and results have survived.

The career of Valentine Greatraks was an exception. Greatraks was a member of the Anglo-Irish 'Ascendancy', as it came to be known. He was a magistrate, and he had influential friends – among them the founder of modern chemistry, Robert Boyle, who was a frequent witness of the stroking, and impressed by its results.

By Greatraks's own account, he first became aware that he had a gift of healing, and then developed stroking as the most effective method, as it put the patients into trances from which they often awoke to say delightedly that their disorders were cured. Coming to England in 1666, Greatraks made an immediate impact not only on the public, but on Boyle's friends, including members of the newly-formed Royal Society. He was even the recipient of a Royal Command, to give a demonstration for Charles II on patients brought from St Bartholomew's Hospital.

Inevitably some witnesses were suspicious; and Viscount Falconbridge decided to try an experiment while Greatraks was treating an arthritic patient. When the patient was in his trance, 'his Lordship thrust a pin of about an inch long, almost to the head, into one of his fingers.' The man did not stir, and the wound did not bleed. When he came out of the trance, Falconbridge found that bleeding began, and the man yelped when he was only lightly pricked.

Mesmer

Exorcism and 'stroking' existed side by side in Europe in the eighteenth century, attracting the attention of the young Franz Mesmer. As a student at the University of Vienna, he had become fascinated with Newtonian physics, and this had set him pondering on the mystery of gravity. As the subject of the thesis which he was required to present to his examiners, he chose 'The physical and mental effects of the planets'; and in it, when he delivered it in 1766, he argued that just as plants reacted to the sun, planetary influences could be affecting the human body. He initially spoke of 'animal gravity'; but he was drawn to the possibility that the force might be magnetic. If a way could be found to harness 'animal magnetism', as he called it, the possibility opened up that the force could be exploited in the treatment of illness.

In the course of his research Mesmer watched two celebrities at work. Johann Gassner, a maverick priest who held public exorcism ceremonies, used to tell people that if they remained unaffected, their disorders must be physical, and they should go to a physician; but those who went into trances and convulsions were suffering from diabolic possession and were suitable subjects for his exorcism. Fr. Hell, Professor of Astronomy at the University, was a 'stroker', using magnets. Mesmer found that the physical effects which Hehl reported could readily be demonstrated; using a magnet, he, too, could increase or decrease the flow of blood from a wound. But he went on to find that the magnet was unnecessary. The flow of blood could be regulated simply by 'passes' of the kind 'strokers' used. Both exorcism and stroking, Mesmer decided, must owe their effects to the existence of a subtle 'fluid', linked with magnetism, permeating everything. Animal magnetism could be concentrated in the magnetizer himself and, through him, passed on to patients, sending them into convulsions and trances which would revive them 'just as a weak magnet may be revived by a stronger'.

Animal magnetism could also, Mesmer came to believe, be concentrated in a tub, a *baquet*, out of which magnetized iron bars protruded which his patients could hold; and this, coupled with his imperious manner and fondness for dressing in robes, was to give orthodoxy its opportunity when, in 1784, a Royal Commission set up by Louis XVI investigated his method. Its membership was one of the most distinguished ever; chaired by Benjamin Franklin, it included Lavoisier, Guillotin, Bailly – the future mayor of Paris, until swept out of office in the Terror, to die like Lavoisier on Guillotin's invention – and the celebrated botanist, Laurent Jussieu. But they were all orthodox in their views. Mesmer, who declined to be investigated – he left that to his follower, Charles d'Eslon – can have been in no doubt that they would be prejudiced against his method; all the more so because it had become very fashionable in Paris, to the irritation of physicians and scientists.

Their report revealed they had been convinced that Mesmer's method worked, in the sense that it induced convulsions which were 'extraordinary by their frequency, their violence and duration', followed by relaxation, languor and drowsiness. Nor could they dispute that patients often claimed to feel great benefit from the treatment. But when trials were conducted with the patients blindfolded, unable to tell whether they were or were not being 'magnetized', nothing happened. Animal magnetism, the Commission decided, was a myth; the *baquet*, spurious. It was simply the imagination of the patients which was responsible for their trances; and the trances themselves, the report warned, were to be condemned – not on health grounds, but because over-heated imaginations constituted a moral danger to women.

The report, hostile though it was, helps to dispose of myths which have established themselves about Mesmer. He was not a hypnotist, in the sense that term has come to be used. There must have been hypnotic influences at work; but basically he was in the shaman tradition, inducing trances and convulsions as a form of treatment. And as Henri Ellenberger pointed out in *The Discovery of the Unconscious* (1970), even his *baquet*, given his premise about the magnetic fluid, was scientific in design. He was trying to find a way to accumulate it in a container 'in the same manner as physicists accumulate electricity in the Leyden Jar'. His theory of a pervasive fluid from the planets, too, derived from gravity, not from astrology. In fact, he condemned astrologers for 'swindling people out of the contents of their purses, thanks to a skill filled with deceit'.

Mesmer had been unlucky. Caught up in the prevailing enthusiasm for the scientific method, he had failed to allow for the power of the patient's imagination. Without his realizing it, his patients were behaving as he wanted them to behave. But the Commission's view that all could be explained by imagination was not justified. In a minority report, Jussieu cautiously dissented from the majority finding that everything that had occurred could be explained by the patient's imagination. Watching carefully, he had seen patients on occasion responding to the mesmerist's pointed finger when they could not have seen the gesture. Suspicious though he was of the theory of animal magnetism, he argued that sufficient evidence had been provided for the Commission's members 'to make us admit the possibility of the existence of a fluid, or agent, which is communicated from one man to another, and sometimes exercises on the latter a sensible action'.

In a perceptive essay on Mesmer in *Mental Healers* (1932), Stefan Zweig suggested that in view of the subsequent discovery of hitherto unsuspected forces in the cosmos, it was conceivable that 'within our own time, or that of our children', research would vindicate him; in any case, 'what right have we to dismiss with contempt the theory of Mesmer and the fluidists that one human being can influence another by some sort of ultra-subtle physical emanation?' A 'more enlightened posterity', Zweig thought, 'was restoring Mesmer's name to honour, and coming at last to recognize how great, how noble, how distinguished a forerunner' Mesmer had been. More than half a century later, there is little sign that greatness, nobility or distinction are terms which leap to the mind whenever Mesmer's name is mentioned. More commonly it is either still associated with charlatanism, or Mesmer is recalled as somebody who made a contribution to the eventual development of hypnotism, but foolishly delayed its acceptance by propounding a misguided theory to account for the induced trances.

The mesmerists

Mesmer had, in fact, relatively little responsibility for mesmerism, as it came to be practised (and called, in English-speaking countries – the French continued to call it animal magnetism). The man mainly responsible for establishing the existence of the mesmeric trance, distinct from shaman-type healing trances, was Armand Chastenet, Marquis de Puységur, a former artillery officer who on his retirement had taken a course with Mesmer, and planned to use the same method to treat his tenants and other locals in and around his estate.

At the time the Royal Commission was conducting its investigation in Paris, one of the peasants on the estate came to Puységur for treatment. When Puységur made his 'passes', Victor fell quietly into a trance, with no convulsions. Fascinated, Puységur began to conduct research into Victor's 'magnetic sleep', eliciting surprising reactions. He had been thought of as 'the dullest-witted peasant in the district'; but in his trances, Puységur did not know 'anyone more profound, more sensible, more clairvoyant'. He could even read Puységur's intentions. Puységur merely had to think 'stop!' and Victor would break off in mid-sentence.

The impact of Puységur's account of his experiments with Victor was remarkable. As Stefan Zweig was to point out in his essay on Mesmer, Puységur was not even a qualified physician; he was 'a human dilettante, inspired with philosophical curiosity'. Yet the distinction of his family name, and the fact that he took no money for providing treatment, made it unlikely that he was a cheat; and the more plausible explanation, that he was a self-deceiver, could be checked by anybody who cared to conduct experiments along the same lines.

Many mesmerists, in France and other European countries, began to conduct them. When Puységur's friend and neighbour J. H. Pététin, a physician and a former President of the Lyon Medical Society, began research into magnetic sleep on his own account he, too, found that a few of his patients enjoyed similar freakish abilities in their trances. Mme de Saint-Paul appeared particularly gifted, and Pététin invited colleagues from Lyon to test her. One of them went into another room, and put substances into his mouth. Asked what it was that he was tasting, she shook her head when chocolate and caramel were suggested, but nodded vigorously when asked whether it was marzipan – as it turned out to be. On one occasion she even correctly guessed where a bottle of wine he had brought with him had come from, which at the time he did not know himself.

These accounts did not excite incredulity. Puységur assumed that the phenomena could be attributed to animal magnetism; Pététin preferred the alternative of animal electricity; as yet there was still a readiness to accept that one or other might be responsible for much that had earlier been taken to be supernatural. 'We are still far from understanding all the agents in nature, and their different modes of action,' Pierre Laplace warned in his *Analytic Theory of Possibilities* (1814), one of the most influential mathematical works ever written. The fact that animal magnetism did not give consistent results should not be used as an excuse to reject the evidence; 'it would display very little of the spirit of philosophy to deny the existence of phenomena only because they are inexplicable in the actual condition of our knowledge.'

That the hard-headed Laplace could take this line indicated that after the trauma of the Revolutionary era, and during the wars that followed, research into animal magnetism had continued. The previous year had, in fact, seen the publication of Joseph Deleuze's *Critical History of Animal Magnetism*. Deleuze's reputation as a botanist was second only to Jussieu's; and in his history he displayed the same methodical thoroughness as he did with plants, surveying the accounts which had been published all over Europe.

The investigators, Deleuze's research revealed, had encountered a variety of manifestations in connection with the induced trance condition; but in general, their accounts confirmed those of Puységur and Pététin, and were in line with Deleuze's own findings. Although convulsions sometimes occurred, it had become clear that they were no longer to be regarded as an indispensable feature; patients could be treated for everyday disorders simply by putting them into light trances, from which they would often emerge feeling refreshed, having got rid of their symptoms.

It was what happened when patients entered deep trance, though, which most intrigued researchers. Some subjects, they had found, were able to go back in time – as Victor could – reliving episodes in their childhood. Deleuze had also found that if he told one of his subjects in a deep trance to return an hour later, wearing certain clothes, the subject would not remember these instructions when he came out of the trance, but would obey them, even at some inconvenience, at precisely the set time.

The 'higher phenomena' of mesmerism, as they came to be known, included 'travelling clairvoyance'. It was not encountered often; some mesmerists never found a subject capable of demonstrating it; but when it occurred, investigators realized that it was easy to test by asking subjects what they 'saw' in another room, or another house, and checking to find if the reports were correct. Sometimes they were. Such individuals, Deleuze claimed, enjoyed faculties absent in their normal lives: 'seeing without the aid of eyes, hearing without the aid of ears, seeing at a distance, reading thoughts, appreciating time with rigorous exactitude and, what is still more astonishing, having a presage of the future.'

He was careful to warn that mesmerized subjects could be unreliable. When questioned, he had found, they sometimes gave answers which he eventually realized were simply designed to disguise their ignorance – much as answers can be in ordinary conversation. But he had witnessed enough to satisfy himself that, in some cases, the faculties were genuine.

The findings from all over Europe confirmed him in this view. Several had come from respected researchers, unaware of what was being done in other countries and reported in other languages, yet describing broadly the same phenomena. Mesmerism, too, was in no sense a cult. Its practitioners believed they were being as scientific as colleagues who were investigating electricity. And they could claim that some, at least, of the curious manifestations they reported were already well-known and generally accepted when they occurred in another form of trance – sleep-walking.

Sleep-walking

The parallel with sleep-walking was so obvious that mesmerized subjects came to be known as *somnambules*. Somnambulism had usually been put in the pathological category, as a symptom of a temporarily disturbed mind. 'I have seen many cases of people groaning and shouting in their sleep,' the writer of one of the Hippocratic treatises had claimed. 'Some choke, others jump from their bed and run outside and remain out of their minds till they wake', when they would be as sane as before. Shakespeare's Lady Macbeth, too, was clearly the portrayal of a woman under intolerable emotional stress. (It has since won the approbation of psychiatrists for what they regard as a clinically satisfying case history.) But in the eighteenth century interest began to be aroused in the fact that sleep-walkers sometimes appeared to have uncannily heightened perceptions, and to do things which they could not have done while awake.

The element of heightened powers had been noted by Lord Monboddo, the eighteenth-century Scots judge whom some of his fellow-countrymen have been inclined to regard as the anticipator, if not the originator, of scientific anthropology. A sixteen-year-old girl would occasionally fall into a trance in the daytime and, in this condition, would suddenly spring around the room she was in with astonishing agility, like a monkey, before escaping (if she could) into the garden where she would run very rapidly, skilfully surmounting the garden wall, to a particular spot in the vicinity which seemed to act as a lure to her. Yet all the time her eyelids were fast closed.

In the course of the century, Ellenberger has recalled, 'marvellous stories were published everywhere about sleep-walkers who would write, swim rivers, or walk over rooftops'; and such tales were to continue, with embellishments, throughout the nineteenth century. Somnambulists whose nocturnal activities lent themselves to research in this way were for obvious reasons hard to come by; but on hearing that a priest in a seminary was known to get up during the night and compose sermons in his sleep, the Archbishop of Bordeaux saw the opportunity to investigate. Tests were made to ascertain whether the priest was seeing what he was writing. When a blank sheet was interposed between his eyes and the paper, he continued to write as freely and as lengthily as before. When he had finished a sermon, he would go back over it and make corrections. The investigators found that if a blank sheet of paper was substituted for the one on which he had written, he would make the corrections on it, in precisely the place where he would have made them on the original page. When he woke up, he could recall nothing of the whole performance.

In Wilkie Collins's *The Moonstone* (1868), young Franklin 'stole' the jewel while he was sleep-walking, his intention being to hide it to prevent it from being stolen; and as he remembered nothing of what he had done, he might easily have lost both his reputation and his loved one, who had seen him do it, but did not realize his intention. A local doctor guessed what had happened and came to the rescue. In Blois, Dr M. Dufay had earlier performed a similar feat in reality. A servant girl had been charged with theft. Hearing that she had been known to sleep-walk, it occurred to him to hypnotize her, to find if she would confess to taking the valuables, and disclose where she had hidden them. In her trance she described how she had been worried to find the valuables lying around, and told him where she had hidden them, intending to tell her mistress. Dufay believed that she really had been sleep-walking, and so did her mistress; when the valuables were found where she had put them, she was released.

Dufay also had a patient who often went into states of spontaneous waking somnambulism. This, he realized, gave him an opportunity to check the differences between her normal and her trance personalities. In her trances, he found, 'Mlle L.' was distinctly more intelligent than in her normal condition (as she realized; she would refer to her normal self as 'stupid'; her normal self had no knowledge of her trance self). Ordinarily Mlle L. had difficulty in threading needles and doing her work in her sewing circle. On entering her trance she would throw away her spectacles contemptuously, and move to get out of strong light. 'If she needs to thread her needle, she throws both hands under the table, feeling in the dark, and in less than a second succeeds in putting the silk through the eye.' Her memory, too, greatly improved. In short, she was a different and superior person.

Mesmerists, too, had often come across examples of subjects who in their *somnambule* state appeared to become different and sometimes superior people. Thomas Mayo, a fellow of the Royal Society and later to be President of the Royal College of Physicians, had witnessed such a change when he had been open-minded enough to watch a demonstration of mesmerism; he noted that the mesmerized subject could move suddenly from one personality to the other, and that 'he has no clear recollection in the one, of subjects which had interested him in the other.' Whether such changes were to a higher or a lower type of person, Mayo thought, was of less significance than the fact that it could happen, which was of profound importance for the future of the treatment of mental illness. 'If mesmerism should help us to a partial removal of this veil, it will have done much,' he wrote in his *Pathology of the Human Mind* (1838). 'The discovery of a cure in disease is most likely to be effective through the discovery of its cause.'

So strong was the evidence that the 'higher phenomena' could occur in sleep-walking that even some rationalists found themselves compelled to defer to it, yet at the same time rejecting very similar accounts of phenomena occurring with mesmerized *somnambules*. This kind of double-think was reflected in Robert McNish's *Philosophy of Sleep* (1830). 'The stories related of sleep-walkers are of so extraordinary a kind that they would almost seem fictitious, were they not supported by the most incontrovertible evidence,' he admitted; 'to walk on the brink of house tops, to scale precipices, and to descend to the bottom of frightful ravines, are common exploits.' Nevertheless McNish contemptuously dismissed the evidence for similar phenomena when they were attributed to mesmerized *somnambules*. It was curious, as Herbert Mayo was to observe in the chapter on trance in his *Letters on the Truth Contained in Popular Superstitions* (1851), that whereas what happened in other induced trances was rejected, sleep-walking 'with all its wonders, being at once undeniable and familiar, has been simply taken for granted'.

Deleuze encountered the same problem. If he had been describing what sleep-walkers could do, he might not have aroused serious dissent; but his descriptions of what mesmerized *somnambules* could do, in his *Critical History* and his *Practical Instruction in Animal Magnetism* (1825), met with hostility. A few eminent scientists – Laplace, Cuvier, Ampère – were impressed by the evidence about animal magnetism; the great majority, largely because of reluctance to accept the 'higher phenomena', tended to dismiss all the findings out of hand, even to the point of declining to accept that the trances themselves were genuine. And the medical profession was even more deeply antagonistic.

It happened that a new 21-volume French dictionary of medicine had been planned for 1825, and the composition of the entry on animal magnetism had been given to one of its severest critics, Professor L. Rostan of the Salpêtrière Hospital. To his colleagues' chagrin, when the volume appeared his article contained descriptions of research with a *somnambule* which had left no doubt in Rostan's mind that the phenomena, including clairvoyance, were genuine, and that they could best be accounted for by animal magnetism.

Rostan's critics were not then in a position (as they were later to be, when the volume went into its second edition) to suppress the article. What could be arranged was another investigation by a commission set up by the Academies, the precaution being taken to ensure that a majority of its members were known to be critical of mesmerism. It went to work with much greater thoroughness than its predecessor, over the period from 1826 to 1831. In particular, it investigated two claims which were of relevance for medicine. The mesmerists had reported that some *somnambules* who displayed clairvoyant powers had been able to diagnose what was the matter with themselves and with other patients, as Victor had occasionally for Puységur. And they had asserted that if a patient could be put into a deep trance, he could be pricked with pins or subjected to more painful procedures, yet feel no pain and remember no pain when he awoke.

A young doctor, P. Foissac, presented the case for clairvoyant diagnosis with the help of 'Céline'. Although she had no knowledge of medicine, she had passed the tests the members of the Commission gave her. In her trance, she correctly diagnosed what was the matter with the patients; she even prescribed remedies which the doctors had to admit were appropriate. In one case, her diagnosis differed from that of the doctor in charge of the case. When, shortly afterwards, the patient died, a post mortem revealed that Céline had been right.

The demonstration of mesmerism's ability to banish pain turned out to be even more spectacular. For several days a practising mesmerist prepared Mme Plantin, aged 64, for an operation to remove a breast tumour. It was performed by a surgeon, Jules Cloquet, taking only twelve minutes. During that time Mme Plantin, who had been terrified at the prospect, conversed calmly with the surgeon, Cloquet, showing no signs of feeling pain. When the wound had been dressed, she was brought out of her trance. Only then, when it dawned on her that the operation she had so deeply feared had been carried out without her being aware of it, was she so carried away by a surge of emotion that she had to be put back, for a while, into her 'magnetic sleep'.

Sceptical though most of the members of the Commission had been, they were impressed by what they witnessed. In their report they affirmed that although in some cases the magnetizing process had no effect, and in others the effects were produced by the imagination, 'it appears that some results depend solely on magnetism, and cannot be produced without it. These are physiological phenomena, and well established therapeutically.' In particular, clairvoyant diagnosis and insensibility to pain had been demonstrated to their satisfaction; further research was clearly needed. The existence of animal magnetism, Deleuze felt entitled to boast in a new edition of his manual, had finally been established beyond doubt.

He was soon to be rudely disillusioned. In 1826, Auguste Comte had given the first of his lectures on positivism; and although they had been interrupted by a bout of mental disorder, they had been resumed, and the first batch published in 1830. They reflected, and helped to promote, a brand of rationalism which found the exploitation of trance for any purpose, let alone to release clairvoyant abilities, repugnant. When it was proposed that the report on animal magnetism should be published, ordinarily a formality, a member of the Academy of Medicine complained that if its findings were accepted they would overturn the currently-held assumptions about physiology. It was agreed that it should simply be noted – not printed. The surgeon, Cloquet, found himself derided. A few years later, a Boston doctor who was visiting Paris decided to find out if the story of the painless surgery was a fabrication. Cloquet, when asked, assured him it was true. Why, in that case, had he not repeated the experiment? Such was the medical profession's prejudice against mesmerism, Cloquet explained, that he had not dared to repeat it. He would have lost both his reputation and his source of income, if he did.

In 1836 the story got around through the newspapers that a dentist, Dr M. J. Oudet, was using mesmerism to extract teeth painlessly. He gave a demonstration to show that the method worked, only to find himself denounced as accessory to a fraud. In England two years later the fashionable London surgeon Sir Benjamin Brodie assured the readers of the *Quarterly Magazine* that even if the mesmeric trance offered patients the certainty of pain-free surgery, which it did not, he would advise them not to accept it, because it would be dangerous for a surgeon to operate on them in that condition. One surgeon actually claimed that pain was 'a wise provision of nature', to hasten post-operative recovery. But the most common attitude among members of the medical profession was simply that the patients who were operated on under mesmerism in demonstrations were lying when they claimed that the operation was pain-free; and in 1840 the French Academy decided that as animal magnetism was spurious, there was no further need to investigate it.

In 1842 the eminent physiologist Marshall Hall told the Royal Medical and Chirurgical Society that he was quite satisfied, concerning a demonstration of mesmerism in the course of which a patient had his leg amputated at the thigh, that the patient was only pretending not to feel any pain; if he had been unconscious the good leg would have twitched, in a reflex action, during the operation. Eight years later he was able to tell the Society that the patient had at last confessed.

In a formal affidavit, the patient flatly denied he had confessed. The operation, he reiterated, had been painless. Asked where the story of the confession had been obtained, Marshall Hall said he had it from 'the most honourable and truthful of men', who in turn stated that *he* had had it from 'a person in whom he had full confidence'. Accepting Marshall Hall's version, the Society declared the matter closed, a verdict which the editor of the *Lancet* welcomed as 'impartial'.

What might have been achieved was being illustrated in India, where the Scots surgeon James Esdaile, in the employment of the East India Company, carried out more than 300 major operations and countless minor ones in the 1840s with the help of a mesmerist; in no case had there been any fatality which could be attributed to the method. He, too, had been denounced as a charlatan by some of his colleagues. As his grateful employer, however, happened also to be effectively the government in British India, they were powerless to damage his prospects; he was promoted Surgeon to the Company in 1846. But by this time ether and laughing gas were being employed as anaesthetics; and they were soon supplemented by chloroform. When Esdaile returned to Britain, he was ignored. The medical journals declined to print his account of his findings.

In the whole history of medicine there is no sadder story than this protracted rejection of what, as Esdaile had demonstrated, would have been an invaluable help to the surgeon and his team, and an incalculable relief to the millions of patients who had had to submit to surgery, ranging from the extraction of a tooth to amputation, without the benefit of anaesthesia, and who might have remained pain-free – or at least (as research was soon to confirm) in more bearable pain, thanks to the soothing component which even a light trance can provide. Yet for over half a century the medical establishment in Europe and America had set its collective face against accepting the evidence that trance can confer insensibility without risk to the patient. Why?

The initial responsibility lay with the 1784 Commission. As the Scots philosopher Dugald Stewart pointed out, it had not been unreasonable for the Commission to reject animal magnetism; but did it follow 'that the *facts* witnessed and authenticated by these Academicians should share in the disgrace?' The symptoms arising from the interaction of imitation and imagination, as the Commission's report had described them, were of much greater interest, he felt, than the issue whether or not a 'fluid' accounted for them. If the method brought results, as the Report had admitted it did, there was no more reason for a physician to refuse to use it than for refusing to use, say, electricity. Certainly imitation and imagination could be exploited for mischief, as the Commission claimed; but so could many other types of medical treatment.

Later, it was rationalism and positivism which were responsible for the rejection of the evidence. Hume's dictum that miraculous events could not happen, because they were contrary to the laws of nature, was accepted. The 'higher phenomena' were deemed to be in that category.

For a time, this presented problems for those who felt the need to avoid conflict with the Church in Catholic countries, or the Kirk in Scotland. For all their admiration for Hume, it was not easy for Scots to deny the possibility of divine intervention. Their let-out was the argument that God had unrestricted powers but, thanks to mankind's development of reason, no longer needed to use them. 'There were times when God held communion with man,' McNish conceded; 'breathing wisdom and foresight over his slumbering spirit gave him a knowledge of circumstances which no human sagacity could have guarded against or foreseen.' But the idea that man still enjoyed supernatural powers thanks to God's intervention could be dismissed; God 'appears no more in vision to warn, to instruct, to solace'; life on earth 'is now, in all cases, governed by the fundamental laws originally made by God for its regulation'.

Having himself encountered examples of what appeared to be prevision of the future in dreams, McNish could not deny that they occurred. But how could people be forewarned in sleep of events which they could not have known about in their waking lives? 'This is the dilemma into which the believers of the prophetic power of dreams are brought; they virtually admit the existence of miracles,' McNish observed. But 'in the present state of the world, the doctrine of miracles is glaringly absurd; and even when they are supported by what appears irresistible proof, no man is justified in believing them.' Although there could be no doubt that dreams occasionally came true, 'this must be regarded as altogether the effect of chance.'

Chance, hallucination, deception, gullibility – one or more of these arguments could always be advanced to explain away any evidence that did not fit positivist preconceptions. With reluctance, Deleuze eventually felt compelled to admit that as animal magnetism could not be fitted into the framework of laws of nature as they existed at the time, real progress would never be made, he feared, by seeking to bring the science of animal magnetism into line with the other sciences; 'it has its own laws, which are not identical with the laws of nature.'

HYPNOTISM

James Braid

In 1843 a book was published which was to help bring about the transformation of mesmerism into hypnotism as it is generally practised today. A Scots surgeon, James Braid, had attended a demonstration by the French mesmerist Charles Lafontaine – hoping, as

Braid was later to admit, to find 'the source of fallacy in certain phenomena I had heard were exhibited'. When he was convinced that the phenomena he witnessed were in fact genuine, Braid turned his attention to seeking an explanation which would provide an alternative to animal magnetism. His patients, he found, could be put into their trances by what he regarded as a straightforward neurophysiological process, getting them to stare at some bright object and soothing them gently into hypnosis, as he called it to distinguish it from the mesmeric trance. There would be no further need, he claimed in his *Neurypnology, or the Rationale of Nervous Sleep*, to look for a fluid or to bother with the mesmeric 'passes' any longer.

Braid's medical background led him to concentrate on investigating what hypnosis could do for patients; and he found it chiefly of value in what had been called the nervous disorders, but were coming to be described as 'functional', in which no organic cause could be traced for the symptoms – rheumatism, headache, skin troubles and so on. He was able to include an impressive list of case histories, to justify his faith in hypnotism; but he knew that he needed to dispel a misconception which had blocked acceptance by his colleagues not just of animal magnetism, but even of the reality of trance, which Marshall Hall and others dismissed as spurious.

In justification, they had been able to cite an experiment which had been made by Thomas Wakley, the formidable founder and editor of the *Lancet*. The mesmerists had claimed that it was possible to put a patient into a trance simply by handing him an object, a coin or a glass of water, which had been 'magnetized' by their 'passes'; and John Elliotson, a physician at University College Hospital, used to give demonstrations. When Elliotson's attention was distracted, Wakley quietly substituted a coin which had not been 'magnetized'. The subject, handed the coin, promptly went into a trance; Elliotson appeared totally discredited; and thereafter Wakley lost no opportunity to deride mesmerism in his journal.

Elliotson, however, had friends who refused to believe he was either a dupe or a cheat. Thackeray was to dedicate *Pendennis* to him; Dickens reposed complete trust in him; Dickens's biographer John Forster was to say of Elliotson that for thirty years he had been 'a synonym for us all for unwearied, self-sacrificing beneficial service to everyone in need'. Braid, too, admired Elliotson, in spite of their disagreement about the reality of the magnetic fluid. Here, then, was the opportunity both to rehabilitate Elliotson, and to show that Wakley's condemnation, though understandable, had been unjust. Braid was able to report that in a series of experiments he had shown that as soon as he was able to hypnotize a patient, a process that sometimes took time, he could subsequently induce hypnosis instantaneously simply by some association – say, a single word, or the production of a coin – which could be used instead of the initial induction method. This, to Braid, clearly proved 'the power of the imagination *on those previously impressed*'. The patients hypnotized themselves simply by seeing or feeling whatever they associated with being hypnotized; 'this readily accounts for the result of Mr Wakley's experiment.'

Wakley remained unimpressed; he continued to denounce mesmerism and its 'brood'. And Braid had another problem to deal with: the evidence for the 'higher phenomena', which irritatingly sometimes reappeared. Braid was spared any encounter with travelling clairvoyance; but he could not dispute that some patients were able to detect and describe objects held behind their backs.

Realizing that to admit the existence of clairvoyance would be fatal for his chance of obtaining recognition for hypnosis, Braid groped for a rational explanation, and found it in the hypothesis that, under hypnosis, some individuals experienced 'extremely exalted sensibility'. They could describe the object held behind them 'not by sight, but by feeling'. And though they could not see when they were being beckoned by the hypnotist from several feet away, they could detect 'the currents of air, which they advanced to, or returned from, according to their direction'.

So implausible a notion would ordinarily have been greeted with ridicule by his fellow-doctors, and by scientists in general. But Braid found an unexpected ally in William Benjamin Carpenter, who had made his name in academic circles with his *Principles of Physiology* (1839), when he was still in his twenties. Carpenter was torn between the two impulses which were to shape his career; his curiosity about the phenomena reported in connection with mesmerism, and later with spiritualism; and his ambition to become the leading physiologist in Britain – and, through his textbooks, in America too.

Braid's experiments presented Carpenter with what must have seemed to him a heaven-sent opportunity to combine the two impulses, by offering him the opportunity to account rationally for phenomena which orthodox scientists had dismissed as contrary to the laws of nature, but which he satisfied himself were genuine: insensibility to pain under hypnosis, enhanced muscular power, and the apparent clairvoyant ability of some subjects. The explanation, Carpenter decided, must be that the human brain functioned on two levels.

Although the idea of a subconscious mind was still unacceptable, Carpenter felt it was safe to shift the issue from metaphysics to neurophysiology, and to propound his theory of 'unconscious cerebration'. The senses, he claimed, were capable of providing a wider range of information when the subject was under hypnosis, passing it to the brain through channels which ordinarily provided signals too faint to attract attention. Carpenter had seen a hypnotized youth trace the owner of a glove from among a party of more than sixty people – clearly, he explained, a demonstration of hyperacuity of the sense of smell. On another occasion the owner of a ring who had just taken it off a finger was similarly detected. This, and some other cases, Carpenter attributed to the exaltation of the sense of temperature – 'very slight differences, inappreciable to ordinary touch, being at once detected'.

Carpenter divided the phenomena associated with hypnotic trance states into three categories: those which could readily be admitted – somnambulism, say – as their existence had never been doubted; those which, like hyperacuity of the senses, were 'not conformable to our previous knowledge', but so long as they did not contravene the established laws of nature could be accepted if the evidence for them were strong enough; and 'those which not only lie *beyond* our existing knowledge, but are in direct contrariety to it'. The evidence for clairvoyance might appear to be just as strong as for hyperacuity. But the 'higher phenomena' which could not be accounted for by hyperacuity of the senses must be rejected, because they contravened the known laws of nature.

Certain by-products of the mesmeric trance, however, Carpenter was prepared to concede had been confirmed by Braid's research. The trance state itself was genuine. In it, insensibility could be induced, so that it was possible to undergo surgery without pain. A form of somnambulism, hardly distinguishable from sleep-walking, could occur. And the muscular system could be excited to a point where the subject would be able to perform feats of strength or endurance far beyond his normal capacity.

Braid was naturally delighted to have Carpenter's support. Earlier he had been polite to the mesmerists; he now blamed them for their extravagance in contending for the reality of the 'higher phenomena', 'pretensions a mockery of the human understanding, as they are opposed to all the known laws of physical science'. But this abrupt change of attitude may have been accounted for less by mean-spiritedness than by his alarm at the spate of reports of trance phenomena which could not be accounted for by hyperacuity of the senses.

Unwittingly, Braid and Carpenter had done mesmerism a service. If doctors and scientists had been wrong to deny the reality of the trance states, of its pain-removing capabilities, and of some of the 'higher phenomena', might they not also be wrong in accepting hyperacuity of the senses on manifestly flimsy evidence? And was it logical to claim that Puységur, Deleuze and others, as well as the second commission of inquiry, had not been telling the truth about some of the phenomena they claimed to have witnessed? They could hardly all have been deceived.

What was impressive about the fresh evidence which the British mesmerists provided was that it came from such a variety of sources, ranging from George Sandby, a country clergyman, to William Gregory, Professor of Chemistry at the University of Glasgow, who enjoyed an international reputation for his research in biochemistry; Alfred Russel Wallace, later to share with Darwin the first presentation of the case for natural selection (though he insisted that the credit must go to Darwin); William Scoresby, the celebrated polar explorer; and Herbert Mayo, who had been Professor of Physiology at King's College, London. None of them made any attempt to sensationalize what they had witnessed. Scoresby, in particular, presented his findings with the same precision as he had used to describe what he had found in his voyages to the Arctic. From all of them, though, the message was clear. A few subjects displayed abilities in their trances which could not be accounted for by hyperacuity of the senses, unless that term was extended far beyond the limitations which Braid and Carpenter needed to impose on it.

The evidence poured out in books, and in *The Zoist*, a journal which Elliotson founded in 1843 to present case histories from different parts of the world; from the United States, where the higher phenomena had begun to attract research in the late 1830s; and from France, where the young Alexis Didier became the first successful professional clairvoyant, attracting clients from all over the country – including Victor Hugo and Robert-Houdin, the first of the internationally re-nowned magicians (from whom Houdini was to take his name). After carefully testing Alexis, Robert-Houdin left 'in the greatest state of amazement,' as he admitted, 'convinced of the utter impossibility of chance or conjuring having been responsible for such marvellous results'.

Most of the investigators had begun sceptically, or at least critically, finding what they had heard about some of the phenomena hard to credit. Nor had they encountered only what they had expected to witness; often they were astonished by what happened, as Scoresby was when he found he could 'will' a lightly mesmerized subject into obeying his unspoken commands. If he ordered her, mentally, not to get out of the chair she was sitting in, she would be astonished to find herself unable to leave it.

Alfred Russel Wallace was a schoolteacher at the time; he used the schoolboys as his test subjects and to his surprise one of them, when mesmerized, reacted to whatever Wallace felt, tasted or smelled as if he were himself feeling, tasting or smelling it. When Wallace formed a chain of boys, with himself at one end and the subject at the other, if in 'perfect silence I was pinched or pricked, he would immediately put his hand to the corresponding part of his own body, and complain of being pinched or pricked.'

It could have been simple to find if hyperacuity of the senses could be held responsible for this 'sympathy' or 'community of sensation', which Scoresby and Gregory explored, by having the subject who was in trance in one room, and the mesmerist, smelling or tasting different substances, in another; but Braid and Carpenter would have refused to credit the accounts. Some of the people who now accepted the reality of mesmeric phenomena, attributing them to hyperacuity, had previously dismissed them as 'mere humbug and imposture', Gregory complained. Had they had the decency to apologize? Of course not! A follower of Braid would now admit the reality of the trance condition, and of insensibility to pain; but 'he rejects (as decidedly as he formerly did those facts) those further phenomena of animal magnetism, such as sympathy, thought reading, community of senses, of taste, smell, etc; the control exercised by the operator over the will and imagination of the subject; and all the force of clairvoyance. In short he repeats, deliberately and recklessly, his former error.'

As Gregory emphasized, too, there could be no question of the mesmerists being duped by clever tricks. Their subjects were not aspiring Robert-Houdins. Most of them knew nothing of mesmerism, let alone the 'higher phenomena'. Often they were unlettered domestic servants – the most readily available category for experiments, as well-off householders usually had several of them.

It was to no avail. The great majority of doctors and scientists remained unimpressed either by the new evidence presented by the mesmerists, or by the work of Braid and Carpenter. It was not so much that they rejected Braid's findings or Carpenter's theory. Physicians tended to regard the functional disorders which Braid claimed to be able to cure much as they had regarded nervous disorders; they were not *real* illness. With anaesthetics available, the use of hypnosis to relieve pain had become superfluous ('this Yankee dodge', Robert Liston, the first surgeon to use ether in an operation in Britain, commented when he had amputated a leg, 'beats mesmerism hollow'). As for the display of hyperacuity of the senses in induced trances, what was the point of it, except in parlour games? When Braid died in 1860, his life's work had left little impression in Britain (and has left little even in his native Scotland: the 'James Braid' in *Chambers Biographical Dictionary* is the golfer). Carpenter resumed his career as a physiologist, switching his critical attention from the mesmerists to the spiritualists, whose principal scourge he was now to become.

SPIRITISM

Table-turning

In the early 1850s the contest between mesmerists and hypnotists was interrupted by the emergence of a new form of contagious trance, self-induced in groups as a pastime. Its original source was the haunting that disturbed the Fox family in their home in Hydesville, near Rochester, New York. The young daughters of the household found they could get the ghost to communicate through raps. Discovering they had strange powers, they moved on to give public performances, in which bemused witnesses found that objects moved around – as had often been reported in poltergeist cases – without the application of any visible force. The pastime developed when it was found that the presence of the Fox sisters was not required. Almost any group prepared to sit for an hour or two in near-darkness, fingers on a table, could hope to elicit some response: raps, and unaccountable movements of the table.

The pastime – variously labelled table-turning, table-tipping, table-rapping or table-tilting – quickly became a craze in and around New York. It had two elements: the actual movement of the tables – along with other manifestations, often startling; and messages which the movements – or sounds, usually in the form of raps – conveyed, in reply to questions (the code became one movement, or rap, for 'Yes'; two for 'No'). As the messages commonly purported to come from people who were no longer alive, they provided – for those who accepted them as genuine – evidence for life after bodily death, giving birth to modern spiritualism. But for the great majority, the antics of the tables were the main attraction, and the craze spread – also as if by contagion.

From New York, in 1853 table-turning spread on to Britain. 'I have no doubt that there are *thousands* of tables turning every night in London,' the science writer Sir David Brewster noted, 'so general is the excitement of the subject.' Even Queen Victoria had sessions at the royal residence at Osborne. She satisfied herself that the movements were not illusory; electricity, she thought, or magnetism must be involved. A number of country clergymen preferred to pin the responsibility on the devil, who had found this ingenious way, they feared, to prove that he was not a myth. A lively controversy ensued in clerical circles on the issue.

From Britain, table-turning moved on to Europe, and everywhere it presented scientists with a problem. 'The facts are undeniable,' one of the most respected of them, Baron Alexander von Humboldt, felt bound to insist; 'it now becomes the task of science to explain them.' Even Faraday, appalled though he was at what he regarded as a recrudescence of superstition, did not care to deny publicly that they were 'facts', for this would have implied that many of his friends and acquaintances were either liars or dupes.

In a letter to *The Times*, Faraday described how he had set up an experiment which had satisfied all those who took part in it that the tables did move – but they moved only because, without realizing it, they had been using physical force. The explanation was 'quasi-involuntary muscular action' – a variant of Carpenter's idea of unconscious cerebration and heightened muscular prowess.

Faraday's table-turning was spurious. It had been achieved with a loose table *top*, easily moved by finger-tip pressure. As a correspondent wrote in protest to *The Times*, this could not account for the movements of heavy drawing-room or dining-room tables. And years later, when extracts from Faraday's correspondence were published, they showed he had conducted the experiment in a far from scientific frame of mind. Horrified at the link between table-turning and spiritualism, he had decided to 'turn the tables on the table-turners', as he put it, without involving himself in an actual investigation.

Dissatisfied with Faraday's research, two distinguished scientists of the time, Count Agenor de Gasparin and Professor Marc Thury, embarked on their own inquiry in Geneva, and reported that they had been left in no doubt that tables and other objects did move, as though pushed or pulled by some as yet unidentified force – 'ectenic', Thury called it. Like Carpenter, Thury sought the explanation in unconscious processes. By analogy with dreams, he suggested, they sometimes produced effects which were not consciously desired. He had to admit this was purely speculation; but the facts, he insisted, were well established. Savants who derided them would be well advised 'to suspend their judgment upon things which they have not sufficiently examined'.

By the time Thury's study of table-turning appeared in 1855, some of the savants who had been derisive were being given an even greater shock. Daniel Dunglas Home had arrived in Europe for the start of what was to be a spectacular career spanning two decades, in which he demonstrated his ability to harness and direct the ectenic forces – soon to be renamed 'psychic' – more regularly and more strikingly than anybody else has since been able to do.

Home went to royal palaces, to the mansions of the rich, and to the homes of the famous – often a welcome guest, as well as a performer. In them, in rooms he had never seen before and with no assistant, he would go into a trance. The other sitters, rarely more than eight of them, would wait until the table around which they were sitting would begin to creak, and produce raps. Then they would watch while it shifted on the floor, turned around, rose up on two legs, and sometimes floated. 'Watch' was the operative term. The sessions were ordinarily conducted in light good enough for all those present to see that Home really was in his trance, and not in any contact with the table.

Home's virtuosity was far too spectacular for scientists' tolerance. Session after session sprang surprises; invisible hands playing musical instruments (and playing them well, though somewhat soupily); or visible disembodied hands which circled the company and could be shaken (but if gripped, they dissolved). Home's spiritualism was another impediment to investigation. His demonstrations, which sometimes included spirit communications, were designed to impress witnesses of the reality of the existence and the powers of the spirits. He was not a performer in the usual sense; he did not accept fees. But when Faraday was finally persuaded to agree to investigate, he insisted as a pre-condition that Home would formally admit 'the utterly contemptible character both of the spirits and their results' – a proposal so insulting that the go-between did not bother to pass it on.

Eventually a few scientists – William Crookes, Coleman Varley and Wallace in England, Alexander von Boutlerow and Nicholas Wagner in Russia – risked the derision of their colleagues. Their investigations satisfied them, too, that Home's psychic powers were genuine. But by then he was near the end of his career; ill-health compelled him to retire.

Almost all those who attended Home's sessions left feeling convinced that the phenomena were genuine. There is no record of any occasion, either during or at the close of a session, when he was accused of cheating; and on the few occasions when he was accused retrospectively, as he was by Sir David Brewster and by Robert Browning, the description of the devices he was supposed to have used was too preposterous to be taken seriously. Ironically, though, the weirder the phenomena reported – when heavy tables tilted, for example, crockery or other objects on them did not slide off – the more difficult it was for people who had not witnessed them to accept them as genuine.

An explanation which a few people who had witnessed them hazarded – the only one which could have brought the phenomena almost within the territory then covered by the laws of nature – was group hallucination. This was a little more plausible in connection with Home's sessions than with table-turning in general, as it could be argued that he was exerting a hypnotic force; and if Faraday was prepared to accept quasi-involuntary muscular action, with Carpenter's delighted approbation, he might have taken the further step and credited Home with the ability, with or without being aware of it, to hypnotize sitters into conjuring up the raps, the hands, and the peculiar antics of the table. It would then have been reasonable for somebody, most probably Carpenter, to attribute the whole table-turning saga to an epidemic of a strange form of mass hysteria – by no means so unlikely a possibility as it may sound today, because the medical profession had just been compelled to admit that another such epidemic had broken out in England, and for a time become widespread, without their recognizing it for what it really was.

Neuromimesis

Sydenham's memory might be revered by the profession, but his views on hysteria had been ignored. Doctors continued to think of it mainly in terms of imitation epilepsy. The characteristic symptoms – the *globus hystericus*, a feeling of a lump in the throat; dizziness; convulsions; foaming at the mouth; and eventual loss of consciousness – were often similar. But this mattered relatively little as there was no effective treatment for organic epilepsy, either. The hysterical version, too, was most easily detectable when it appeared to be 'put on' – a tantrum; and doctors did not regard this as an illness.

Sometimes, however, they were deceived, as Sydenham had warned they would be, by mimicry of other disorders. In a way, such cases resembled possession; the victims behaved as if they had been taken over – not by a demon, but by a more subtle infiltrator who sapped their volition and their conscious control, causing them to produce symptoms of a kind that so perfectly imitated the real thing that they would be looked after and fussed over, rather than told to stop being nuisances. And the most commonly encountered form had been paralysis.

In *Hysteria* (1867), F. C. Skey, a former President of the Royal Medical and Chirurgical Society, recalled that in the early part of the century, 'all the sea-side towns were crowded with young ladies between 17 and 25 years of age and beyond it, who were confined in the horizontal posture, and were wheeled about on the shore in Bath chairs, on the supposition that they were the subjects of organic disease.'

Skey was gently intimating that there had been an epidemic of hysterical paralysis, which doctors had failed to recognize. They must learn to live with the clinical fact that every part of the body was capable of becoming 'the seat of an apparent disease that in reality does not exist, with an exactness of imitation which nothing short of careful and accurate diagnosis can distinguish from the real disease'. He went further. The profession had been wrong, he thought, to continue to believe that hysteria was a woman's disease. Impressionable girls in their teens or early twenties were the most susceptible; but this should not be allowed to leave the misleading impression that it was not a real disease – it was, and could be serious – and that it was confined to the weaker-minded. 'It will often select for its victim a female member of a family exhibiting more than usual force and decision of character, of strong resolution, fearless of danger, bold rider, having plenty of what is called "*nerve*".'

Skey found a formidable ally in his campaign to rescue hysteria from the obloquy into which it had fallen; Sir James Paget, already renowned as a trenchant lecturer, soon to become surgeon to Queen Victoria. 'To call a patient hysterical is taken by many people as meaning that she is silly, or shamming, or could get well if she pleased,' he observed; but often hysteria was serious, 'making life useless and unhappy, and not rarely shortening it'. Nothing could be more mischievous, he asserted, 'than a belief that mimicry of organic disease is to be found only or chiefly in silly, selfish girls'; on the contrary, it was more likely to be found 'among the very good, the very wise, and the most accomplished'. It was time, he suggested, to give up using the term hysteria. It had become confusing, owing to the colloquial identification with hysterics – tantrums. He proposed 'neuromimesis', instead.

The medical profession showed no inclination to take Skey and Paget seriously. The distinction between organic disorders, on the one hand, and functional, nervous, or hysterical symptoms, on the other, had been hardening, with doctors increasingly inclined to assume that their business was to concentrate on diagnosing and treating the organic variety. Hysteria in its neuromimetic form was consequently coming to be regarded with increasing irritation: a snake in the clinical grass. And it had another disturbing component, unmentionable in polite society, and rarely referred to even in medical circles: latent sexuality.

This had attracted the attention of a young medical practitioner in an English country town, Robert Brudenell Carter. *On the Pathology and Treatment of Hysteria* (1853), published when he was only 25, put the case for recognizing suppressed emotions, and in particular sexual urges, as the root cause of hysteria. 'It is reasonable to expect that an emotion which is strongly felt by great numbers of people, but whose natural manifestations are constantly repressed in compliance with the usages of society, will be the one whose morbid effects are most frequently witnessed,' he argued. And this was borne out by the facts: sexual passion was more repressed in women, and the injurious effects of that repression were familiar.

Even if erotic passion was not included, he went on, the relative power of the emotion was clearly greater in women than in men, 'partly from that natural conformation which causes her to feel, under circumstances where the latter thinks, and partly because the woman is more often under the necessity of endeavouring to conceal her feelings.' If sexual desire was also taken into account, the emotional pressures on women, particularly those who were unmarried, were far greater than on men. Men had 'facilities for its gratification'. Whenever they were excited by the desire, 'it is pretty sure to be speedily exhausted through the proper channels.'

Carter was later to became well-known as an ophthalmologist. His treatise on hysteria appears to have been ignored; probably, as Ilsa Veith observed in her *Hysteria, the History of a Disease* (1965), because it was 'too embarrassingly perceptive for his Victorian compatriots'. And because of the embarrassment, the medical profession in Britain did not care to confront the unpalatable evidence that well-brought-up, prim Victorian young ladies were apt to suffer not only from relatively civilized forms of hysteria – paralysis, fainting, 'going into a decline' – but also from nervous attacks in which they would talk and behave like trollops, perhaps making indecent advances to their doctors.

On the continent of Europe there was a greater readiness to face and deal with hysterical outbreaks of the kind. As hysteria was still quite generally assumed to be a disorder of the uterus, its sexual manifestations were often treated by drastic physical measures, drugs and even surgery. The then celebrated gynaecologist Alfred Hegar advocated hysterectomy, advice which his students accepted. Another group, Veith has recalled, 'followed the renowned neurologist Nikolaus Friedreich in cauterizing the clitorises of those patients whose sexual needs and demands they deemed immoderate'. And although P. Briquet warned in his *Traité de l'Hystérie* (1850) that it was not simply sexual frustration that gave rise to the symptoms – deprivation of love and affection, he believed, were of greater significance for sensitive individuals – few of his contemporaries bothered to make his distinction. The safest place for hysterics, surely, was hospitals such as the Salpêtrière, where they could be effectively controlled, and cease to be an appalling embarrassment to their families and friends.

There, they could have fallen into the charge of Jules Falret, soon to be President of the Paris Medico-Psychological Society. His belief was that hysteria was a form of moral insanity. The patients were 'veritable actresses'; they took pleasure in deception. Outwardly they would pretend to be pious, 'while at the same time abandoning themselves to the most shameful actions'; at home, they would use obscene language in front of their husbands and children.

Falret's treatise on hysteria appeared in 1866. Three years before, another doctor with an interest in hysteria had joined the Salpêtrière staff, and his patients were having a decidedly more enjoyable time. They were, in fact, about to become the talk of Paris, when Jean-Martin Charcot put them on public display to demonstrate the effects of hypnotism, and to illustrate his new theory to account for them.

4

TWO DECADES OF RESEARCH

THE 'CHARCOTERIE'

'Hystero-epilepsy'

Jean-Martin Charcot had felt it was safe for him to experiment with hypnotism because 'Braidism', as it was called on the continent of Europe, had managed to circumvent what had amounted to the interdict imposed by the Academies. He appears to have been influenced by the work of the young Charles Richet who, though by training a physiologist – he was later to receive a Nobel Prize for his work on allergy – refused to accept segregation between the academic disciplines; he had undertaken psychological research, investigating hypnosis in the course of it, and publishing an account of his findings in 1875. Four years later Rudolf Heidenhain, the influential Professor of Physiology at the University of Breslau, came out on the same side after watching a professional hypnotist, Carl Hansen. Heidenhain arranged for a test on his own younger brother. Put into a trance, young Heidenhain not merely swallowed some ink with every expression of pleasure when told it was beer; he put his hand into a flame, showing no sign of feeling pain; 'and with scissors so unmercifully cut off his whiskers, which he had assiduously cultivated for a year, that on awakening he was greatly enraged.'

By 1880, Charcot was in any case so securely established, internationally as well as nationally, as the leading neurologist of the era that he could afford to shrug off criticism. His fellow-doctors, he knew, would think he was foolish to waste his time investigating animal magnetism (as it was still generally described in France) and treating hysteric patients; but they were not in a position to undermine his massive reputation. And his research with the patients, using hypnotism, provided results which amply justified his hope that he would be able to confound critics. In their trances, his hysterics developed certain symptoms associated with epileptic seizures. Such seizures were notoriously hard to distinguish from their hysterical counterparts. The explanation, Charcot assumed, must be that hypnosis was an induced form of seizure to which only hysterics are susceptible.

At the same time, he managed to convince himself and his followers that hysteria was a neurological disorder. Hysterics were not malingerers; they were suffering from a form of brain degeneration. In view of the well-established facts about the hysterical mimicry of organic symptoms, this might have been difficult; but, as it happened, there were materialist theories in circulation which for a time blurred the distinction between organic and hysterical disorders. Consciousness, T. H. Huxley had asserted, 'would appear to be related to the mechanism of the body simply as a collateral product of its working'; it was 'as completely without the power of modifying that working as the steam-whistle, which accompanies the work of a locomotive engine, is without influence on its machinery'. Mental processes, epiphenomenalists insisted, were real, but could be accounted for in exclusively neurophysical terms.

In 1882, Charcot presented a report on his Salpêtrière research to the Academy of Medicine. Although on the last occasion on which its members had investigated animal magnetism they had agreed that the subject should never again be brought to their attention, Charcot could reassure them; his paper was not on animal magnetism, but on hystero-epilepsy – a brain disorder, induced by neurological processes, mimicking another brain disorder, hysteria, which itself, in seizures, mimicked epilepsy.

There could hardly have been a hypothesis more acceptable to the medical Establishment. It established hysteria as a real disease, which doctors need no longer be embarrassed at having to diagnose. Yet it also spared them the problem of treating it: this, clearly, could be left to the specialists – neurologists and alienists – at the Salpêtrière and other such hospitals. Above all, Charcot had put animal magnetism and 'Braidism' in their place. He had demolished the pretensions of the mesmerists and hypnotists, in particular their claim that the trance state could be used therapeutically. 'Facts are denied until a welcome interpretation is offered,' as William James remarked. 'Then they are

admitted readily enough.' In its new pathological form, the mesmeric
or hypnotic trance was at last given recognition.

It was also recognized, and welcomed, even by the Church authorities. In an essay entered for a religious competition in Salamanca,
a Jesuit, H. Hahn, recalled the evidence from Saint Teresa's autobiography, showing how she had suffered from heart pains, nausea,
tongue-biting, fits, the *globus hystericus*, trances, paralyses and hallucinations – the very symptoms of hysteria which Charcot's patients at
the Salpêtrière had been demonstrating. 'We are in the presence of an
instance of organic hysteria as characteristic as possible,' he felt
justified in claiming. 'The disease reaches in truth its highest limit.'

For Teresa to have accomplished so much, Hahn was arguing, in
spite of her sufferings, showed that she was a more remarkable figure
even than hagiography had made her out to be. His thesis won an
award. Only when the Vatican authorities later realized that such
symptoms were not going to be accepted as organic, after all, and that
medical opinion was reverting to its earlier beliefs about hysteria, was
Hahn's paper put on the Index.

The Nancy School

Hardly had the Academy delivered its favourable verdict than Charcot's assumptions were shown to be fallacious, largely due to the work
of an obscure country doctor practising near Nancy. A paper which
Braid had written in 1860, shortly before his death, had attracted A.
A. Liébeault's attention, and he had begun to follow Braid's method
in treating everyday disorders, taking advantage of 'the parsimonious
character of the French peasant', as J. Milne Bramwell, who was to
become the leading exponent of hypnotherapy in Britain, was to recall.
Liébeault's patients had absolute confidence in him, Bramwell found
when he paid him a visit; but naturally they expected to be given the
usual drug treatment. So he would say to them, 'If you wish me to
treat you with drugs I will do so, but you will have to pay me as
formerly. On the other hand, if you allow me to hypnotize you I will
do it for nothing.'

Liébeault's ruse worked, as did his very simple form of treatment.
He would make soothing, sleep-promoting suggestions – followed,
when his patients were in their trances, by further suggestions designed
to remove their symptoms. So successful did the method prove that it

attracted one of Professor Hippolyte Bernheim's dissatisfied patients, and when Bernheim heard that Liébeault's treatment had succeeded where his had failed, he went in some wrath to investigate. Converted by what he witnessed to the realization that Braidism worked, Bernheim adopted it in his Nancy hospital; and, annoyed that Charcot's theory had been accepted, he began to demonstrate to doctors who came to visit Nancy that to equate hypnosis with hystero-epilepsy was nonsense. Patients by the hundred were receiving his and Liébeault's care who had never shown any sign of hysteria or epilepsy; yet they could easily be put into a trance, light or deep, without displaying hysterical symptoms. They appeared to go to sleep; and while they were in that condition, it was possible by suggestion to cure them of a wide range of common disorders.

Hypnosis, Bernheim claimed, *is* sleep – a particular form of sleep, in which the sleeper's attention, instead of being scattered, is fixed in relation to the hypnotist, so that his suggestions are followed. 'Suggestion rules the greater part of hypnotic manifestations,' he asserted, 'because of special concentration of mind in the hypnotic condition.'

Gradually it became obvious that whether or not Bernheim's theory was correct, his practice at Nancy showed that Charcot at the Salpêtrière had been misled by the fact he was using hysterics in his experiments. Being highly suggestible, they had demonstrated whatever Charcot wanted them to demonstrate. This might have been expected to embarrass the members of the medical Establishment who had endorsed Charcot's theory. Had they wished to overturn it, they could have done so, as they had in the third investigation half a century earlier. But they had no such wish. Hypnotherapy as practised by Liébeault and Bernheim was a threat to the profession's peace of mind; it required no medicines. Worse, it often cured disorders which had been regarded as organic; and at medical schools students were being assured this was impossible. Charcot's version was clearly preferable.

The experimenters

In one respect Charcot had performed a signal service. It at last became possible for psychologists to begin to extricate themselves from the departments of philosophy in the universities. They were able to conduct research into hysteria and hypnosis without damaging their reputations. Again and again, they found and described phenomena which had been encountered and described by the early mesmerists, but which for a century had been rejected by orthodox scientists and physicians. And as some of the researchers were scientists and savants of established reputations, the positivists, dominant though they still were in some universities, were unable to stamp out the revived heresy.

Whether the Salpêtrière or the Nancy version of hypnosis was accepted, one of the heretical contentions had to be conceded even by the positivists. The reactions in the trance condition were real, not faked; and they could display a range of abilities that neither the subjects nor their friends had any inkling of from their everyday lives. Some of those abilities, too, would be of obvious potential value, if a way could be found to make them available to people on tap, as it were, rather than only when they were hypnotized.

One which particularly intrigued the investigators was that a hypnotized subject could tell the time not only when she was under hypnosis, but later, provided the suggestion was made while she was still in her trance (not all the experimental subjects were women, but most of them were). If the suggestion was implanted that at a given time, after she had come out of her trance, she would take a certain course of action, the likelihood was that she would perform the act, and at the given time, even though she had no conscious recollection of what had been suggested.

That the mind in sleep had a time-clock was already established; as Frances Power Cobbe had noted, people had often found that if they told themselves when they went to bed to wake up at a certain time the following morning, they could rely upon waking up at that time. The researchers now found that suggestion under hypnosis could perform a similar task, at a greatly increased time-span. In 1886, Joseph Delboeuf, Professor of Philosophy at the University of Liège, conducted a series of trials designed to discover how far ahead, and how accurately, his subjects—his two sisters, and his domestic servants – would carry out trivial tasks. Some were jokey – pulling his son's ear, or the cook's nose; some were simply unusual – harnessing a donkey; going to bed at a different hour. The time difference between the making of the suggestions and the undertaking of the tasks ranged from 350 to 3300 minutes. Out of fourteen trials, six were completely successful: the tasks were carried out at the right time or the impulse to do them was recognized and reported. In the others, the tasks were carried out, or the impulse reported, but not quite at the suggested time.

The servant girls, poorly educated, were hardly able to tell the time from a clock, and lacked the ability consciously to make the calculations which would have told them when to conform to the suggestion. Impressed by Delboeuf's findings, Milne Bramwell began to experiment with a patient who agreed to co-operate in a series of tests which he would give her in the course of her treatment. They were on the same lines as Delboeuf's, except that 'Miss D.' had only to make a cross and, before looking at a clock, write down the time she believed it to be. Not merely did she always get the time right when she made the cross, at intervals from between 320 minutes and 7200 minutes after the suggestion had been made under hypnosis; on one occasion she actually knew, when a friend of hers told her what the time was, that the friend's watch was four minutes late.

How did she do it? Bramwell asked her, while she was under hypnosis. She insisted that no calculation was involved, while she was in her trance; and she did not remember the suggestion, between awakening and the carrying out of the instructions. When the correct time came, she simply felt an impulse to take a pencil and make the cross and write down the time, before finding what the time was.

The researchers also found it was relatively easy to induce hallucinations by suggestion under hypnosis. The subject could be made to 'see' somebody who was not present. Occasionally, hallucination could even be induced by post-hypnotic suggestion. In one experiment, Bernheim suggested to a former army sergeant while he was in a deep trance that he should visit Liébeault's house on a given date. There, he would meet the President of the Republic, who would give him a medal and a pension. Although the sergeant remembered nothing of the instruction when he awoke, 63 days later he went to Liébeault's, entered the library, saluted, and made a short speech of thanks. Asked by Liébeault who was being thanked, the sergeant replied 'The President'.

Although light-hearted experiments of this kind were common, they sometimes had a serious purpose; and one of the results was temporarily to rescue hallucination from the odium into which it had fallen. 'The cocksure commonsense of the years from 1660 to 1850, or so,' the Scots polymath Andrew Lang recalled, 'regarded everyone who had experience of an hallucination as a dupe, a lunatic or a liar.' Even the great William Osler could argue, at a conference in 1892, that nobody who saw a hallucinatory figure could be said to be in good health; the mere fact of having a hallucination implied some serious organic disturbance. Under hypnosis, however, it proved easy to induce harmless hallucinations. If a subject was told that the bird embroidered on her apron was real, and she was asked to look at it, Alfred Binet noted, 'as soon as the words are uttered she sees the bird, she feels it in her hands, and she sometimes even hears it sing.' Similarly if a hypnotized subject was told *not* to see somebody in the room, he would see everybody in the room except that person.

Insensibility to pain in the trance state, whether in hysteria or hypnosis, was also frequently confirmed; and Delboeuf took the knowledge of the mind's power over pain to a further stage in what later came to be called a 'controlled' experiment. He branded a hypnotized subject on both arms with a red hot iron bar, suggesting that she would feel pain only in her left arm. She duly complained of pain only in her left arm. He then bandaged the arms. The next day, when the bandages were removed, the left arm was blistered. Her right arm, though it showed the outline of the iron bar, was not. Suggestion had not merely relieved the pain; it had inhibited the development of the symptoms which normally would have followed the burn.

Even more surprising was the discovery that suggestion under hypnosis could *create* the symptoms of burns, or other injuries. Within the medical profession the dogma was that the mind could not exercise causal effects on the body of any kind, in ways which could be held responsible for organic disorders. Hack Tuke had done his best to show his colleagues that this was nonsense in his *Illustrations of the Influence of the Mind upon the Body in Health and Disease* (1872), citing examples from cases (and incidentally coining the term 'psychosomatic'), but without appreciable effect. Fifteen years later his contentions were confirmed by Pierre Janet, investigating hysterics in Le Havre. With one of them, he was able to produce under hypnosis what to all appearances was a real burn, with a blister, and eventually a scab. The marks sometimes even reflected the hysteric's assumption of what they would probably be like. When Janet put an imaginary mustard plaster on her stomach, he was puzzled to observe that the reddening which followed there was in the form of a rectangle with the corners cut off. She explained that this was the size and the shape of the mustard plasters she was accustomed to using.

These discoveries not only had significant implications for medicine; they helped to account for the appearance of stigmata on saintly men and women. A great many cases had been collected and preserved, as they formed part of the case for beatification and canonization; but to the positivists, they were simply another example of the way in which such evidence was faked.

In 1855, Alfred Maury – himself a positivist, but anxious to find rational explanations for well-attested accounts, rather than simply reject them – had put in a plea that cases of stigmata, when they occurred, should be studied by doctors as 'the most striking proof of the influence of the imagination upon the body'. This influence, he suggested, was 'truly a miracle, in the sense of being one of those marvellous effects of thought, whose secrets escape and whose extent confounds us'. Doubtless imposture and exaggeration had occurred in connection with accounts of the stigmata, but he thought that the symptoms were usually an extension of the process, often noticed by doctors, by which dreams of injuries were sometimes followed by inflammation and ulceration; 'just so with visionaries, under the power of the imagination; by the concentration of the attention, the blood is directed to the place where they fancy they are affected.' And in *La Magie et l'Astrologie*, five years later, he suggested that the stigmata were symptoms of hysteria, brought on by the rigours of monastic life.

The stigmata were still too closely linked with superstition in the minds of positivists for this to have an influence. When in the 1860s the stigmata of the young Louise Lateau aroused international curiosity, public opinion quickly hardened into two opposing camps: either they were miraculous, or they were fraudulent. However, in the 1870s M. H. Biggs, a doctor practising in San Francisco, became irritated at the way in which the Church exploited a Catholic girl who every Friday went into a trance and displayed the stigmata. It must be a form of auto-mesmerism, Biggs decided; he began to experiment with hypnosis; and in 1870 he found a subject who, after a course of post-hypnotic suggestion, could produce a pink patch on her chest in the shape of a cross. Henceforth it was possible for manifestations of the stigmata to be attributed to hysteria; there was no further need to assume when they occurred that they could only be explained by fraud.

In much the same way, one of the mysteries of the great witch-hunt era was resolved. In 1603 a physician, Edward Jorden, had written a treatise on witchcraft, following a trial in which he had appeared for the defence. The woman had been found guilty, which had prompted him to point out that its symptoms were often the same as hysteria: convulsions, and the loss of sensation in parts of the body. If pricking with pins caused no pain, therefore, it could be symptomatic of hysteria. Hysterics, the Salpêtrière team found nearly three hundred years later, often had 'islets', patches of skin which could be pinched or pricked without the subjects realizing what was being done to them, though if they were pinched or pricked in places only a couple of centimetres away, they would react. Here, then, lay an explanation for the 'witch-marks' which the witch-hunters had probed for, and so often found.

At the same time, the researchers found indications of the kind the mesmerists had often reported, showing how some sorcerers might have won their reputation. Where Scoresby had used hypnosis to render his subjects incapable of moving from their chairs, Binet and his Salpêtrière colleagues experimented with the traditional technique of the sorcerer, drawing a 'magic circle' around a hypnotized subject, and informing her she could not leave. No great depth of trance, they had found, was necessary for the subject to find it impossible to move from the encircled zone.

Nor was it necessary for the process of hypnotic induction to be repeated on each occasion. Whatever technique was used – mesmeric passes; making the subject stare at a bright object; or simply suggesting 'sleep . . .' – when a subject had been hypnotized for the first time, she could often be put back into a trance by some simple signal, a word, a gesture, or a sound. At the Salpêtrière they used a gong, whose effects were instantaneous. On one occasion it trapped a hysteric in the act of pilfering; her hand was transfixed into catalepsy, half-way into a drawer.

Dual personality

The mistake that Charcot had made in assuming that only hysterics could be hypnotized turned out to have been understandable. The similarity between the symptoms which could be induced in suscep-tible subjects under mesmerism or hypnotism, and those long associ-ated with hysteria, were too close to be attributed to chance. And at this point it was realized that they both sometimes displayed the symptoms of what had been regarded as diabolic possession, but could now be attributed to the existence in an individual of more than one personality.

The prejudice against mesmerism had meant that the evidence about dual personality had been ignored; but Eugène Azam, professor of surgery at the Bordeaux Medical School, followed it up out of curiosity when he was giving a woman patient mesmeric treatment for headaches. Ordinarily 'Felida X.' was dull and taciturn; but on recovering from a headache she was transformed into somebody who was jolly, vivacious and intelligent. In this state, she knew all about her life in the other one; but the dull Felida knew nothing of the bright one. When the dull one came to consult Azam about an enlarged abdomen, the bright one broke through and told him *she* knew she was pregnant – as she turned out to be. She married her lover, and for a time took over.

Later the dull one started coming back. She was gloomy, disliked her husband, and was often ill, though never seriously – whereas the bright one was healthy. Eventually, however, the appearances of the dull one became infrequent; the bright one re-established herself as the dominant personality, though with occasional embarrassing episodes when the dull one would re-emerge. As she remembered nothing that had been arranged she would find herself at, say, a funeral with no idea why she was there, or who was being buried.

When Azam's detailed case history of 'Felida', *Hypnotisme, Double Conscience*, was published in 1887, it was with an introduction by Charcot. It established dual personality as a neurological curiosity; but its implications were far wider. Accounts of the symptoms of both hysteria and neurosis strongly suggested the existence not just of split personalities on the Felida model, but also of potential personalities hidden in the unconscious unless they were released. And the similarity of the symptoms further suggested that what had been regarded as attacks of hysteria should be considered as a trance condition – as they were at the Salpêtrière. For Bernheim to equate trance with sleep, and to attribute its associated phenomena simply to suggestion, was an over-simplification.

The existence of the close links between the two forms of trance, spontaneous and induced, was soon confirmed by William James, investigating the case of Ansel Bourne. In his childhood Bourne had been subject to fits of an epileptic type, and to periods of deep depression, until what had been diagnosed as sunstroke led to a religious conversion, and he decided to spend the rest of his life as an evangelist preaching in Rhode Island. One morning he disappeared, and two months passed before he awoke to find himself keeping a small shop in Norristown, Pennsylvania, under the name of A. J. Brown. None of his customers, apparently, had noticed anything strange about him, and apparently he had had no previous experience of the work and could not remember how he had done it. His case was investigated by James and Richard Hodgson on behalf of the American Society for Psychical Research. They found that under hypnosis they could get Bourne to remember details of his life as A. J. Brown, though he had no recollection of them in his resumed life as Bourne.

The most thorough of the investigations of dual personality in this period was carried out by Pierre Janet. His uncle Paul had established himself as France's leading philosopher; and he appears both to have inspired and helped his nephew to make his name in psychology, then branching out from philosophy into its own academic discipline. After passing through the Ecole Normale Supérieure with distinction, Pierre Janet became a professor at Le Havre when he was still only 21; and there he met J. H. Gibert, a doctor who had been using hypnotism to treat hysteric patients. Among these was 'Mme B.'

When in her normal state, Janet found, 'this poor peasant woman is a serious and rather sad person, calm and slow, very mild with everyone, and extremely timid; to look at her one would never suspect the personage which she contains.' The moment she was hypnotized, a striking change came over her, even over her features. 'She is gay, noisy, restless, sometimes insupportably so.' She even showed a taste for irony and cruel jokes, particularly about people who, out of curiosity, had come to watch when she was hypnotized. Her eyes were closed, but she seemed to develop greater acuteness in her other senses; when the visitors left, 'she gives a word-portrait of them, apes their manners, claims to know their little ridiculous aspects and passions, and for each invents a romance.'

'Léontine', as this secondary personality insisted she should be called, despised 'Léonie' (Mme B.): 'She is too stupid!' Janet for a while was puzzled because she acknowledged her children, but not her husband, who she insisted was Léonie's, not hers. Later, however, Janet found that hypnosis had been used in her first *accouchement*; in later ones she had slipped into the hypnotic state without assistance.

When Léonie was put into an even deeper trance, a third personality appeared. 'Léonie 3', as Janet labelled her, was serious and grave, reflecting both Léonie – 'a good but rather stupid woman, and not me!' – and 'Léontine' – 'How can you see anything of me in that crazy creature?' In other words, there could be multiple personalities, each sufficiently well established in the subliminal mind to be identifiable when it surfaced. But this was rare. Far commoner were the dual personalities who only came to light under hypnosis. Commonest of all were the temporary personalities which, by this time, stage hypnotists – following Hansen's example – had learned to induce in volunteers, getting them to behave in silly and humiliating ways to amuse spectators.

Audiences were often so startled to watch an ordinarily respectable citizen demeaning himself in this way that they were tempted to think he must, for some inscrutable reason, be in league with the hypnotist. Numerous experiments now revealed that the ostensible powers of suggestion under hypnosis were genuine – as even Braid, who had originally been sceptical, had eventually recognized. A committee set up by the newly-formed Society for Psychical Research in 1882 – just before hypnosis completed its transition to scientific acceptance – watched while a subject ate a tallow candle under the impression it was sponge cake, and 'drank a spoonful of vinegar with much relish, believing it to be cream'. They found, too, that his reactions were what were to be expected if the substance was what he *thought* it was – not to the actual substance. 'When white pepper was blown up his nostrils, he being under the impression it was mignonette, not only did he not sneeze, but his eyes did not water to any appreciable extent.'

Directing the committee's research, Edmund Gurney found that sometimes the subject would be dimly aware that what he was doing was silly. Afterwards 'he perfectly recalls not only the actions but the feelings of passive acquiescence, or of surprise, or of repugnance, with which he performed them.' Sometimes he would explain to Gurney that 'he felt as if he had *two selves*, one of which was looking on at the involuntary performances of the other, without thinking it worth while to interfere.' One subject who had been terrified by a 'ghost' while under hypnosis 'described himself as having in a sort of way known that it was only a handkerchief which the operator was flourishing, and yet was unable to resist the ghostly terror'. The explanation, Gurney decided, must be that hypnosis could develop a kind of double consciousness, in which one personality was aware of the behaviour of the other – much as Surin had found when he was possessed at Loudun.

In a paper on 'Duplex Personality' in 1889, Thomas Barkworth put the case for recognizing this ability of the mind. He himself had a form of trance which, he had found, enabled him to do two things at once: one consciously, the other without conscious control. When he had to add up columns of figures, 'by degrees it is possible to cease thinking of the figures, and by constant practice to be able to add with great ability and correctness while the mind is far away and busily engaged on other subjects.' This could not be explained away by instinct and habit. It required 'a succession of independent mental actions which are not foreseen'.

Barkworth put musical improvisation in the same category. 'Not only is no decision formed as to the theme or its modifications, but there is not even any knowledge of what the next bar will be,' he had come to realize. 'Thus I have constantly sat and listened to my own improvisations with as much interest, and with no more knowledge of, what was coming than another listener would have, and this statement applies not only to melody or theme, but to the most elaborate modulations of harmony' – effected, he insisted, independently of a theoretical knowledge of music.

The hypnotherapists

By the close of the 1880s it seemed as if the new psychology, derived from the discoveries about the unconscious mind from research into hysteria and hypnotism, was securely establishing itself, particularly in medicine. Max Dessoir's *Bibliography of Modern Hypnotism* (1888) contained over 800 titles, and this without including newspaper or magazine articles; an International Congress on Hypnotism in Paris the following year attracted a distinguished range of physicians, psychiatrists and psychologists. Most of the speakers were followers of Bernheim; and it was by this time obvious that it was his methods, based on Liébeault's, that had come into medical practice all over the Continent, and to a lesser extent in Britain and the United States.

The extent to which hypnotherapy had caught on was to be shown in two surveys published in 1889, both entitled *Hypnotisme*, one by Professor Albert Moll of Berlin; the other by Professor Auguste Forel of Zurich. Both provided useful surveys of the research, and its findings.

Forel had made his reputation as a young man first by studying ants, on which he established himself as the world's leading authority, and then as a brain anatomist, which led to his appointment to the Chair of Psychiatry at Zurich University. At this stage, as Ellenberger has recalled, Forel was a positivist. But in his capacity as supervisor of a Zurich mental hospital his confidence in positivism was shaken in much the same way as Bernheim's had been; in Forel's case, by the discovery that a local quack was treating alcoholics successfully, which Forel himself was unable to do. When asked why, the quack told him, 'I am an abstainer, while you are not.' Forel took the pledge, and decided to visit Bernheim at Nancy; impressed by what he witnessed there, he set up an out-patient department in Zurich providing hypnotherapy. Considering his involvement, his book was written with admirable detachment – as, indeed, was Moll's.

Hypnosis, Moll showed, was still chiefly used in the treatment of illnesses which had been diagnosed as hysterical, functional or nervous; but this constituted a wide range, including sleep-walking, agoraphobia and writer's cramp. Forel's list was even more comprehensive, including arthritis, digestive problems, sea-sickness, erratic menstruation and impotence, as well as addiction to alcohol. The best results of all had been obtained by obstetricians, using it to ease childbirth, and by physicians who had to handle children, who found it invaluable in banishing afflictions ranging from nail-biting to bed-wetting.

There was general agreement that hypnotherapy had no obvious contra-indications, and was remarkably safe. Simply getting rid of the symptoms, admittedly, could be risky unless the cause was found; but this applied equally to the stock alternative form of treatment, drugs. In extensive reading of the literature, Bramwell found only one instance where death had been reported following hypnotherapy, and the *British Medical Journal* had conceded that this had been coincidental.

Hypnosis was also being extensively used in this period to treat disorders which the medical profession classed as organic, but which Hack Tuke maintained could be psychosomatic. For the profession to draw an arbitrary line between organic and functional was foolish, John F. Woods pointed out in a paper in 1898. Heart disease, for example, might be organic, yet it might become dangerous only if patients worked themselves into a nervous state. Hypnotism, he had found in hundreds of cases, would exercise a calming influence, remove pain, and at the same time reduce the risk of a heart attack.

If the successful treatment of minor disorders had been the only accomplishment to their credit, the researchers into hysteria and hypnosis could have congratulated themselves on a notable

achievement. Yet what they had discovered was of much greater significance, as Binet noted; the indications of two or more forms of
consciousness were of profound importance, he claimed, for the future
of psychology and psychiatry. In the past, doctors had assumed the
existence of a single consciousness; symptoms suggesting there were
others had been taken to be indications of mental disorder. Now, it
had to be recognized that even when the symptoms appeared to be
pathological, they might be calling for the recognition of the needs of
a secondary self.

This discovery could be exploited for social purposes, as well as in
the treatment of ill-health, as one of the Salpêtrière physicians showed
in 1884. 'Jeanne S.', a patient there, was a hard case, a criminal
lunatic, filthy in her habits, violent, a chronic thief. Dr August Voisin
had taken charge of her. At first he had used hypnosis simply to
suggest she should undertake simple chores, such as cleaning her
room. When this worked, he used it to persuade her to give up her
criminal ways. Two years later, he was able to report that she had a
job as a nurse in another Paris hospital, where her conduct was
irreproachable.

The researchers, too, though chiefly interested in the therapeutic
potential of hypnotism, were often impressed by the emergence of
secondary personalities which revealed that, in their trance condition,
patients could display talents they ordinarily showed no signs
of possessing. 'A splendid dramatic performance!', Janet noted of
one subject; no actress could have done it 'with such perfection'.
One of Bramwell's subjects ordinarily could play only a few dance
tunes from the music – and only when she was sure no stranger
was listening; 'when hypnotized, blindfolded and deprived of her
music, she played the same tunes much more brilliantly in a room
full of people.'

A striking testimonial to the effect of suggestion under hypnosis was
to come from Rachmaninov. After the humiliating failure of his first
symphony, he fell into a deep depression which lasted for over a year
until, early in 1900, he began to have daily sessions with a doctor who
hypnotized him and repeated, over and over again, 'You will begin to
write your concerto . . . you will begin to write your concerto . . . you
will work with great facility . . . the concerto will be of excellent
quality.' About the 'excellence' of the second piano concerto, dedicated
to the hypnotist, critics have differed; but it was unquestionably a
resounding success when it was first performed.

THE RESURGENCE OF THE 'HIGHER PHENOMENA'

Phantasms

Even before the century ended, however, it had become clear that all was not well with the new psychology. The split between the Nancy and Salpêtrière schools never entirely healed, and a new division had arisen which was also to be damaging. In the early 1880s, reports which suggested that researchers were again encountering the 'higher phenomena' of mesmerism could be shrugged off by those psychologists who did not care to credit them; they might well be accounted for, the general impression was, by trance effects, hyperacuity of the senses and hallucination, along Carpenter's lines. But this was to prove over-sanguine.

The chief responsibility lay with the Society for Psychical Research, and in particular with Frederic Myers. His main concern was not with the evidence which hypnosis experiments were giving for the subliminal mind, or even for the subliminal self, but with the implications – as the full title of his book, when it came out posthumously, was to show: *Human Personality and its Survival of Bodily Death*. How far, he wondered, did the evidence which the research was providing point to survival?

As he was later to recall, he had realized from the start of his own research in the 1870s that the issues 'must be fought out in a way more thorough than the champions either of religion or of materialism had yet suggested'. The champions of religion had relied on faith, propped up by metaphysics; the materialists had relied on *a priori* assumptions, in particular the existence of unbreakable laws of nature. If there was anything discoverable about the Unseen World, Myers had decided, 'it must be discovered by no analysis of tradition, and by no manipulation of metaphysics, but simply by experiment and observation – simply by the application to phenomena within us and around of precisely the same methods of deliberate, dispassionate and exact inquiry which have built up our actual knowledge of the world which we can touch and see.'

Although Myers was clearly anxious to approach the research in a scientific spirit, for most scientists this involved a contradiction. It was manifestly *un*scientific, they assumed, to investigate 'that wretched superstition of animal magnetism, table-turning and spiritualism, and mesmerism and clairvoyance and spirit-rapping', as Sir William Thomson, the future Lord Kelvin, described it in a lecture in 1883. He himself might be a 'seer', as his biographer was to describe him, in the sense that his ideas constantly sprang into his mind through no conscious process of cogitation; but he totally rejected the explanation that clairvoyance could be responsible. Clairvoyance was 'the result of bad observation mostly; somewhat mixed up, however, with the effects of wilful imposture'.

A crucial division existed between what could, and what could not, be accepted by the scientific Establishment. A subliminal self capable of presenting information to consciousness through the mechanism of intuition, or even of hallucination, was permissible; a subliminal self capable of picking up information through second sight was not. And the first major project launched by the Society for Psychical Research after its foundation in 1882 brushed aside that barrier. It was conducted mainly by Edmund Gurney, joint Honorary Secretary with Myers to the Society; and its findings were published in 1886 in *Phantasms of the Living*, with an introduction by Myers.

Seldom can a book have had a more misleading title – as, in effect, Myers admitted. The book was concerned with 'all classes of case where there is reason to suppose that the mind of one human being has affected the mind of another,' he explained, 'by other means than through the recognized channels of sense'. The first of the two volumes was largely devoted to the evidence, anecdotal and experimental, for the reality of telepathy. As part of the evidence came from accounts of apparitions – hallucinations of people, sent in to the Society – and as they had shown that the hallucinations were not necessarily visual, it had been decided to use 'phantasm'. When something appears to a percipient as real, Gurney explained, whether visually or through a voice, yet nothing is actually there, 'what is presented is a phantasm'. And whatever form the experience might take, 'there can be no mistake as to its generic characteristics; it is a *hallucination*'.

Apart from the use of 'phantasm', which did not catch on, this was a promising beginning. Rationalists would find it easier to accept the existence of apparitions if they could be shown to be hallucinations. As it happened, a well-known rationalist had just prepared this ground. In his *Inquiry into the Human Faculty* (1883), Francis Galton described how, much to his surprise, he had found that 'a notable proportion of sane persons have had not only visions', but actual hallucinations, 'of sight, sound or other sense, at one or more periods of their lives'. A

distinguished authoress had told him that one of the principal characters in her novels had appeared through a door, and come up to her:
'It was about the size of a large doll, and it disappeared as suddenly
as it came.' Another lady, the daughter of an eminent musician, often
'heard' her absent father playing.

Galton had made his name as one of Britain's foremost scientists.
His discovery of how commonly hallucinations were experienced could
have formed the basis, alongside Gurney's research, for a valuable
reappraisal of the significance of ghost stories and folklore – fairies,
goblins and so on. But this was not Gurney's aim. 'It is naturally only
with one particular species of the great family of hallucinations – the
veridical species, which psychology has so far not recognized – that I
am directly concerned.'

Gurney was working on the assumption that psychologists *had* now
recognized that apparitions were hallucinations, and that they were
not necessarily pathological, as they were being safely conjured up
under hypnosis. He wanted to persuade doubting psychologists that,
in some cases, the hallucinations carried messages which could later
be confirmed as telepathic, or as corresponding to something which
had actually occurred; as illustrated in a case investigated in 1887 by
Richard Hodgson, who vouched for the integrity of the informant and
the other witnesses. 'Mr F. G.', a Bostonian, recalled how ten years
earlier he had been sitting in a hotel room when he turned round and
saw his sister who had died ten years before. 'So sure was I that it was
she, that I sprang forward in delight, calling her by name, and, as I did
so, the apparition instantly vanished.' When he told the story to his
parents, on his return home, his father was inclined to pooh-pooh it; but
when he added that he had distinctly seen what looked like a scratch on
his sister's face, his mother fainted. She herself had unintentionally
made the scratch, she explained when she recovered, while laying out
the body. Shocked, she had obliterated all sign of it with powder, and
nobody else had known about it. For the mother it was an indication
that 'she would rejoin her daughter in another world'.

Veridical hallucinations, Gurney's research showed, were not
merely far more common than had been realized; they had been
experienced by people who were in good health at the time, and who
did not regard themselves as in any way psychic. What most impressed
both Myers and Gurney was the quality of the accounts that flowed
in. They were not presented as ghost stories in the usual melodramatic
sense. Few of them came from people who had been carried away by

'silly supernatural notions'. They were related as though what had been seen or heard had been a natural but inexplicable occurrence – usually an isolated one, once in a lifetime.

That so many people contributed accounts, trusting the Society to preserve their anonymity, was largely due to the esteem in which so many of the Society's leading figures were held. The President, Henry Sidgwick, had been a Fellow of Trinity College, Cambridge, until his doubts over the doctrines of the Church of England, which Fellows were formally called upon to accept, had prompted his resignation – a proof of the integrity which had increased the respect he had won as a philosopher. The Society's vice-presidents included Arthur Balfour, the future Prime Minister; the eminent physicist Lord Rayleigh; and – to calm possible Protestant worries – a pillar of the Church of England, the Bishop of Ripon. Amongst the honorary members were Wallace, Ruskin, Tennyson and Gladstone, who in 1885 claimed that what the Society had begun to do was, in his opinion, 'the most important work in the world'. Among the corresponding members were Bernheim, Hartmann, James, Janet, Liébeault, Richet, and Taine.

People who ordinarily would have thrown Gurney's request into the waste-paper basket, or hesitated to give him their experiences, felt it was safe to reply. What also impressed Gurney and Myers was the consistency of the evidence for veridical hallucinations. Although it was impossible to rule out coincidence in any individual case, the fact there were so many examples, so well-attested, gave 'the strength of a faggot' to the collection.

The faggot was made all the stronger by the pains Gurney took to check the positive replies – over seven hundred of them, out of a total of 5700. Myers and Frank Podmore investigated some cases, but it was Gurney who did the bulk of the work. Alan Gauld, preparing *The Founders of Psychical Research* (1968), realized how prodigious Gurney's efforts were: 'in the course of following up cases he would not infrequently write fifty or sixty letters in one day, and in his own hand', and these were often accompanied by personal visits, so that he could assure himself that the sources were to be trusted. There must be no hint of exaggeration, Gurney told William James in a letter describing his task in categorizing and analysing the results; 'I feel that every sentence written on these matters ought absolutely to *reek* with candour.' And as Andrew Lang was to confirm, Gurney was not a man to be easily imposed upon.

Gurney's untimely death in 1888 did not stop the flow of accounts of veridical apparitions coming in to the Society; and following the first International Congress of Experimental Psychology in 1889, it was decided to mount a fresh inquiry which would be more carefully designed to allay psychologists' fears about getting mixed up with occultism. The initial aim would be to provide a statistical base by asking a single question: 'Have you ever, when believing yourself to be completely awake, had a vivid impression of seeing or being touched by a living being or inanimate object, or of hearing a voice; which impression, so far as you could discover, was not due to any external cause?' Those who answered 'yes' or 'perhaps' were invited to provide further details about themselves and their experiences.

The Census of Hallucinations, as it came to be known, was taken between 1889 and 1892. About 17,000 replies were collected and tabulated. Those which were in the affirmative were checked, and if doubt arose, transferred to the negative category. The remainder, those which were considered to provide reasonably convincing evidence for a hallucinatory experience, constituted about one in ten of the sample.

The report of the Census committee showed that its members were under no illusions that the sample was representative of the adult population. For a start, nine out of ten of those who replied came from the professional classes, or were of an equivalent educational standard. Nevertheless the findings were of considerable interest – as they remain because, as the report predicted, the labour involved in the collection, and the care that had to be taken in vetting the replies, made it 'very doubtful whether an equally extensive inquiry into the characteristics and conditions of this class of phenomena will ever again be under-taken'.

One of the most clear-cut of the findings was that hallucinations were most likely to occur when the percipient was in a state of light trance – in repose, in a reverie, or waking after sleep. The report drew attention to the way in which this linked up with the research into hallucinations induced under hypnosis. Myers related them both to the way in which ideas generated below the threshold of consciousness could break through to 'flash upon the inward eye', and to the way in which '*the inspirations of genius* – Raphael's San Sisto is the classical instance – may present themselves in hallucinatory vividness to the astonished artist.'

This report, too, should have helped to bring about a reassessment of hallucinations. It strongly suggested that they were not necessarily pathological, and that they could be regarded as an evolutionary device to enable the subliminal mind to break through into consciousness for a variety of purposes, some valuable. But again, the main interest of the Society lay in the hallucinations which fell into the veridical category; and the proportion which did was too high, relative to those which had no veridical component, to be explained by chance. The explanation, Gurney had suggested, might be that an endangered or dying person might transmit a cry for attention or sympathy which could be picked up by percipients telepathically, hallucinations forcing the message through to them. Myers thought another explanation possible: that the people who experienced crisis apparitions did so through their psychic antennae – sweeping around much as radar receivers were later to do – picking up the distress signal.

Either way, though, a sixth sense must be involved. This was in line with Myers's hopes, because evidence for the existence of communications which did not come through the five senses in the ordinary way helped to undermine the hitherto secure foundations of materialism. Veridical hallucinations could not be accounted for in the light of the laws of nature, as they stood. If their existence could now be no longer rejected, well, the 'laws' would have to be revised.

It was a forlorn hope. True, as Myers could reasonably claim, until Gurney had begun his inquiry 'this wide, important subject was treated, even in serious textbooks, in a superficial and perfunctory way.' Largely owing to Gurney's efforts, the facile assumption that hallucinations were pathological, and other confusions, were being cleared away. But Gurney's admission that 'naturally' he was primarily concerned with veridical hallucinations meant that the evidence would be unacceptable. It would entail having to accept telepathy. Few scientists were prepared for acceptance because, if it existed, their materialist edifice would appear to have been built on sand.

Mediumship

Even more damaging for the prospect of trance remaining in the mainstream of psychological research were its links with spiritualism. Several of the founder members of the Society for Psychical Research were spiritualists, and although most of them soon broke away, unhappy at the brusque manner in which some of the Society's researchers decided, after brief scrutiny, that certain well-known mediums were frauds, a few of the investigations came up with evidence that a medium enjoyed psychic powers.

There was no clear-cut distinction between 'mediums' and 'psychics', but most mediums credited their psychic powers to a spirit 'control'. The process resembled hysterical possession: the medium would go into a trance – sometimes spontaneously, sometimes brought on deliberately – and 'a more or less complete substitution of personality', Myers believed, would occur. The 'control' would take over, talking through the medium in a voice different from hers, either giving information for sitters, or introducing 'communicators' who would provide it. The 'controls' might or might not identify themselves as having lived on earth; the communicators usually presented themselves as deceased friends or relatives of sitters, conjured back from the spirit world to provide reassurance that there is no death, only a transition.

The investigators of mediums had three main objectives; to ascertain whether any of the information provided by 'controls' or 'communicators' in fact came *ab extra*, from some outside source, other than the medium's conscious knowledge; and, if so, to decide whether it was obtained telepathically, or from the spirit world.

On the first of these issues the investigators were left in no doubt. Whether the information provided by mediums in their trances was coherent or nonsensical, valid or spurious, and whatever its nature, the state itself was as real as the mesmeric or hypnotic trance.

Mediumship had, in fact, occasionally been reported by the early mesmerists. Deleuze had noted that what one of his *somnambules* said appeared to be dictated by an inner voice, so that in his trances he regarded himself as 'an organ of a superior intelligence'; an intelligence so superior that some witnesses were persuaded that it came from the spirits. The trances of mediums, too, often had effects similar to those encountered by hypnotists. The 'control', in some cases, appeared to be considerably more intelligent than the medium, as in the case of some secondary personalities emerging under hypnosis. 'I have heard an uneducated barman, when in a state of trance, maintain a dialogue with a party of philosophers on "Reason and Foreknowledge, Will and Fate" and hold his own against them,' the barrister Edward Cox recalled in *What Am I?* (1875). 'A quarter of an hour afterwards, when released from the trance, he was unable to answer the simplest query on a philosophical subject.'

It was possible, too, to suggest to a medium that she would not feel anything when she was pinched, or that something hot applied to her skin was cold, and she would react according to the suggestion as if under hypnosis. Although the medium 'speaks, writes or acts as if animated by a foreign person,' Willliam James asserted, 'mediumistic possession in all its grades seems to form a perfectly natural special type of alternate personality, and the susceptibility to it in some form is by no means an uncommon gift, in persons who have no other obvious nervous anomaly.'

On the second issue, whether or not any of the information reached mediums *ab extra*, a careful investigation was made by one of the leading psychologists of the time in Europe, the Swiss Theodore Flournoy – 'my revered and fatherly friend', as Jung was to describe him.

In 'Hélène Smith', Flournoy had the advantage of conducting research with somebody whom he felt sure he could trust. She was not a professional medium. Having discovered her powers, she had developed them mainly out of interest, and for the benefit of her circle of friends, 'many of whom', Flournoy knew, 'were persons of much intelligence and cultivation'. In her everyday life he found her 'in every respect a capable and altogether admirable person', who successfully occupied a responsible position in a large business firm; and he could think of no possible reason why she would want to risk her reputation by deceiving him or anyone else.

If she *had* wished to deceive him, the information with which she provided him in her trances would surely have been of a different character. As it was, her trance communications came through 'Leopold', her 'control', who thought of himself as Cagliostro in the spirit. He took charge of the proceedings, explaining that Hélène had had two previous lives, one as the wife of a Hindu prince 500 years before; the other as Queen Marie Antoinette. In addition, 'Leopold' introduced Flournoy and the rest of the group to a 'communicator' who claimed to be living in the spirit on Mars.

The Martian language, Flournoy was able to work out, turned out to be a curious kind of old French. Some of Marie Antoinette's statements were easily checked, and found to be unreliable. The sources of all the information, Flournoy decided, must be a secondary personality which Hélène had carried with her since her childhood, and whose vivid imagination provided her, in her trances, with 'dream fictions, fantastic subdivisions of her hypnoid consciousness'.

Flournoy related his findings in *From India to the Planet Mars* (1900). Sceptical though they had left him, he had to admit that the Indian episode was not easy to account for. He had taken the trouble to check the details, and found to his surprise that many of them were accurate. The only way she could have learned about some of them was in an old and extremely rare book, which she certainly could not have read as a child, and which she would hardly have forgotten if she had sought it out and read it as an adult.

The idea that she could have read it, Flournoy had to admit, was difficult to accept. Yet, 'though there is scarcely any choice, extravagance for extravagance, I still prefer the hypothesis which only invokes natural possibilities to that which appeals to occult causes'; he settled for 'cryptomnesia', the reappearance of a forgotten memory, as the most likely explanation.

Nevertheless it was important, he believed, for psychologists to keep an open mind on the issue of psychic phenomena. To refuse to investigate them on the *a priori* ground that they were contrary to the laws of nature, he was to claim, was 'the philosophy of the ostrich' – the philosophy to which the opponents of Galileo had clung when they refused to look through his telescope for fear that what they saw would prove him right. It was a philosophy which, he feared, 'is still entertained by many brains petrified by intemperate reading of works of popularized science, and by unintelligent attendance at university lectures, the two great intellectual dangers of our time'.

With this contention William James, who was to enjoy as warm a relationship with Flournoy as the great distances which usually separated them permitted, would have been in entire agreement. He, too, had been persuaded to investigate a medium – a Boston housewife, Leonore Piper. Her 'control' in her trance was 'Dr Phinuit', who claimed he had been in practice in France earlier in the century. This was easy to check, and 'Phinuit' was revealed as a liar.

The information he provided, however, was also easy to check; and it was often uncomfortably accurate about matters which, James recalled, Mrs Piper could not have known about. It was difficult, he admitted in his report to the SPR in London in 1890, to present the evidence as he would have wished, because so much of it concerned domestic intimacies. She could describe the contents of letters which he and his wife had just received, for example, and make caustic and entertaining comments on the writers. There was no way, he had satisfied himself, in which she could have tapped his correspondence;

and no way in which she could have provided a flow of information about intimate domestic affairs in the James household. There was nothing spectacular about the information she provided; it was the accumulation of trivia that had finally convinced him. 'Taking everything I know of Mrs Piper into account, the result is to make me feel as certain as I am of any personal fact in the world that she knows things in her trances which she cannot possibly have heard in her waking state.'

Richard Hodgson remained unconvinced. He was seconded to the American Society for Psychical Research when it was threatened with collapse, for lack of active researchers – illness, travel and other labours, including the Giffard Lectures which were to be published as *The Varieties of Religious Experience*, were to combine to reduce James's activity, though he continued to write on psychic phenomena until his death. Hodgson, who had made a formidable reputation as a debunker of claims for psychic powers, had decided that Mrs Piper must be employing agents; so he countered by setting up his own spy system to catch them. There turned out to be no agents; Hodgson was eventually reluctantly convinced that her psychic powers were genuine.

In England Oliver Lodge, already one of the country's leading physicists, reached the same conclusion. He had one doubt: might not Mrs Piper be picking up clues and feeding back information which was in the sitter's mind, and which by word or gesture he might have unwittingly disclosed? In his own case, he was able to satisfy himself that he could not have prompted her in this way; some of the information she gave him about his family was unknown to him, but was confirmed by an uncle later.

The third issue, whether the psychically-obtained information came through some form of telepathy or from the spirits, remained unresolved. Flournoy's research made it difficult for psychical researchers to accept uncritically that 'communicators' really were the people they claimed to be, even when they came through the medium in astonishingly lifelike ways. The 'control' was often even harder to take seriously. In America, James observed, he was 'either a grotesque, slangy and flippant personage ("Indian" controls, calling the ladies "squaws", the men "braves", the house a "wigwam", etc. etc., are excessively common)', or 'he abounds in a curiously vague optimistic philosophy-and-water, in which phrases about spirit, harmony, beauty, law, progression, development etc., keep recurring.' The odd thing about this, James felt, was that so many people who had not been exposed to spiritualism behaved *like* spiritualist mediums, if they happened to become entranced. It was as if a single author was responsible for the scripts, 'no matter by whom they are uttered'.

In spite of the respect that most psychologists had for James, they found it hard to reconcile his trust in Mrs Piper with his revelations about the eccentric mechanics of mediumship. A few, investigating for themselves, became convinced spiritualists. Others accepted that mediums in their trances had psychic powers, but decided that the 'controls' and 'communicators' were fantasies. The majority declined to investigate the issue, treating the published results of his work with Mrs Piper as an embarrassment, best ignored.

Eusapia Palladino

There was an even greater source of embarrassment to those psychologists who wanted to keep their research scientifically respectable: the reports of investigations of 'physical mediums', as they were described. Usually they, too, had 'controls' who could sometimes conjure up 'communicators'; but they were distinguished from mental mediums by their ability to produce telekinetic phenomena – action at a distance without the use of physical force, ranging from moving small objects to the production of ectoplasmic materializations.

The leading exponent of positivism on the Continent at the time was Cesare Lombroso, Professor of Forensic Medicine and Psychiatry at the University of Turin, founder of the science of criminology, and a caustic critic of spiritism (the term ordinarily used in Europe) and everything associated with it. The recollection of the resistance his own ideas had encountered, however, led him to ask light-heartedly in an article he wrote in 1888 whether he and his friends 'who laugh at spiritism, are not also in error?' In an open letter to him in a newspaper Ercole Chiaia, who had been a dashing cavalry officer under Garibaldi, issued a challenge to Lombroso to find whether or not he was in error by investigating what a Neapolitan girl, Eusapia Palladino, could do in her trances.

Lombroso at first ignored the challenge; but three years later, as he admired Chiaia, he decided that he was being cowardly. He found that Eusapia – thirty years old and illiterate – could produce the phenomena Chiaia had described. She could move objects at a distance, levitate tables, and cause musical instruments to play (though not as well as they had been reported as playing for Home). 'I am quite ashamed and grieved at having opposed with so much tenacity the possibility of the so-called spiritist facts,' he wrote after the demonstrations had finally convinced him that trickery (though she used it, incompetently, if she could get away with it) could not account for what he had witnessed. 'I say the facts, because I am still opposed to the theory. But the facts exist, and I boast of being a slave to facts.'

In the 1890s several teams of scientists investigated Eusapia; and the only one of the reports to assert that all her phenomena were faked was largely the work of Richard Hodgson, who had claimed she was a fraud even before he had tested her. His 1895 report, though, was based on the assumption that if she was allowed to cheat by using physical force, and took advantage of the opportunity, this sufficed to discredit her; a view which was rejected by Lombroso and other investigators, notably Charles Richet, who pointed out that the only results which could be regarded as acceptable were those from tests where her hands and feet had been securely controlled.

It had taken a number of such trials before Richet allowed himself to be convinced. He had assumed that the phenomena of physical mediumship could only be produced by conjuring tricks. Then he had witnessed Eusapia in action for himself, and agreed with Lombroso that they were facts. But 'after we have witnessed such facts, everything concurs to make us doubt them', he told the SPR in his Presidential Address in 1899. 'May it not all have been an illusion? May I not have been monstrously deceived?' In such investigations, results that seem so convincing at the time become ever more uncertain, 'and we end up by letting ourselves be persuaded that we have been the victims of a trick.'

Myers also had wavered. Initially impressed by trials which he attended with Richet, which left both of them certain that the movement of objects at a distance from Eusapia could only be accounted for by telekinesis, he allowed himself to be overruled by Hodgson, and to agree that trickery must be the explanation. Yet when, in 1898, Richet persuaded him to resume tests with Eusapia, he realized that this had been a mistake. Flournoy, too, was present, hoping to detect how Eusapia had duped so many scientists. He was unnerved to feel himself being slapped and pinched – one of the ways in which Eusapia teased sceptics – when he was sitting some distance away from her. 'Unless we are to distrust the combined testimony of sight, hearing and touch,' he felt bound to admit, he had been left with no room for doubt. The only alternative was that Richet, Lombroso and the other scientists were all 'wicked aiders and abetters of the farce enacted by this charming Neapolitan lady'.

Myers did his best to offer a plausible explanation. Automatism, he suggested, could manifest itself in a number of ways, which he defined roughly in order of increasing specialization. There were urges – promptings of a vague kind which compelled people to do something or go somewhere, without knowing why. There were subliminal motor impulses of the kind which produced automatic writing and drawing. And there were telekinetic effects. Some unexplained force must be responsible for automatic writing, or the movements of a planchette; might it not also be able 'to emit some energy which can visibly move ponderable objects not actually in contact with my flesh?'

Why, if a telekinetic power existed, was it so seldom encountered? One possibility, Myers thought, was that it was a product of the evolution of the subliminal self, which the parallel development of the conscious self had prevented from establishing itself – the same process that prevented one of Janet's patients, Célestine, from displaying in tests on a dynamometer the strength which in trances enabled her to lift heavy chairs with ease. It could further be surmised that certain people in the hysteric condition might exert telekinetic force without necessarily being aware of what they were doing. If so, this would help to explain the phenomena traditionally associated with poltergeist-type hauntings reported throughout history from all parts of the world; objects flying or floating around as if propelled or carried by human hands.

Motor automatism

There were two other types of motor automatism – as Myers called the physical activities initiated in the subliminal mind, to distinguish them from sensory automatism, such as hallucinations – which were to reinforce the split in the research movement: automatic writing, and dowsing.

Janet and some of the Salpêtrière group had been intrigued to find that some of their subjects while under hypnosis could compose and write coherent and legible sentences, sometimes passages of prose, without being aware that they were writing, let alone *what* they were writing. This was welcome additional evidence for the existence of secondary personalities, emerging during trance; because often, as Myers put it, they would 'write down matter quite alien from the first personality's character'. But Myers went on to add, from his own experience, that this might be matter 'which the first personality never knew'. His main interest was in finding cases where the information in the writing could only be accounted for by assuming the existence of some psychic channel (as the leading practitioner in Britain, the Revd Stainton Moses, assumed; his communications through automatic writing came, he believed, from some high-minded spirits). But to the Salpêtrière group, and to most of those who followed Bernheim, secondary personality seemed the more reasonable explanation.

Liébeault was an exception. Initially he had scoffed at spiritism, but in 1868 one of his patients in Nancy whom he was treating with hypnosis, 'Mlle B.', found she could produce information through automatic writing. 'I have seen her rapidly writing page after page of what she called "messages" – and all in well-chosen language and with no erasures – while at the same time she maintained conversation with people near her,' he wrote in reply to a question from Gurney. She had no knowledge of what she was writing, and 'believed a spirit must be responsible'.

Liébeault assumed that the messages came from a secondary personality; but one day 'she felt a kind of need, an impulse which prompted her to write – it was what she called a *trance*', and she rushed off at once to her large notebook. The message on this occasion was that a former school friend of hers, Marguerite, was dead. Liébeault, consulted, agreed that they should find out whether Marguerite had in fact died. 'Mlle B.' wrote to a teacher at the school in Coblenz where Marguerite was working, taking care not to indicate the reason for the letter. In her reply, the teacher enclosed an announcement of Marguerite's death. It had occurred, Liébeault realized, about the time of 'Mlle B.'s' trance.

An episode of this kind did not need to be credited to spirits; but it was hard to attribute it to chance, and for Gurney, it was a significant addition to his collection of veridical trance communications. But the Salpêtrière researchers – and in this context most of the Nancy school, too – preferred to keep automatism free from either spiritist or psychic connections.

In one respect, some fresh evidence about dowsing was even more of an embarrassment to them. It was quite a familiar spectacle in most countries in the form of water divining, though a few practitioners claimed also to be able to detect seams of ore or buried metal. 'At first sight few subjects appear to be so unworthy of serious notice and so utterly beneath scientific investigation,' the physicist William Barrett commented in 1897, 'as that of the divining rod.' The rod itself was usually a forked hazel twig; and the sight of a dowser walking over fields holding it out in front of him, waiting for it to twitch when he was over water, provoked incredulity; 'the widespread belief of a sceptical public is, of course, that the dowser intentionally twists the forked twig when he fancies he has reached the subject of his quest.'

At this time Professor of Physics at the Royal College of Science in Dublin, Barrett had trained under Tyndall at the Royal Institution where the atmosphere, as he was to recall, was 'entirely opposed to any belief in psychical phenomena'. But while he was there he went to stay with a friend in Ireland; and he witnessed experiments with a child who, when hypnotized, demonstrated 'community of sensation'. Incredulous, Barrett took careful precautions to ensure that she could not detect what he was doing; but if he tasted sugar, she would enjoy its sweetness, and if he held his hand over a candle, she would cry out that her hand was burnt.

In 1876, Barrett tried to persuade the British Association for the Advancement of Science that communication of this nature should be investigated; but without success. He was instrumental, six years later, in bringing together the men who were to be the founders of the Society for Psychical Research, and in 1884 performed the same service for the American Society. His investigation into dowsing, which followed, remains the most comprehensive survey of the historical, anecdotal and experimental evidence that has ever been undertaken.

In order to operate successfully, Barrett found, a dowser needed to 'set' himself, 'rendering himself as far as possible oblivious to the ordinary stream of sense impressions, making his mind as passive, as effortless, and as much a *tabula rasa* as he can'. In other words, he had to enter a trance condition, light in some cases, deep in others, to allow the mechanism which was responsible for the rod's twitches to come through: 'the good dowser is largely an automatist.'

Barrett noted another significant feature of dowsing. Some of its practitioners felt symptoms of the kind associated with hysteria. One had found that whenever he walked over an underground stream he was seized with violent trembling; his son, also a dowser, actually had convulsions. Others reported that dowsing gave them a feeling of malaise. It was yet another example of the similarities which the various manifestations of trance displayed, pointing to a common evolutionary source.

Barrett's research, as he admitted, left several questions unanswered. Were the rod's twitches generated by hyperacuity of one or other of the senses – smell, perhaps – over water, or by clairvoyance? Were they the result of unconscious muscular actions, or telekinesis? If telekinetic, what was the source of the influence?

It was not difficult, Barrett found, for dowsers to demonstrate the twitches were genuine. People who did not themselves feel them usually felt them immediately, and often powerfully, the moment a dowser put his hand on their arms. Many initially sceptical individuals, too, were prepared to testify to their reality, as Edward Tylor did in *Nature* in 1883. When he had tried dowsing for himself, he had felt the twitches (though only when he allowed his attention to wander from what he was doing) and the rod had moved 'in a way so lifelike that an uneducated person might well suppose the movement to be spontaneous'.

On the second issue, Barrett would have been prepared to accept clairvoyance. But he drew the line on telekinesis: 'few will dispute the proposition', he claimed in his report, 'that the motion of the forked twig is due to unconscious muscular action.' If he had established that hyperacuity of the senses, operating through unconscious muscular action, could account for the movements of the rod, dowsing might have eased into acceptance as another form of motor automatism – and a very useful one. But there were snags. Some dowsers who had impressive records in the field came badly out of tests: their 'will' to do well was usually blamed. And many dowsers flatly disagreed with Barrett over the role of unconscious muscular action. The rod, they claimed, twisted around in the hands in ways which could not be thus accounted for. If they tried to stop it, it would break.

A correspondent, Edward T. Bennett, pointed out in the Society's *Journal* that in nine of the descriptions which Barrett himself had cited, what the dowser or the witness of the dowsing had written made 'a strong *prima facie* case in support of the view that some of the movements of the "divining rod" may be attributable to a cause of quite another kind than muscular action.' The same force which had been

encountered in table-turning, Bennett suggested, was a possible alternative. But this, Barrett feared, could only mean that spirits would be
held responsible, which he thought ridiculous. When a Theosophist,
A. P. Sinnett, had suggested that the dowsing force came through
some 'elemental' agency, a view with which Wallace had agreed,
it was also too much for Oliver Lodge; did Wallace really believe
that 'a deceased person comes and bobs the stick?' Barrett agreed:
even if 'these creatures' might 'swarm in the neighbourhood of
mediums and dowsers', this was not an explanation likely to convince
scientists.

This was unfair. Sinnett and Wallace were not arguing that spirits
hung around dowsers to activate the divining rods; they were simply
claiming that it was a spirit-derived force working through the medium
of the dowser. Yet the possibility that the force could not be accounted
for by unconscious muscular action – leaving aside whether spirits
might be responsible – was enough to ensure that the problem of the
source of the rod's movements would not be investigated by orthodox
scientists who wanted to keep their reputations untinged by association
with psychical research.

The tests at Le Havre

The experiments by which Barrett had satisfied himself that 'community of sensation' could be demonstrated by certain individuals
under hypnosis were easy to set up, provided that suitable subjects
were available. Several such trials were conducted in the 1880s: the
results varied, but in some of them reasonably clear-cut evidence was
provided of the ability of a few subjects to pick up mental as well as
spoken suggestions. On one occasion Liébeault and a colleague mentally formulated an instruction to a subject that when she awoke,
she would find her black hat had been transformed into a red one.
She burst out laughing when she came out of her trance, accusing
them of playing a trick on her by substituting somebody else's red hat
for hers; and she had to be put back into the trance to convince
her that the hat would again be black when she awoke the second
time.

In England, Henry Sidgwick and his wife Eleanor conducted several
trials of a more elaborate nature which gave positive results; but the
experiments along these lines which had the most unexpected outcome

were those conducted at Le Havre in 1885 with 'Léonie', reported in a paper read at a meeting of Charcot's *Société de Psychologie Physiologique* – its name reflecting his determination to keep the new psychology firmly within the bounds of physiology.

It was read by Paul Janet, on behalf of his nephew Pierre. Pierre's friendship with Dr Gibert, and their common interest in his hysteric patient Léonie, had led them to conduct tests on her for 'community of sensation'. Over a period of three weeks they were able to satisfy themselves that in her trances Léonie not only could pick up and execute suggestions which they made mentally, but that she could also be hypnotized from a distance, without her being aware of what was happening.

So startling was this revelation that it was received with incredulity – though in silence, perhaps out of a respect for Paul Janet – apart from some general observations by Charcot. Julian Ochorowicz, who was in the audience, was disturbed. He would have to go to Le Havre and find out for himself, he decided, what the facts were.

As assistant professor of Philosophy and Psychology at the University of Lemberg, Ochorowicz had devoted much of his time to research into hypnosis, initially in the hope of exposing it as spurious; later, when he became convinced the trance condition was genuine, to seeking explanations for the phenomena along Carpenter's lines. From time to time he would encounter what appeared to be instances of the 'higher phenomena', which hyperacuity could not account for; but always he was able to rationalize them away. Even when he found that one of his subjects could read his thoughts, and feel pain in the part of her body where he was pinching himself, he refused to accept the possibility that her power was psychic. The explanation, he decided, must be some form of localized vibrations set up through the brain.

This theory, he realized, might pass muster when hypnotist and subject were close to each other; but 'vibrations' could hardly account for the transference of thought and feeling at the distances Janet had reported, and it was this that he was anxious to test at Le Havre – as were several other researchers, including Richet and Myers. Together with Gibert and Janet, they began a series of trials in the winter of 1886. They were chiefly designed to find whether Léonie could be hypnotized from Gibert's house while she was somewhere else, usually in another building a kilometre away where her reactions could be watched; and also to ensure that neither Gibert nor Janet nor any of the other investigators could disclose to her, consciously or unconsciously, the times when she would be 'endormed'. Out of 25 tests, 18 were completely and four partially successful.

For Myers, these results were naturally a welcome confirmation of his belief in telepathy. Nevertheless he realised that its implications were going to irritate many researchers. They would have difficulty in casting doubt on the reliability of the findings; the fact that the experiments had not been easy to run, each involving the co-operation of a number of people, had at least ensured that there would be several witnesses, some of whom would have been relieved had the results been negative. But if the reality of an induced trance at a distance was conceded, it showed that hypnotism could not be simply a matter of soothing subjects into sleep and putting verbal suggestions to them, as the Nancy school were insisting.

For Ochorowicz, the Havre experience was traumatic. 'I left Havre with a profound emotion,' he recalled in his *Mental Suggestion*, published the following year. 'I had at last witnessed the extraordinary phenomenon of action at a distance, which upsets all the opinions currently received.' He checked his notes again and again, in case he could have been deceived; he did his best to think of some explanation along the lines of hyperacuity; but in the end he was forced to accept that action at a distance was a reality. He was to spend much of the rest of his career in careful research into psychic phenomena with, among others, Eusapia Palladino.

For Pierre Janet the results were also disturbing, but for a different reason. The incredulous reaction to his paper on Léonie and, still more, the publicity his work attracted in the newspapers, worried him. He began to study the history of hypnotism, reaching back into mesmerism, finding much that he and Gibert had observed with Léonie had been commonplace, and that some of the reported higher phenomena had been even more startling. This was not a safe branch of psychology, he decided. In *L'Automatisme Psychologique* (1889) he described in detail some of the work which he and Gibert had done with Léonie, but omitted the experiments with hypnosis at a distance. From this time on, according to René Sudre, he had a 'holy terror' of psychic phenomena. In his writings he either avoided the subject or, in dealing with mediumship, attributed it to 'a certain moral state which can develop into hysteria or madness'.

THE TIDE TURNS

Scepticism

In retrospect the Le Havre affair was decisive. From 1886, the division between those researchers who were prepared to accept the reality of psychic phenomena and those who were not began to develop into a fissure. The experiments with hypnosis at a distance were published in the *Revue Philosophique* for August 1886; but by the end of the decade the psychical researchers felt compelled to bring out their own *Annales des Sciences Psychiques*, if they wanted space for their contributions.

Reports of the higher phenomena continued to flow in to the *Annales*, including one from M. Gibotteau, a Paris doctor, following up the Havre tests. He had a patient, Berthe, who like Léonie came from Normandy, and who could be hypnotized at a distance. Berthe, though, claimed she could reciprocate; and Giboteau found that she could exercise a disturbing effect on him. He would suddenly, for no reason, feel frightened, or have some minor hallucination. 'This is one of Berthe's tricks!' he would tell himself, and by discreet questioning when he next saw her, he would extract from her the admission that she had 'willed' him to be frightened at the time.

Berthe also showed Gibotteau how she could make people fall down. She would stroll up behind somebody in the street, mimicking his walk and, as she put it, 'charging' him, which Gibotteau took to be her way of describing how she was able to hypnotize people without their knowledge. 'Then, you must visualize a string stretched across the road a few steps in front of him,' she explained. 'At the moment when he reaches the imaginary string, you yourself intentionally stumble, and the poor man is forced to tumble down.'

Inevitably, accounts of this nature alarmed those doctors and psychologists who wanted to ensure that their work with hypnosis secured scientific and academic recognition. This was a regression, surely, to the superstitious belief in sorcery? For a time, efforts continued to explain such phenomena in Carpenter's terms; one distinguished physician, according to Myers, actually claimed that Léonie must be picking up, 'by auditory hyperesthesia', every change in the condition of Dr Gibert's arteries 'caused by his concentrating himself upon the act of *willing*'. But when it had to be stretched so far, hyperacuity of the senses became an embarrassment.

Yet it was difficult for those psychologists who knew and sometimes had worked alongside the psychical researchers to dismiss their evidence out of hand. Their reports showed that they had been just as methodical as those who had concentrated on the straightforward trance effects; and it was difficult to claim that men of the standing of Sidgwick, Gurney, Myers, Lodge, Richet, Liébeault, James, Lombroso, Flournoy and Ochorowicz were to be trusted only so long as no psychic component could be detected in their offerings, and must be regarded as sadly gullible if they reported telepathy or telekinesis. Some doubters took what seemed the safest course and looked the other way. Others agreed that the evidence was strong but continued 'subjectively', as Moll admitted, to resent it.

Some members of the younger generation, however, claimed the right to ridicule the evidence for psychic phenomena on *a priori* grounds. The appointment in 1892 of Hugo Muensterberg to take on James's work at Harvard, while James took a sabbatical, foreshadowed the future. Muensterberg, from the University of Freiburg, was by training and temperament in the mechanistic tradition, concentrating on laboratory research – which was why James, who disliked laboratory work, chose him. They might have formed a balanced team, but James's ill-health and frequent absences when he was travelling left Muensterberg to his own devices, and he soon initiated a course on natural science 'with special reference to the theories of evolution and materialism'.

Physiology, Muensterberg taught, is the fundamental basis of psychology. 'The psychologist insists that every perception of occurrences outside one's own body,' he claimed in an article in the *Atlantic* in 1899, 'and every influence beyond one's own organism, must be intermediated by an uninterrupted chain of physical circumstances.' In case readers might not grasp what this implied, he went on to denounce mediums and mediumship: 'the facts, as they are claimed, do not exist, and never will exist.' It was to be the first shot in a protracted campaign to discredit psychical research, which was to sadden James. 'Buffoon article', he noted in his diary in 1910 a few months before he died, after reading one of Muensterberg's more eccentric outbursts in the *Metropolitan Magazine*.

Joseph Jastrow, Professor of Psychology at the University of Wisconsin, was even more outspoken in his denunciations of psychical research. Belief in telepathy, he claimed in 1901, was part of a complex conglomerate of symptoms, including hysteria, conscious and unconscious fraud, chance, collusion and hallucination, compounded by 'defective observation, falsification of memory, forgetfulness of details, bias and prepossession, suggestion from others, lack of training and of a proper investigative temperament'. All these, he explained, conspired to 'invalidate and confuse the records of what is supposed to have been observed.'

Hypnotism in decline

Because so much of the research which had resuscitated the higher phenomena had been conducted with the help of hypnotized subjects, research into hypnosis itself gradually became suspect by association. At the same time, the heady enthusiasm of the 1880s evaporated as doctors, in particular, began to find that hypnotherapy was not so simple a matter as Bernheim and others had maintained.

Some patients, they complained, could not be hypnotized. Estimates of the proportion of patients who could be hypnotized varied considerably; and it was coming to be realized that they were misleading, because the process depended not only on the patients but also on the hypnotist, and on the degree of rapport he was able to establish in individual cases. Failures might occur because the hypnotist was impatient, or distracted by some worry, or for some reason had lost confidence. Remarking on this, Ochorowicz observed that he himself had been lucky. When he began to experiment with hypnotism, he found he could easily make subjects insensible to pain, and his confidence transmitted itself to his patients; but 'operators who have begun with a mishap always therefore have a fear which influences their subjects.' However skilled and experienced, too, a hypnotist might find that he could not induce certain symptoms. Even Deleuze had had to admit that he could not induce areas of anaesthesia in his patients, though less accomplished mesmerists found that relatively easy.

Hypnotherapists were also disturbed by the controversy which arose over whether patients could be hypnotized if they did not wish to be. Bernheim insisted that nobody could be hypnotized against his will. Ochorowicz replied that on the contrary, he had hypnotized subjects who had resisted 'with all their might'.

The explanation for the contradiction, Ochorowicz suggested, was that resistance could arise at two levels, conscious and unconscious;

and somebody who was consciously resisting might be unconsciously submitting. This, however, only brought up another problem: could the submissive unconscious be persuaded to take some action which the conscious individual would baulk at? Could a hypnotist use suggestion under hypnosis to seduce a patient? Could he persuade a subject, through post-hypnotic suggestion, to commit a murder?

There was no evading these issues, as occasionally they came up in court cases which inevitably attracted massive publicity. In one, a swindler hypnotized a baroness, persuaded her that he wanted to marry her, and succeeded in having sexual intercourse with her. Another culminated in a trial for murder in Paris in 1890. Gabrielle Bompard confessed that she had lured a bailiff to her apartment so that she and her lover, Michel Eyraud, could kill him and take his money; Eyraud, she claimed, had hypnotized her into collaborating in the deed. Eyraud was sentenced to death; Gabrielle was given a twenty-year prison sentence.

The case, hypnotists argued, could not be regarded as settling the issue whether or not hypnotism could be held responsible. Bompard was a woman of low moral character, who might have responded to her lover's suggestion without the need for hypnotic reinforcement. Efforts were consequently made to set up tests which would show whether subjects could be persuaded to do under hypnosis what they would not do in their ordinary conscious state. They gave confusing results. Researchers found there was little difficulty in persuading hypnotized subjects to act – or try to act – in ways they would have considered irresponsible, or criminal, in their ordinary lives. Yet they might refuse to do something they would willingly do when conscious.

Gurney had a subject who was willing to carry out all manner of suggestions under hypnosis, but drew the line at being asked to carry a telegram. He had been a telegraph boy, and had loathed the job. Even when told that delivery was a matter of life and death, and offered £20 to take it, he still refused. Yet his conscious self would have delivered the telegram unhesitatingly for the money.

This aspect of hypnosis intrigued Myers. From his extensive study of the evidence he had found that it often seemed easier to induce subjects to commit 'some great imaginary crime – say, to put arsenic in his aunt's tea' – than to perform 'some trifling act of manifest *inconvenience* – such as taking off his boots in public'. The most plausible explanation for this paradox had been that 'somewhere within him there must be a shrewd suspicion that the supposed arsenic really came out of the sugar basin.' The hypnotized subject might be persuaded to behave in anti-social or immoral ways, but only because he was aware – as Moll had asserted – that it was play-acting.

Even if an unscrupulous hypnotist could in theory seduce a patient, Forel pointed out, or get her to commit a crime, the risk was small because every experienced hypnotist knew that patients sometimes suddenly and unexpectedly woke up, if asked to behave in some way they did not approve of. There was also the possibility that even if the patient had no recollection of what had happened, the memory of it could return when she was hypnotized by somebody else. That there was so little evidence of hypnotism's use for illicit purposes, Forel assumed, was due to recognition of the risks involved.

Trilby

These controversies inevitably had an effect on the public. The widespread impression at the time, largely due to the reports of the court cases and of experiments such as those at Le Havre, was that hypnotism worked through the transmission of a 'fluence' – a term then in common colloquial use – transmitted by the hypnotist to control the subjects. This was understandable, as the trance effects which members of the public were most likely to see were those induced by stage hypnotists, using the routines which Hansen had developed, hypnotizing volunteers from the audience and getting them to behave as if totally under the hypnotist's control, doing whatever he told them to do, however humiliating.

Most hypnotists agreed that this was misleading. These subjects had voluntarily relinquished their willpower. The public, however, was fed by stories implicating hypnotists in dubious practices; and in particular by George Du Maurier's novel *Trilby*, published in 1895. Trilby was ordinarily a wretchedly bad singer; but when hypnotized by the sinister Svengali, she sang with a voice 'immense in its softness, richness, freshness', making her a music-hall favourite until, at the start of a concert, Svengali died of apoplexy. She then began to sing in her old way, 'as she used to sing it in the Quartier Latin – the most lamentably grotesque performance'.

Trilby was a best-seller, and although the extent of its influence cannot be assessed, it may well have been considerable. Certainly

'Svengali' has remained in colloquial use to this day, to describe somebody who has contrived deliberately and unscrupulously to dominate another individual. The portrait must have helped to confirm readers in the assumption that hypnotists did, or at least could, use a 'fluence' to achieve such control.

The story as Du Maurier wrote it was not, in fact, entirely remote from reality. Carpenter had described the case of a factory girl whose musical ability was ordinarily limited, but who was able under hypnosis to provide an imitation of Jenny Lind's singing; she followed 'the Swedish Nightingale's songs, in different languages, so instantaneously and correctly, as to both words and music, that it was difficult to distinguish the two voices'. To test her powers, Jenny Lind herself had 'extemporized a long and elaborate chromatic exercise, which the girl imitated with no less precision'. The impression Du Maurier left, however, was not of Trilby's talent being uncovered and allowed to flourish, but of Svengali's wicked exploitation of a lovely innocent girl.

The BMA investigation

To the medical profession, the growing public mistrust of hypnotism came as a relief. Such was Charcot's reputation that the initial reaction of neurologists had been to accept his theory, and to try to describe hysteria and hystero-epilepsy in plausible-sounding physiological terms, 'functional disturbance of the cerebral cortex', 'dislocation of the nerve fibres', or 'cerebral anaemia'. Soon, however, the researchers at the Salpêtrière and elsewhere were making the organic hypothesis untenable, for example through inducing 'glove anaethesia' by suggestion under hypnosis. The subject's hand would be anaesthetized as if all feeling had been cut off by a wrist bracelet; 'he seems to attend to the popular conception of the organ,' Janet commented, rather than to its actual anatomy.

Doctors who did not use hypnosis, or who tried it and found it unsatisfactory, were also made uneasy by the realization that if there were hypnotists who could treat the commoner disorders as easily and successfully as the Nancy school were claiming, there was nothing to stop people with no medical qualifications from joining in. By 1886 members of the Academy of Medicine in Paris were campaigning for a law to be passed forbidding the practice of hypnotism except by members of the medical profession. This could be expected to happen whenever there was a conflict between mystics and scientists, James sarcastically commented, if the mystics were proved right. The facts of animal magnetism had been 'dismissed as a pack of lies by academic medical science the world over' until a non-mystical theory was found for them. Then, 'they were admitted to be so excessively and dangerously common that special penal laws, forsooth, must be passed to keep all persons unequipped with medical diplomas from taking part in their production.'

The British Medical Association was slow to realize the threat which hypnotherapy posed to conventional medical practice; but in 1891 it despatched a team to Nancy 'to investigate the nature of the phenomena of hypnotism, its value as a therapeutic agent, and the propriety of using it'. Of its eleven members only one, Hack Tuke, could have been accounted a committed supporter of hypnotherapy, on the strength of his *Illustrations of the Influence of the Mind upon the Body in Health and Disease* (1870). Yet its members unanimously reported that the induced trance state was genuine; and that it was frequently effective 'in relieving pain, procuring sleep and alleviating many functional ailments'.

Even though the pill was sugared by the predictable recommendation that the practice of hypnotism for therapeutic purposes should be confined to qualified doctors, the BMA Council could not bring itself to accept the committee's embarrassing verdict. Its members were asked to have another look. They did. In 1893 they presented the same report, with an appendix giving further evidence of the value of hypnosis in treatment. When the new report was handed in, a motion that it should 'lie on the table' was rejected in favour of another, that the report should merely be 'received' – thereby exonerating members of the Council from the need to read it.

The Establishment's worry about medically unqualified practitioners using hypnotherapy soon evaporated. The main reason, in all probability, was the impact of Pasteur's discoveries about germs, and Koch's identification of the tubercle bacillus. Might not almost all types of illness be carried by germs? With the discovery of more varieties, and then of viruses – some accounting even for the common cold – the idea that suggestion under hypnosis could deal effectively with them began to sound foolish.

Sigmund Freud

In retrospect, the doctor who was ultimately most responsible for the downgrading of both hysteria and hypnosis was, paradoxically, Freud, who owed to them his start in psychiatry.

Freud had fallen under Charcot's spell while working for him as a student at the Salpêtrière in the winter of 1885. 'Charcot', he wrote at the time, 'is both one of the greatest of physicians and a man whose common sense is of the order of genius' – a view which he saw no reason to modify when he came to write Charcot's obituary in 1893.

Freud was impressed by the use Charcot made of hypnosis to establish hysteria as a neurological disorder. Some members of the profession in Austria had continued to regard it and treat it as a disorder of the uterus, and consequently experienced only by women; by demonstrating conclusively that it was 'the result of specific ideas holding sway in the brain of the patient', and disclosing the mechanism by which the ideas had their effect, Freud contended, Charcot had rescued hysteria from the ill-repute into which it had fallen, restoring dignity to the disorder. Gradually 'the sneering attitude which the hysteric could reckon on meeting when she told her story' was given up; it was realized that she was not a malingerer, 'since Charcot had thrown the whole weight of his authority on the side of the reality and objectivity of hysterical phenomena'.

At the time, Freud still firmly believed that there must be a physio-logical basis for all mental processes, which would eventually lead to a fusion between neurology and psychology. To have established hysteria's reality and objectivity was, for him, a necessary preliminary stage in making the correlation. As his biographer Ernest Jones pointed out, it was not until almost the close of the century that he gave up the idea. In giving it up, he was admitting that he had been mistaken, too. Hysteria could not be brought into the neurological fold.

Freud also abandoned hypnotism. Initially he had been impressed by its potential, not only from witnessing its use in Paris, but by a remarkable case history in Vienna. In the 1870s he had become friendly with Joseph Breuer, who had a reputation as a scientist as well as being a well-known physician. In 1880, Breuer had begun to treat 'Anna O.' – the 21-year-old Bertha Pappenheim, who at the time was suffering not only from a range of stock hysterical symptoms, such as paralyses and constricted throat, but also from personality changes: sometimes she would behave normally, sometimes it was as if she had turned into a naughty child. Chance led Breuer to a discovery: when Bertha was recalling the first occasion on which she had suffered from one of her symptoms – inability to swallow – she gave vent to the disgust she had felt on that occasion, but had then been too inhibited to express. They both grasped that this might be significant; Breuer encouraged her to try to get rid of her other symptoms by the 'talking cure'; and hypnosis, he found, was a help in eliciting episodes which she had forgotten.

Breuer's account greatly intrigued Freud. When he tried out the talking cure on his own patients, putting them under hypnosis, he satisfied himself that it worked. Soon, however, he decided it was unnecessary to put them into a trance. By his own account, hypnosis appeared to block the process by which they were able to uncover their repressed traumas; but it has often been surmised that he was an indifferent hypnotist – not surprisingly, as the psycho-analytic method he adopted involved distancing himself in various ways from the patient, such as sitting out of the patient's line of vision. His disciples followed his advice and example, and Freudian psycho-therapy parted company from hypnotherapy.

At the same time, Freud was advancing a concept of hysteria which undermined Charcot's. By 1895 Freud had decided that all the neuroses had a common source, the subject's sexual life, 'whether they lie in a disorder of his contemporary sexual life, or in important events in his past life'. The significance of this proposition, he wrote the following year, was that it elevated sexual influences 'to the rank of specific causes'; and in a lecture he gave on the aetiology of hysteria he elaborated on his theory that psychoneuroses were caused by sexual abuse in childhood, and would develop into hysteria in those cases where the child had suffered the abuse passively.

As Freud became the dominant force in one of the main channels which psychotherapy was to take, it was his theory of the unconscious that came to be accepted within that catchment area. Disciples who broke away were not inclined to return to the starting-point, and reassess the role of trance. His influence, too, was to extend far beyond the narrow circle of his followers. Even psychiatrists who thought themselves immune from his influence often accepted his 'Id', or something very similar, as their model of the unconscious.

Much of what had been regarded and loosely diagnosed as hysteria now came to be attributed to psychoneurosis; and psychiatrists who were not Freudians reclassified some of the rest as schizophrenia, or as manic depression. Mimetic hysteria reverted to its former unpopularity, partly because it could be so difficult to identify when the mimicry of the organic disorder was effective, partly because it so often resembled malingering that the doctor was inclined to tell patients to stop wasting his time.

Even somnambulism found itself in this malingering category. In Thomas Stedman's monumental encyclopaedia *Twentieth Century Practice* (1897), the recommended prescription for the treatment of somnambulism in children was revealing. If a young lad walked in his sleep he should be told if he did it again he would get 'a sound raw-hiding'. Should this fail, the chastisement should be immediately applied, and 'occasion for a second recourse to it will seldom be demanded.'

A vision fades

In *Principles of Psychotherapy* (1925), Janet was to recall the remarkable, if melancholy, course which psychology had taken during the last quarter of the nineteenth century. He gave the initial credit to Richet who, as a young doctor, had risked his reputation to establish that the hypnotic state was genuine. This had not been given the recognition it deserved because his solid contribution had soon been overshadowed by those of the two rival schools, the Salpêtrière and Nancy, 'less interesting from the scientific point of view,' in Janet's opinion, 'but much more conspicuous'.

The impact had been astonishing. From being denounced as part superstition, part fraud, hypnotism – and in particular hypnotherapy – had blossomed. It had its own reviews, as well as a place in the neurological, medical and philosophical journals. 'In a great number of medical theses, and in numerous volumes, were set forth the stories of innumerable cures of all possible maladies by simply verbal suggestion.' Then, quite suddenly, hypnotherapy had virtually disappeared. 'In medical circles hypnotism was not denied. No one doubted the acknowledged power of suggestion. It was simply no longer discussed.'

Janet might have added that nothing quite like this had ever happened before in history. On innumerable occasions fashions in science and medicine had burgeoned, only to fade away when it was realized that their promise had been illusory. In connection with hypnosis the opposite had occurred. Not merely had the existence of induced trance been established, along with several of the side-effects, such as insensibility to pain and post-hypnotic suggestibility; the research had liberated psychology from its earlier status in the academic world, as a despised offshoot of philosophy, giving it instead independence and a firm base, in the form of university chairs, on which to make a fresh start in the sciences, away from the arts.

The researchers, too, had helped to account for much that had been baffling in history, in connection with shamanism, witchcraft and hagiography. And for all the problems that confronted hypno-therapists, there could be no disputing that suggestion under hypnosis was capable of dealing with a wide range of common symptoms more effectively, quickly and cheaply than the alternative drugs – most of which, at that time, were, at best, placebos.

A potentially healthy infant, therefore, had been thrown out, largely because of dirt in the bath water – trance's occult associations. And the main responsibility lay with the development of a secular religion: materialism, derived from positivism, permeated with reductionism in science and organicism in medicine; soon to spawn other 'isms' – neo-Darwinism in biology, behaviourism in psychology, logical positivism in philosophy.

FREDERIC MYERS

Human Personality

There was to be one notable casualty as a result of the collapse of interest in trance: Frederic Myers. He bore some of the responsibility for it because of his determination to pursue psychical, if necessary at the expense of psychological, research; and, unlike James, he made no attempt to keep the two separate. As a result his legacy, the posthumous *Human Personality* – 'a first immature attempt', he admitted, 'to bring some kind of order out of a chaotic collection of strange and apparently disparate observations', was soon forgotten, in spite of a perceptive testimonial from James.

Myers 'took a lot of scattered phenomena, some of them recognized as reputable, others outlawed from science, or treated as isolated curiosities', James wrote in his obituary notice of Myers in 1901. 'He made series of them, filled in the transitions by delicate hypotheses or analogies, and bound them together in a system by his bold inclusive conception of the Subliminal Self, so that no one can now touch one part of the fabric without finding the rest entangled with it.' Myers had at least established the phenomena as deserving of research; 'I cannot but account this as a great service rendered to Psychology.'

James initially had reservations about the subliminal self, as he had about theories of the unconscious in general. He liked to keep his own theorizing within the limits of consciousness. Nevertheless he conceded that psychologists for half a century accepted that there were unconscious mental processes. What they had attempted to do was provide a map of the region. Myers had confronted this problem; which, after him, 'it will be impossible to ignore'.

The map which Myers had constructed with his hypothesis of a subliminal self was derived from the research into trance. It had been accepted that instinct and habit played a considerable part in people's lives, and it had been possible to ignore the evidence for a subliminal self by giving them the responsibility for 'unconscious cerebration'. What people do through instinct or habit, however, can be recalled. Instinct and habit could not account for the fact that if it were suggested to a hypnotized subject that he would take a certain course of action at a certain time, after he had come out of his trance, he would take the action without knowing why he was taking it.

But was it correct to say that the subject had 'come out of' his trance? Myers was the first to emphasize that trance can not be considered a condition wholly distinct from normal consciousness. 'I hold that in all the varied trances, lethargies, sleep-walking states, to which hypnotism introduces us we see the subliminal self coming to the surface,' he explained, displacing only as much of our consciousness 'as may from time to time be needful for the performance of its own work'. To come to the surface, the subliminal self used whatever channels it could.

The most familiar were sleep and dreams. 'We cannot treat sleep – as it has generally been treated – in its purely *negative* aspect,' Myers insisted. 'We must treat sleep *positively*, so far as we can, as a definite phase of our personality, co-ordinate with the waking phase.' Sleep, he had himself found, could sometimes have a profound effect: consciousness had only to depart for a few moments and it was as if there had been a release, which could 'change a man's outlook on the world'.

Dreams were capable of providing insights and inspiration – he cited R. L. Stevenson's account of the way in which he had learned to exploit his dreams to provide himself with his stories. And there was the strange phenomenon of somnambulism, which bore to normal sleep something of the relationship which hysteria bore to normal life, bringing into play 'resources which are beyond ordinary reach'.

Messages from the subliminal self reached consciousness through three channels, Myers explained: vague or anomalous feelings – intuition, inspiration, premonitions; passive, or sensory, automatism – visions, dreams, hallucinations; and active, or motor, automatism – somnambulism. Sensory and motor automatism could also operate in collaboration, as in automatic writing. Their existence was clear evidence 'that a stream of consciousness flows on within us, at a level beneath the threshold of ordinary waking life, and that this consciousness embraces unknown powers'. Thanks to the research with hypnosis, it had become possible actually to demonstrate some of them, by inducing them. The ways in which they emerged spontaneously, though, as in intuitions, suggested that they must be coming from some established agency, capable of presenting them as if from an intelligent source.

This theory, Myers believed, could account for much that previously had been inexplicable, and regarded as occult superstition. Witchcraft was one example. Edmund Gurney had combed through the available accounts, coming to the conclusion that there was 'a total absence of respectable evidence, an almost total absence of any first-hand evidence at all, for those alleged phenomena'. The evidence came almost entirely from confessions, most of them extracted under torture; from accusers; or from witch-hunters. But though the evidence *for* witchcraft could be discounted, the evidence *about* witchcraft – the beliefs, the methods used to detect witches, the confessions – was extensive; and it could be readily accounted for in the light of the discoveries about hysteria, and the subliminal self.

The tendency has been for historians to blur the distinction between the actual evidence for, and the beliefs about, witchcraft. Even the great William Lecky in his *History of Rationalism* (1865) failed to differentiate between, say, the accounts of witches riding on broomsticks to sabbats, and the accounts of finding 'witches' marks' on suspects' bodies so that they felt no pain when pricked. The sabbat was derived from fantasy and hallucination, the insensibility to pain was symptomatic of hysteria. 'The part of the case for witchcraft which is now exploded superstition had never, even in its own day, any real evidential foundation,' Gurney had concluded. 'The part which had a real evidential foundation is now more firmly established than ever.'

At the other extreme, Myers believed that the evidence could also help to account for the flashes of inspiration which far surpassed the products of consciousness, both in intensity and co-ordination. For these flashes to be conspicuous, however, it was often necessary that the 'glare' of consciousness should be 'deadened by sleep or trance'. One of trance's most important functions was to facilitate the transmission of messages from the subliminal self to consciousness.

The content of the messages inevitably reflected the condition of the subliminal self. If the personality was divided, so that there were, in effect, two individuals at loggerheads – as in the case of 'Felida' or Ansel Bourne – there would be no collaboration; either one or the other would be dominant. If the subliminal self was not integrated, its messages would be confusing, though not necessarily foolish; there were many examples of people suffering from severe mental disorder who had latent periods during which fine poems or music might be composed. But where the subliminal self worked in harmony with consciousness the 'most admired forms of achievement', as in the arts, were most likely to be found.

Such harmony was rare. Ordinarily the subliminal self had to force its way through. Sometimes it arrived in the form of inspiration: a witticism, an idea for a story, a line of verse – perhaps a whole poem. It could come in a reverie, or in a dream, or in the condition described as ecstasy. Inspiration consisted of 'a subliminal uprush', as Myers put it, an emergence into the current of a man's ideas of others which had not been consciously originated, 'but which have shaped themselves beyond his will, in profounder regions of his being'.

The subliminal self, Myers was careful to insist, was not necessarily inspired – as, indeed, hypnotism demonstrated: the readiness of a hypnotized subject to eat a tallow candle thinking it was cake showed a profound subliminal control of the mechanism of taste, 'but not a *wise* control'. Similarly, automatic writing could provide messages of higher moral import than the writer could consciously produce; but they could also be incoherent, and sometimes so false that the temptation was to ascribe them to the devil, 'though in reality it is not a devil but a dream'. There were also individuals in whom the contents of the subliminal uprush varied between the trivial and the sublime. But at its best, it was to work done with its help, Myers felt, 'that the word "genius" may be most fittingly applied'; work that had to satisfy two quite distinct requirements: 'it must involve something original, spontaneous, unteachable, unexpected; and it must also in some way win the admiration of mankind.'

The explanation for genius, Myers believed, was that evolution in man had been taking a different course from evolution in animals, because of the development of his far more complex mind. If consciousness had worked so great a change in such a relatively short period, in evolutionary terms, was it not reasonable to suppose that the subliminal mind had been evolving, too? If so, genius could be explained by the ability of those who were credited with it to reach down, 'by some self-suggestion which they no more than we can explain, to treasures of latent faculty in the hidden self'.

To illustrate his contention, Myers shrewdly chose infant prodigies who had demonstrated remarkable mathematical skills. They ranged from some children who had briefly become celebrities and were then forgotten, to others who had eventually become famous scientists – Ampère, Gauss – or who had been successful in other fields, such as Richard Whately, who had become Archbishop of Dublin, and G. P. Bidder, whom Myers had known, and who had been a Queen's Counsel.

What was manifest from the accounts of these prodigies was that they had not made their calculations in any of the ways that young children are ordinarily taught to add, subtract, multiply and divide. Whately had recalled that around the age of five or six he could do the most difficult sums, 'always in my head, for I knew nothing of figures beyond numeration', and he could do them much quicker than anybody else. He never made a mistake – until he went to school, where he was found to be 'a serious dunce' in conventional arithmetic. Bidder 'had an almost miraculous power of seeing, as it were intuitively, what factors would divide any large number, not a prime'. Given the number 17,861, he would instantly say '337 × 53'. He was unable to explain how he did it, except that the answers to such questions seemed 'to rise with the rapidity of lightning'; the ability continuing, in his case, into adult life.

Efforts had been made to account for prodigies, but without success. For Myers they clearly showed 'that the main and primary achievement had in fact been subliminal'. The same subliminal process, he suggested, was at work with prodigies as with hypnotized subjects who were able to calculate, without being aware of it, exactly when to respond to a post-hypnotic suggestion. It would also account for the ways in which inspiration reached so many writers, artists and composers through hallucination. He cited de Musset – 'one does not work, one listens; it's as if an unknown one speaks into your ear'; and Lamartine – 'it is not I who think; my ideas think for me.' The 'flashes' of calculation which a prodigy displayed might seem 'a mere curiosity', Myers concluded, 'but without the type of faculty which that boy has shown, the inspiration of a Shakespeare or a Raphael would never have arisen to bring joy to mankind.'

Myers agreed that from one point of view the way in which genius manifested itself bore a resemblance to hysteria. In both, the screen between the subliminal and the conscious mind was readily permeable. But whereas in hysteria the subliminal uprushes resisted voluntary control, in genius they co-operated with voluntary effort, and enriched the conscious self's output. Hallucinations were common in both, but in connection with genius they represented 'an advance in integration'.

This was an even more challenging view than it sounds today. The general view still was that, except in cases of lunacy, hallucinations did not happen – as the first writer to put the case for studying them, the Boston doctor Edward H. Clarke, lamented in *Visions* (1878). According to his friend Oliver Wendell Holmes, who wrote the introduction, when Clarke learned that he had a terminal illness he decided to devote what remained of his life to surveying the evidence. Considering that such very different personalities as Saint Paul, the Buddha, Muhammad, Joan of Arc and Luther had seen visions, and that they were also seen by hysterics, drug-takers and alcoholics, their existence, Clarke argued, ought surely to be taken for granted. Not so; visions were regarded, not only by scientists but by the public, as 'very much like ghosts, as unrealities' – as delusions. Yet 'the persistence with which the truthfulness of visions had been affirmed, at all times, everywhere, and by such a variety of individuals, is itself a significant fact, and one that deserves consideration'; and Clarke presented a series of case histories, most of them occurring to people he knew, emphasizing that they were not mentally disordered – on the contrary, they 'were all persons of more than ordinary intelligence and cultivation'.

Myers's contention about hallucinations' value also had support from two decidedly unexpected allies. One was Henry Maudsley, the leading London psychiatrist of the time. Hard-headed though he was in most respects, Maudsley despised the materialism he saw prevailing in his profession because it left little or no place for the authority of the mind.

In particular, he claimed in 1897, it was absurd to regard halluci-nations simply as the product of some brain disease. When it was considered how great a part hallucinations have played at critical periods of human history, admittedly, 'the cynic might triumph – and the believer in the hopes of mankind might despair – were it necessary to believe that human progress ever rested entirely on so rotten a basis.' But 'if a person has been fired by a fervent faith and, so inspired, has done epoch-making work in the world, what matters it that he had a helpful hallucination?' He took William Blake as an example; 'how inestimable, then, the service sometimes rendered to mankind by the few who can think and, thinking, do differently from the herd.'

Myers's other ally was even more surprising. George Henry Lewes – remembered by posterity mainly as George Eliot's lover, but an influential literary figure in his lifetime – was a positivist, with a sceptic's contempt for those who believed in the possibility of com-munications from the spirits, or from any source other than through the five senses. He had consequently been disturbed to find that his friend Dickens's characters flashed into the novelist's mind's eye as clearly as if they were real. 'I have never observed any trace of the insane temperament in Dickens's works, or life,' Lewes insisted, 'they being indeed free even from the eccentricities which often accompany exceptional powers.' Yet when Dickens imagined a street, he saw it not in the ordinary way of imagination, but as if he *was* actually seeing it: 'the action of the imagination in hallucination'.

More than that: 'Dickens once declared to me that every word said by his characters was distinctly *heard* by him.' This surprised Lewes; but he could not believe that Dickens would deceive him. The expla-nation, he decided, must be that Dickens hallucinated his material thanks to an extraordinary development affecting the brain. Lewes was not altogether happy about the results; he felt that characters such as Pecksniff, Micawber and Mrs Gamp were unreal, speaking a language 'never heard in life'. But this was because Dickens saw and heard them in hallucinatory form; 'he, seeing it thus vividly, made us also see it.' So powerful was the imagination 'that even while knowing it was false we could not help, for a moment, being affected, as it were, by his hallucination'.

Positivism, though, still had far too strong a hold for hallucination – or, for that matter, genius – to be accepted on those terms. In 1891,

Otto Jahn in his biography of Mozart referred to the celebrated letter which Mozart had written to 'Baron von P.' describing his way of composing. The music appeared to pour into him, he claimed. 'Nor do I hear in my imagination the parts successively, but I hear them as it were all at once.' It was as if the composition took place for him in a lively dream. This letter, Jahn insisted, was 'incontestably a fabrication'.

Jahn gave no reason for this assertion. The most likely is that he was unable, as a positivist, to accept that Mozart 'heard' his music in his imagination, because such hallucinations of hearing were regarded as degenerative psychosis, as Lombroso explained in *The Man of Genius*, also published in 1891. Great wits were not simply to madness near allied; genius was an actual by-product of insanity.

Although in the closing years of the century positivism was being superseded by its offspring materialism, materialists were even more dogmatically opposed to many of Myers's ideas, in particular his willingness to accept the possibility that the information which came in the subliminal uprush might be obtained from sources other than those which memory and the senses provide.

There were four possibilities, he suggested. They could come from the percipient's own mind, 'from the resources of his ordinary memory' – occasionally dramatized, as they were in dreams. They might be picked up telepathically from the mind of somebody else. They could come from 'some unembodied intelligence of unknown type' – not all spiritualist 'guides' or Christian angels had necessarily once lived on earth. Or they could actually come, as they sometimes seemed to come, from the deceased.

Myers accepted that the great majority of communications from the subliminal were in the first category. His inclusion of the other three, however, not merely aroused the derision of materialists, but set him apart from the growing number of psychologists who wanted to detach their discipline from psychical research. In some cases – notably Bernheim and Bramwell – their main interest was in psychotherapy. Others, such as Binet and Janet, realized that their chance of establishing psychology as an academic discipline would be jeopardized by the existence of any psychic element. And this, as events were soon to show, meant that hysteria and even hypnosis also had to be ditched.

5

MATERIALISM IN CONTROL

CO-CONSCIOUSNESS

Mind and brain

It has largely been forgotten how influential positivism was in the
nineteenth century. The entry in *The Oxford Companion to the Mind* reads
simply, 'See Comte'; and gives Comte only a couple of inches. It is
not easy to assess the full extent of his influence, admittedly, because
it became so pervasive in intellectual circles, particularly in and around
science, that it ceased to be identified with positivism – much as today,
materialist assumptions are still widely held by people who would not
consider themselves to be materialists. But Comte's disciples hoped
that the process by which society was escaping from the clutches of
superstition, theology and metaphysics, to a recognition that only
positive facts and observable phenomena and laws derived from them
were important, would produce a new secular religion.

Some eminent scientists, believing that matter alone could provide
the foundations, endorsed the idea. 'By an intellectual necessity I cross
the boundary of the experimental evidence,' John Tyndall, Faraday's
successor at the Royal Institution, told the audience in his Presidential
Address to the British Association for the Advancement of Science in
Belfast in 1874, 'and discern in that Matter which we, in our ignorance
of its latent powers, and notwithstanding our professed reverence for
its Creator, have hitherto covered with opprobrium: the promise and
potency of all terrestrial Life.'

Tyndall's sermon had all the greater impact because it was delivered
in Belfast, where the British Association happened that year to hold its
annual gathering; he was by upbringing an Irish Protestant preaching

heresy in the heart of Protestant Ulster. Thirty years later, one of Bernard Shaw's characters in *Man and Superman* could say, 'Nothing has been right since that speech Professor Tyndall made in Belfast', and still be confident that the audience would get the allusion. On the Continent, Ernst Haeckel had taken up the crusade, founding an association with the aim of eliminating superstition from Christianity and fusing what remained into science to become the religion of the future.

There was no inherent reason why even a psychology basing itself on materialism should not have recognized the importance of trance, if trance could have been established as a by-product of chemical processes in the brain. As it happened, though, the materialists were themselves divided on the subject of the ways in which the brain produced mental effects. 'Parallelists' asserted that mind and body could not act on each other, as they ran on parallel tracks; 'epiphenomenalists' preferred the theory that the body acts on the mind, but not vice versa. In the light of everyday experience, parallelism sounded a regression to metaphysics, and epiphenomenalism absurd. The research into hypnosis, in particular the discoveries about the effects of post-hypnotic suggestion, made both of them untenable except by comical contortions. And this should have left the field open to the 'interactionalists', who accepted that mind could act on body, as well as body on mind.

The problem confronting the old guard of researchers into hypnosis, Janet, Binet and others, was how to keep 'mind' within the confines of the increasingly dominant materialist model of the universe. Binet tried. Overshadowed though he was by Janet, who had defeated him in the election to a chair at the Collège de France, he had done valuable pioneering research into the workings of the mind, particularly in connection with hypnosis. Mechanistic by temperament – he invented the first IQ test – he nevertheless found it impossible to accept the materialist contention that thought, mind and sensation must all eventually be accounted for in terms of matter; the attempt to equate a thought with a block of stone defeated him. Introducing *The Mind and the Brain* (1905), he explained that it was an attempt to distinguish between mind and matter; 'nothing is more simple than to realize this distinction when you do not go deeply into it,' he asserted, but 'nothing is more difficult when you analyse it a little.'

Binet hoped to mollify the materialists by accepting that mind cannot exist without matter; but this did not satisfy them. They wanted to get rid of mind, as an active agent, altogether. And increasingly psychologists, still more of whom were hoping to obtain formal academic recognition, were compelled to realize that if they were to complete the transition for which James had initially set the example, from the arts to the sciences, the psychology they offered would have to be trimmed to persuade scientists to accept them. They must concentrate their research on projects which could be justified as producing objective evidence, ignoring, and if necessary disparaging, those areas where a subjective component could not be avoided.

The pace was set by John Broadus Watson, who launched behaviourism in a series of lectures at Columbia University in 1912, and in the space of twenty years made it the most influential movement within psychology in the United States. 'The raw fact that you, as a psychologist, if you are to remain scientific, must describe the behaviour of man in no other terms than those you use to describe the behaviour of the ox you slaughter,' he observed in 1930, 'drove and still drives many timid souls from behaviourism'; but this, he insisted, had from the start been his fundamental principle. Psychologists must deal only in what they could observe. 'Now, what can we observe? We can observe *behaviour – what the organism does or says.*' Only by obeying this rule could the psychologist aspire to be a scientist: 'his sole objective is to gather facts about behaviour – verify his data – and subject them both to logic and mathematics.' He must forget about such concepts as consciousness, or the unconscious. They could not be observed. The behaviourist had to drop from his scientific vocabulary 'all subjective terms such as sensation, perception, image, desire, purpose, and even thinking and emotion as they were subjectively defined'.

Creativity also had to go, except as an example of 'stimulus and response'. A question often raised was how poems came to be written. 'The answer is that we get them by manipulating words, shifting them about until a new pattern is hit upon.' The stimulus could be provided by, say, a loved one or a publisher; the poems emerged through random shuffling of words until they seemed ready to obtain the desired response, the loved one's kiss, or publication.

By the 1930s, Watson was able to boast, 'no university can escape the teaching of behaviourism.' It had its critics, but he had always refused to answer them; a precept which his disciples were pleased to follow, as many of them would have felt uneasy at having to justify so grotesque an explanation of creativity. They were also spared the need to take trance into consideration. In so far as it appeared to be a manifestation of the unconscious, it was a delusion.

'To explore the most sacred depths of the unconscious, to labour on what I have just called the subsoil of consciousness, that will be the principle task of psychology in the century which is opening,' Henri Bergson had claimed. 'I do not doubt that wonderful discoveries await it there, as important, perhaps, as have been in the preceding centuries the discoveries of the physical and natural sciences.' Yet by the 1930s, curiosity about the most sacred depths was all but extinguished. Freudian psychoanalysts continued to probe them, but primarily with the aim of releasing repressed material, of no intrinsic interest. Jung was moving towards a new vision of the unconscious, in which it had access to a collective source; his followers, though, were mainly preoccupied by psychotherapy, and were often uneasy about his growing interest in the occult. Psychiatrists, infected with the organicism that was dinned into them during their medical student days, were pinning their hopes on physical treatments: insulin coma therapy in the 1920s; brain surgery – lobotomy and leucotomy – and electroconvulsive therapy in the 1930s. And in the medical profession, organicism took complete charge. There were functional disorders, it was conceded; but they were not taken seriously. 'Functional' was no more than a label for symptoms which could not be traced to an organic source; it had come into use initially, according to W. H. R. Rivers in his *Instinct and the Unconscious* (1920), 'as a means of avoiding the word "hysteria".'

Hysteria downgraded

That the medical profession should have felt compelled to avoid the diagnosis of hysteria was the measure of organicism's dominance. For a while, Janet had fought to rescue it from the odium into which he could see it was falling. In a lecture he gave to the Harvard Medical School in 1906, he put in a plea for recognition of the value of trance conditions, even when manifested by people who appeared to be insane. The great French psychiatrist Moreau de Tours, he recalled, had been in the habit of claiming that all the world's great achievements had been accomplished by people who were mad. This might be an exaggeration, Janet admitted, 'but it is nevertheless true that most great creeds have spread by means of the emotion caused by surprising phenomena' – invariably related to hysteria. 'Hysterics' had visions; they saw and heard what others could not see or hear. Sometimes beatified, sometimes burned as witches, they had played a decisive part in the development of the religions of the world.

Janet even tried to restore faith in Charcot's theory that in so far as hysteria was pathological, it was a real illness. Humanity should do homage to him, Janet urged, for the countless number of patients he had saved from surgery by establishing hysterical symptoms as 'real'; 'do not try to count the number of arms cut off, of muscles in the neck incised for cricks, of bones broken for mere cramps, of bellies cut open for phantom tumours.' By a singular irony, thousands of bellies were about to be cut open precisely because Charcot's theory had had to be rejected.

In the 1920s, the pressure to offer an identifiable organic cause for symptoms of the kind that had been labelled hysterical, and were now in the uneasy functional or neurasthenic categories, led to the proposition being put forward that most of them could be traced to focal sepsis: toxic matter accumulating in the intestines, or the jaw. The theory bore a striking resemblance to the one held by the surgeon Cutler Walpole in Shaw's *The Doctor's Dilemma* (1906); 95 per cent of the human race suffered, Walpole claimed, from blood poisoning. 'Your nuciform sac is full of decaying matter – undigested food and waste matter – rank ptomaines,' he asserted, prescribing surgery to remove it.

The nuciform sac was a figment of his, and Shaw's, imagination; but in a weird case of life imitating art, the similarly spurious concept of focal sepsis – a source of toxicity, either in people's intestines or in the roots of their teeth – was taken up gratefully by surgeons in the 1920s, and hundreds of thousands of people were actually relieved to be reassured that there was an organic cause of their symptoms, which could be removed by a simple operation to extract part of their gut, or all of their teeth. The focal sepsis fashion was still in full swing when the psychiatrist William Sargant was a medical student at St Mary's Hospital in London in the 1930s; he was to recall that it 'made large fortunes for several members of the staff; staff members were even elected because of their work in it; and stayed on working at it for years after it was discredited.' (In some private hospitals, it was still being diagnosed as late as the 1950s.)

The operation became fashionable because the public had been brainwashed into sharing the medical profession's organicism. Doctors did not care openly to diagnose paying patients' illnesses as functional, let alone hysterical. As a result, a diagnostic label which carried a suitably organic implication could be exploited – as the novelist A. J. Cronin found, and later admitted in his autobiography.

When Cronin 'put up his plate' as a general practitioner in London, for a while he had a hard time of it, with very few, and very poor, patients. Then he had the good fortune to be called upon, in an emergency, by a rich woman. The introductions he received as a result of her gratitude began to bring him many women patients, often 'rich, idle, spoiled and neurotic'. He told them they had 'asthenia' – quietly dropping the 'neur-', which had become suspect owing to its Freudian links. They told each other that Cronin had found they were really ill. And to confirm that they were suffering from a genuine organic disease he treated them with courses of injections; 'again and yet again my sharp and shining needle sank into fashionable buttocks, bared upon the finest linen sheets.'

It was simply hocus-pocus, he had to admit, yet it had been 'surprisingly, often amazingly, successful'. The patients wanted to believe they were really ill; the diagnosis delighted them, particularly if their doctors had told them there was nothing the matter with them; and the injections – of placebos in effect – completed the cure.

As a consequence, hysteria tended to be diagnosed only if a doctor wanted to get rid of a patient, or when the symptoms were manifestly those of classical hysteria of the epileptic type. Then, the patient would be referred to a psychiatrist. Because hysterical symptoms could be represented as a form of unconscious malingering, designed to help the patient to escape from some unwelcome situation, they ceased to give that help; if the diagnosis was confirmed, it could lead not to sympathy but to being 'certified' as a lunatic, and locked up in an asylum. Not surprisingly, the incidence of diagnosed hysteria in the population fell almost to vanishing point.

The growing influence of Freud did nothing to restore hysteria's reputation. Hysterical symptoms are simply the memory symbols of traumatic experiences, he argued in a paper 'Hysterical Phantasies and their Relation to Sexuality' (1908). They served the purpose of sexual gratification, being 'equivalent to the recurrence of a form of sexual gratification which had been really experienced in infantile life, and been repressed'; they provided a compromise between the impulse to enjoy the experience and the need to suppress it. The essence of a hysterical symptom, he reiterated, is the realization of an unconscious phantasy; and though in time the symptoms may come to represent various non-sexual impulses, 'it cannot dispense with some sexual significance.'

Eventually Freud fused 'conversion hysteria' into the theory of neurosis which he expounded in 1917. Although, as he admitted, it did not satisfy him, it caught on with the public in a garbled version, so that 'neurotic' took over colloquially to describe physical and behavioural symptoms which suggested some underlying emotional disturbance. So far as Freud and his disciples were concerned, though, it simply indicated the existence of repressed material which psychoanalysts had to uncover and release. There was nothing of value to be mined from the 'Id'.

Georg Groddeck

Freud borrowed the term 'Id' from Georg Groddeck – 'that neglected genius', as Lawrence Durrell was to describe him. Freud's version, though, was very different from Groddeck's which was closer to Myers's subliminal self. Germs and viruses, Groddeck argued, dictate what form an illness will take; but they are not the cause of the illness. Our Id, he insisted, dictates whether they are going to be allowed to make us ill. The Id is perfectly capable of providing us with protection from bacteria; 'or by the same token, it may, when illness seems advisable, produce conditions in which the pathological germ can be permitted to be effective.'

There had been some striking evidence earlier that this view was justified; as when Max von Pettenkofer, to demonstrate his disbelief in the theory that it was a bacillus which caused cholera, swallowed a beakerful of bacilli taken from a dead cholera victim and suffered nothing more serious than diarrhoea (the bacilli were retrieved in his stools). Even Pasteur admitted, on his deathbed, that he had been wrong to place so much emphasis on germs rather than on the reception that they encounter in the human body; 'the terrain', he told a friend who was visiting him, 'is everything.' But this had been forgotten.

Illness, Groddeck argued in a paper in 1917, is a by-product of hysteria. We are all hysterics; all capable of generating not just mimetic symptoms, but also organic disorders, by aiding and abetting the activities of invading germs – much the same as the theory that has recently surfaced in connection with auto-immunity. The virus, or bacterium, associated with a disease, it is now realized, cannot necessarily be regarded as *the* cause, because it can co-exist peacefully enough with the human body; but if the host's auto-immunity breaks down, it will be there to identify the disorder for purposes of treatment.

Swimming as he then was against the organicist tide, Groddeck made little impression. Freud's theories, rooted as they were in neurophysiology, could more easily be accepted; although his contention that hysteria and neurosis were derived from repressed sexual phantasies was embarrassing, their reality as behavioural disorders could be conceded. Not so an 'Id' capable of making people *really* ill.

Carl Jung

Jung's influence was not to be widely felt until later; but it was in this period that he was establishing himself as a leading analyst in Europe, and he owed his choice of career, as he recalled in *Memories, Dreams, Reflections* (1973), to experiences of the 'higher phenomena', and to a study at first hand of trance mediumship. While he was a medical student, Jung was sitting at home one day when 'something happened that was destined to influence me profoundly.' It was a sound like a pistol shot; the 70-year-old walnut table-top in the next room had suddenly split. A couple of weeks later there was another deafening report; the blade of the breadknife in the sideboard had split in several places. These inexplicable, poltergeist-type explosions compelled him to realize that earlier materialist assumptions needed to be discarded, making it possible for him 'to achieve a psychological point of view'.

A few weeks later Jung heard that some relations of his family, who liked to have table-turning sessions, had found a young spiritist medium; and when he went round to witness her performance, it occurred to him that he might conduct the same kind of investigation that Flournoy had carried out with 'Hélène Smith'. In 1900 he presented his findings in his inaugural dissertation for his medical degree, 'On the Psychology of so-called Occult Phenomena'; and it was to be his first published work (1902).

The symptoms he was dealing with, Jung explained in his introduction, were certain rare states of consciousness whose meaning had yet to be understood: trance states, such as narcolepsy, automatism, amnesia, dual personality, somnambulism, pathological dreaminess, and pathological lying. These were sometimes attributed to epilepsy, sometimes to hysteria, sometimes to exhaustion of the nervous system – neurasthenia – and 'sometimes they may even be accorded the dignity of a disease *sui generis*'. But these terms, Jung had already come to realize, were meaningless. A patient with one of the symptoms might go through 'the whole gamut of diagnoses from epilepsy to hysteria and simulated insanity', according to the preconceptions of his psychiatrist. One psychiatrist, Paul Steffens, had in fact laid down that there was no dividing line between epilepsy and hysteria; they could be distinguished only in extreme cases.

Jung classified the case of 'Miss S. W.' as somnambulism taking the form of spiritist mediumship. He had no doubt that the trance condition she entered at sessions was genuine. Her personality changed, and she became much brighter and livelier, with the ability to perform entertainingly as a mimic. She even acted the dead, bringing them back to life so effectively that she deeply impressed even people who were not easily influenced. She also spoke literary German fluently, something she could not do in her normal state; and her movements acquired 'a noble grace'.

Jung did not concern himself, at this stage in his career, with whether or not the medium had genuine psychic gifts in her trances. It was enough for him to watch and record the change of character and its effects. For a time his collaboration with Freud kept him from further exploration; but then in 1909 came the extraordinary episode – an echo of the explosions at his home years before – when Freud irritated him by dismissing psychic phenomena in shallow positivist terms. Jung felt as if his diaphragm was red-hot, 'a glowing vault'; and suddenly there came 'such a loud report in the bookcase, which stood right next to us, that we both started up in alarm'. Jung attributed it to 'exteriorization'; Freud replied that this was 'bosh'; Jung promptly predicted that it would happen again and 'sure enough, no sooner had I said the words than the same detonation went off in the bookcase.' To the end of his life, he could not explain what gave him the certainty; but the episode left him in no doubt of the ability of the unconscious to 'exteriorize', and to create physical effects.

'Sally Beauchamp'

Another exception to the general trend for orthodox psychologists and psychiatrists to cease to concern themselves with hysteria, hypnosis and other forms of trance was a protracted investigation carried out into a case of dual, or multiple, personality by Morton Prince – who, paradoxically, was by temperament a hard-line organicist. As a medical student in the 1870s, Prince had written a graduation thesis, which he was to enlarge and have published as *The Nature of Mind and Human Automatism* (1885), whose aim was to bring the growing evidence for unconscious – or as he preferred, automatic – processes into line with materialist dogma. 'Today the weight of authority is in favour of a material basis for all mental phenomena,' he had claimed. 'It is generally conceded the mind depends upon the development of a peculiar matter, the brain, for its existence.'

This proposition had caused some worry, Prince admitted, because of a fear that it put a limitation on the freedom of human thought. Not so: we all know we can make a choice between two courses of action, and take it. But when we say we have that power, 'what do we understand by this term *we*?' There was no evidence, Prince insisted, for a directing agent distinct from the brain; or even for an Ego uniting mind and body. What was thought of as *a* personality, he suggested, is actually a compound of states of consciousness, directed by the state which happens to be dominant at the time.

Far from personality being all-important, he pointed out, it can disappear almost completely, as it does in trances, in reveries and in daydreams, only returning when deliberation is required. There was no clear distinction between them; it was impossible to say where reverie ends and deliberation begins. Nor could it be claimed that the states in which personality is active are superior to those in which it is passive – where people become, in effect, automatons. 'Mozart's genius was automatic,' Prince asserted, citing the letter to 'Baron von P.' as evidence. And there was no need to invoke spirits or any outside source: unconscious cerebration did the work. Nor was there any longer a need to regard mind as a kind of independent directive force. There was simply cerebration, unconscious or conscious. One by one, Prince claimed, supernatural phenomena had been weeded out by science, 'and now but one remains. This is mind. This, in its turn, must go. It only remains to decide whether it shall be today or tomorrow.'

Orthodox scientists might approve of his defence of materialism, and agree that 'mind' was an unnecessary abstraction; but they were still reluctant to regard themselves as automatons, or to accept that they did not have single, identifiable personalities. It was not until the late 1890s that Prince, practising in Boston as a specialist in nervous diseases, came across a patient who fulfilled his expectations by behaving much as Azam's 'Felida' had behaved, displaying all the signs of having more than one personality.

'Miss Beauchamp' had come to him suffering from headaches and a general feeling of malaise. She was an intelligent, conscientious woman, he found, admired by her friends, and clearly not a malingerer. When she told Prince she had occasional fugues, in which for a while she lost track of what she was doing – she could find herself walking in a different direction from the one she had set out on – he diagnosed hysteria, and decided to treat her by suggestion under hypnosis.

The treatment seemed to do her good. But it also uncovered two, and eventually three, additional personalities which were quite distinct from each other. Prince was sufficiently familiar with the research which had been done into hysteria and hypnosis to feel able to handle the problems this would pose, and he was pleased to be able to present a case history which would show his peers that he had been justified in his theory of automatism. But this, he was to find, he could not do. His paper was entitled 'A contribution to the study of hysteria and hypnosis', both of which by 1898 had gone out of fashion. By a nice irony, when it appeared it was in the *Proceedings of the Society for Psychical Research*, which was full of reports of phenomena of the kind he contemptuously dismissed as supernatural. As it happened, though, his research continued to bring up material of a kind sufficiently fascinating to interest a New York publisher. *The Dissociation of a Personality* (1906) made Morton Prince's name, and has remained in print ever since.

'Miss Christine L. Beauchamp', Prince explained in the introduction, 'is a person in whom several personalities have become developed; that is to say, she may change her personality from hour to hour, and with each change her character becomes transformed and her memories altered.' As well as her normal self, she could turn into any one of the three different persons with different opinions, beliefs and tastes – different memories, even. Two of her personalities had no knowledge of each other, or – except what they were told, or inferred – of the third. The third – Sally – knew about the others, and was a bizarre character far removed from them.

Miss Beauchamp – the name, pronounced 'Beecham', had been chosen in jest to describe the composite personality – was a real-life example, Prince thought, of imaginative creations such as

R. L. Stevenson's – though there was a trace in only one of them of the malevolent 'Mr Hyde' aspect. And although the personalities came and went in kaleidoscopic succession, several changes often being made in the course of a single day, each of the different personalities was capable of leading what appeared to be a normal social life; 'as a matter of fact, each personality leads its own life, like any other mortal.'

'Sally' was the most interesting, though she was a practical joker. She was scathingly contemptuous of Miss Beauchamp as too prim and proper; and as she knew Miss Beauchamp's thoughts, she could make her life a torment – for example by smoking cigarettes, which Miss Beauchamp thought a nasty habit. On one occasion 'Sally' removed herself, leaving Miss Beauchamp to 'come to' with a lighted cigarette burning her fingers. On another, she left a 'present' for Miss Beauchamp which turned out to be a box full of spiders.

After about five years of complicated psychotherapy – each of the personalities had to be treated in her own right – Prince managed to establish a reasonable fusion into the 'real' Miss Beauchamp, as he called her. By 1905, when he was preparing his account of the case, she had been in more or less continuous existence for several months, with only brief losses of control in times of illness or stress.

The most important aspect of the case, Prince thought, was that it established the existence of 'co-consciousness', as distinct from 'the unconscious'. The unconscious, he claimed in his book of that title in 1914, is merely a repository, 'that which is devoid of the attributes of consciousness'. It must not be confused with what had emerged as a result of the Beauchamp inquiry: 'there are *very definite states of co-consciousness*' – consciousness 'of which the personal consciousness is not aware'.

Not the least interesting outcome of this research, Prince added, was his discovery that the different personalities had different disorders. 'One would imagine that if ill-health were always based on physical alterations, each personality must have the same ailments, but this is not the case.' Miss Beauchamp had the worst health record, 'Sally' the best – 'she does not know what illness means.' Significantly, too, she did not feel pain. She was a 'hypnoid personality'.

Prince had hopes of bringing hallucinations back into respectability as a subject for research, as they fitted quite well into his theory of co-consciousness. The visions and the voices of Christian saints and others, he pointed out, which had been interpreted as supernatural, were in reality the product of the subject's own thoughts, running in the co-conscious stream which breaks through in dreams, and occasionally in waking life. And this should not be regarded as pathological, he warned in *The Unconscious*. He could cite numerous cases displaying 'intelligent constructive imagination, reasoning, volition and purposive effort' expressing themselves in a variety of forms of automation which 'either solve a disturbing problem or carry to fruition a subconscious purpose'.

Psychologists were prepared to tolerate Prince's account of his research with Sally Beauchamp as a curiosity, but few went along with his co-consciousness theory, let alone his views on trance, which were too reminiscent of the 1880s for comfort. Their reaction disturbed the editor of the *British Journal of Medical Psychology*, T. W. Mitchell. The knowledge which had been achieved of dissociation, splitting of consciousness into dual or multiple personality, he recalled in 1925, had been mainly derived from the research into hysteria and hypnosis. But by 1925 hypnosis was no longer taken seriously, and hypnotherapy was frowned on. There was a danger, he feared, that research into the varieties of dissociation might cease, and that the results which the research had achieved would be forgotten.

In America, Prince had the support of William McDougall, who in 1921 succeeded Muensterberg in James's old Chair of Philosophy at Harvard. 'Consciousness', he suggested in his *Abnormal Psychology* (1926), is the normal condition of man. But agreeing with Prince (and, without realizing it, echoing Myers), McDougall expressed the view that his own self – the one which he, and those who knew him, thought of as his self – was 'only the dominant member of a society, an association, of similar members'; and there were several purposive activities within his organism for which the associates were responsible.

On the whole, the association worked reasonably well, McDougall felt, as they all thought they were working for the common good; 'but when I relax my control, in states of sleep, hypnosis, relaxation and abstraction, my subordinates, or some of them, may continue to work and they are apt to manifest their activities in the forms we have learned to call sensory and motor automatism.' In cases where the dominant member was weak or irresolute, the subordinates could get into conflict; in extreme cases, one of them might be sufficiently insubordinate to acquire increasing influence and eventually to challenge the dominant self – as illustrated by 'Sally'.

Ordinarily Prince would have been gratified to have such support, in view of the lack of interest shown by his fellow-psychiatrists (and also by the Freudians: Prince had originally been quite well-disposed to them, but Freud thought him a man whose friendliness masked bad intentions, and declined to accept the theory of co-consciousness). But there was a catch. Both Mitchell and McDougall were involved in psychical research, and both had been Presidents of the SPR. Prince had been ready to use the Society's *Proceedings* when he had no other outlet; but the success of his book enabled him to found the *Journal of Abnormal Psychology*, in which psychical research rarely featured, because of its continuing links with mediumship and other phenomena which he still dismissed as superstition.

Worse: impressed by the fact that 'Sally' was able to tap the thoughts of Miss Beauchamp, McDougall argued that this could only be explained by a kind of telepathy. What other form of communication was there, that co-conscious personalities could enjoy? Prince, craving orthodox recognition, backed away.

'Patience Worth'

In *The Nature of Mind and Human Automatism*, Prince had written that he could not understand 'how any right-minded person, how anyone who truly seeks after knowledge, can have any sympathy with those who refuse to accept a doctrine, however strong may be the evidence on which it is based, simply from fear that when carried to its logical consequences, it may antagonize preconceived notions.' He was now himself to be confronted with another case of multiple personality which was providing strong evidence against his belief that 'mind' was the last of the supernatural phenomena, destined to be disposed of by the march of science.

Mrs Pearl Curran had grown up in the American Middle West, where she had received little formal education. Outwardly she was an undistinguished housewife until, at the age of 31, she was invited to join in ouija-board sessions. The planchette worked well for her; but nothing of interest appeared until one day a 'communicator' announced her presence. Although Mrs Curran was not a spiritualist, she was prepared to allow 'Patience Worth' to take over; and 'Patience' was promptly to display literary talents far in excess of Mrs Curran's meagre capabilities. All that Mrs Curran had to do was to keep her hand on the planchette, while holding a conversation with others who were present. Meanwhile 'Patience' would be busy; answering questions put to her, often wittily; composing verses, of no great merit but not to be sneered at; and eventually producing full-length novels which attracted praise from the critics, and sold well, in their own right – not as curiosities.

Mrs Curran did not need to go into a recognizable state of trance for her ouija sessions. It was enough if she could achieve a degree of abstraction from what her hand, on the planchette, was doing. It was as if 'Patience' simply needed to be free from any interference from Mrs Curran whom she despised; when Mrs Curran tried to claim some of the credit for what was appearing, 'Patience's' response was scornfully dismissive.

Most trance-transmitted writings could without too much difficulty be attributed to the wanderings of the writer's subliminal self within the bounds of his acquired knowledge – as they could be in the case of Stainton Moses. This explanation did not fit Mrs Curran's. 'Patience' was not merely far cleverer; she was able to write in ways which were outside Mrs Curran's reach.

The novel *Telka*, for example, about a girl living in Anglo-Saxon Britain, was written almost entirely in words with Anglo-Saxon roots, with hardly any Norman-French or other accretions. An expert would have found it difficult to match the performance. Yet doubters who probed Mrs Curran's background were compelled to admit that she could not have acquired the knowledge through her education, or in her married life, without detection. In any case, the sheer speed with which the novel appeared, testified to by those investigators who watched her at the ouija board, ruled out any possibility of deliberation.

In the mid-1920s, Morton Prince's namesake Walter Franklin Prince made a careful investigation of Mrs Curran, coming rather diffidently to the conclusion that 'Patience' could not be accounted for simply as a co-conscious personality, in the sense that the term could have applied to 'Felida' or 'Sally'. 'I know of no proof that a secondary personality, subliminal or alternative, can show ability so tremendously in advance of the primary or normal consciousness,' he concluded. Either the stock concept of the subliminal mind would have to be radically revised to include hitherto unrecognized powers, 'or else some cause operating through, but not originating in, the subconsciousness of Mrs Curran must be acknowledged'.

It was arranged that Morton Prince would investigate Mrs Curran and 'Patience'; but when 'Patience' answered his questions elliptically and in her *Telka* dialect, Prince took the opportunity to insist that he would not continue unless Mrs Curran allowed herself to be hypnotized. Fearing that if she consented, she might lose 'Patience', Mrs Curran refused – sparing Prince from the embarrassment which evidence of her mind's ability to roam in time would certainly have caused him.

Auto-suggestion

The rapid decline in the practice of hypnotherapy after 1900 left the few remaining practitioners unable to arouse interest in their findings. In Sweden, Sydney Alrutz, a lecturer in psychology at the University of Uppsala, conducted experiments which provided further evidence for the reality of a 'fluence'; but when he died in 1925 they had made no lasting impression. In America, Clark Hull, Professor of Psychology at Yale, conducted an investigation in the 1930s with the aim of bringing hypnotic phenomena into line with behaviourist doctrine, in what he believed were carefully controlled scientific experiments. In retrospect, all that they succeeded in demonstrating was that the performances of hypnotized subjects tend to conform to the expectations of the hypnotists, as they had to Charcot's, the experiments being flawed and the 'controls' – as Hull feared – inadequate.

Almost the only useful contribution to the understanding of induced trance came from William McDougall, in his *Outline of Abnormal Psychology* (1926). Recalling an experience related by Janet of a girl who under hypnosis appeared willing to commit murder, but who awoke in wrath when asked to take off her clothes, McDougall surmised that under hypnosis there is a temporary splitting of the personality: 'while one part accepts absurd suggestions and acts them out in systematic fashion, another part silently watches, aware that the whole thing is as it were a game'. If the game threatens to go too far, overstepping the limits imposed by the subject's moral conditioning, 'this part becomes active, steps in, and puts an end to the game by terminating the hypnosis and effecting the re-integration of personality.'

McDougall looked for an explanation in evolutionary terms. Human behaviour under hypnosis, he suggested, is linked to the instinct of submission in gregarious species of animals. 'We see some members of a herd or flock submitting tamely and quietly to the dominance, the leadership, the self-assertion of other members' – and not necessarily from fear. The human race, he believed, retained this instinct. With the development of language and intellect, words became the means of evoking and directing submission; along with prestige – 'the power of using suggestion, of compelling bodily and mental obedience or docility, without evoking fear'.

The ordinarily dominant self was ready to relinquish control of its actions under hypnotism, McDougall suggested, because it realized that the control was being handed over to subordinates who were better able to carry out the instructions which suggestion would give. The subordinates were capable, in ways of which the dominant conscious self was incapable, not just of receiving and understanding but of remembering and executing instructions which were given when the conscious mind had not registered them or had forgotten them.

The most promising development, though, to emerge from the earlier research into hypnotism was auto-suggestion – a form of induced trance which came into use in the 1920s as a by-product of the Nancy school. It was offered as psychotherapy by Johannes Schultz in Germany, and by Emile Coué in France. Schultz's method attracted little attention at the time, except among his circle of patients; its importance lay in the future, half a century later, when it was to form the basis of bio-feedback training, but Coué's method became for a while internationally celebrated.

The story goes that Coué, a chemist in Troyes, one day substituted coloured water for a drug which a patient demanded but which he was not permitted to prescribe. The patient's symptoms duly disappeared. Could it be, Coué wondered, that the imagination within certain limits can perform the same function as a drug? He made a pilgrimage to Nancy in 1885, and came back to Troyes convinced that suggestion under hypnosis was very effective; but he had not hypnotized the patient to whom he gave the placebo – the coloured water. The patient's own imagination must have supplied the cure. Surely, then, psychotherapy's objective should be the training of patients to heal themselves, through auto-suggestion?

This was far from being an original idea. Even before the Nancy school had made its name, some practising hypnotists had recommended it. In the curiously named *Statuvolism* (1869) a Chicago hypnotist, W. B. Fahnestock, had described how he taught patients how to enter a trance 'at pleasure, independent of anyone'. Moll and Forel had both stressed the significance of auto-suggestion as a component of hypnotic suggestion, as had Myers; hypnotism, he had insisted, was simply a name 'for a group of empirical practices by means of which we can manage to get hold of the subliminal faculty, allowing it to emerge in a more persuasive manner than it ordinarily does'. He could not bear to use 'auto-suggestion' – a linguistic barbarism, he complained; but self-suggestion – suggestion 'conveyed to the subject himself from one stratum of his personality to another without external intervention' – must, he felt, be the vital component. Suggestion from without could be no more than an aid.

It was left to Coué, however, to popularize auto-suggestion by offering a simple way through which anybody could learn to exploit it, derived from the earlier research into hypnosis. We have first to recognize the existence of our two selves, he explained, conscious and unconscious; and to understand that the unconscious, though full of potentially invaluable resources which the conscious self lacks or remains unaware of, is remarkably credulous. The unconscious is in charge of our automatic functions. If something goes wrong, therefore, suggestion should be directed at the *un*conscious to put it right.

It was at this point that Coué diverged from an earlier assumption about auto-suggestion. In their report on the Second International Congress on Experimental Psychology, held in London in 1892 – it had proved to be the last gathering at which induced trance and its related phenomena took a major part – Sidgwick and Myers noted that the debates on hypnosis had shown there was general acceptance of three propositions: that suggestion under hypnosis could be therapeutically effective; that the existence of susceptibility to suggestion while in the trance was not an indication of morbidity; and that independent investigators were agreed on the 'great importance of self-suggestion in all forms of psycho-therapy'. But as Delboeuf had emphasized, when auto-suggestion worked 'in perhaps every case the patient's cure was effected merely by a firmer reliance on his own powers of will.'

This, Coué argued, was where hypnotherapy had gone astray. It is not the will but the imagination that is crucial. Often they are in conflict; and when they are, 'the imagination invariably gains the day.' Coué cited as an example a plank thirty feet long and one foot wide. Place it on the ground, and anybody can walk along it. Lift it to the height of a cathedral, 'who then will be capable of advancing even a few feet along this narrow path?' Why the alarm? 'Simply because in the first case you *imagine* that it is easy to go to the end of the plank, while in the second you imagine that you *cannot* do so.'

Coué cited other examples, as did his followers: the will cannot produce salivation or sexual arousal – they depend on the imagination. And recognition of the imagination's supremacy, Coué pointed out, was of vital importance not just for individuals, but for society. Alcoholics often claim in all sincerity that they want to give up drink, but that they lack sufficient will-power. What they in fact lack is control over the imagination. Some criminals claim they commit their crimes in spite of themselves; 'something impelled me'. The drunkard and the criminal are telling the truth: 'They are forced to do what they do, for the simple reason they imagine they cannot prevent themselves from doing so.' They are puppets until they learn to control their imaginations.

But how can the imagination be tamed, and trained? It was for this purpose that Coué devised his formula: 'Every day, in every way, I get better and better.' He had originally used it with patients in a light trance, telling them they were getting better; then he had told them to use it themselves, after first ensuring they were in a relaxed mood. They were to repeat it twenty times in a monotonous voice, emphasizing 'in every way' in order to remind the imagination that the aim was not just to remove some unwanted symptom, but to stir the life force into action to promote better health in general.

The formula, therefore, was not designed as an exhortation, but as a childlike litany, or a mantra. Its purpose was to dissolve conscious-ness of self, in much the same way as Tennyson had learned to do, to liberate inspiration. In a letter to a friend, Tennyson had described how he used to put himself into a trance with the help of an unusual type of mantra: his own name. He would repeat it to himself, silently, 'till all at once, as it were out of the intensity of the consciousness of individuality, the individuality itself seemed to dissolve and fade away' – not into a confused state, 'but the clearest of the clearest, the surest of the surest, the weirdest of the weirdest, utterly beyond words'.

Coué remained chiefly concerned to demonstrate the power of the imagination in preventing and curing disease. Patients flocked to him, as they had to Liébeault; his mantra could be heard in different languages all over Europe; his name, if not his face, was as well-known internationally as Al Capone or the Prince of Wales. The medical profession, however, felt justified in dismissing him as a quack, without medical qualifications, and with so poor an understanding of physiology that he could believe in the exploded myth of the power of the imagination to cure organic disease.

Yet ironically, the validity of Coué's thesis was being busily exploited by the medical profession, with lucrative results. Cronin's 'asthenia' patients were demonstrating the power of auto-suggestion – the belief that their illness, now that it had been diagnosed, would be cured – coupled, perhaps, with a touch of his hypnotic effect. Not that he would have felt any need to make them aware of his influence; that would have weakened their faith in the organic nature of asthenia. But by his own account he was exploiting his personality, as well as his clinical method, to impress them.

Cronin, though, did not think of what he was doing as a contribution towards restoring suggestion and auto-suggestion to a respected place in orthodox medicine. 'I was, I assure you, a great rogue at this period,' he recalled, 'though perhaps not more so than many of my colleagues.' So ingrained had the dogma of organicism become that it would have been disastrous for him and his colleagues to admit the deception, and to point out that suggestion and auto-suggestion were actually more potent than the drugs available at that era.

A handful of doctors, usually under the influence of Freudian theory, tried to warn that organicism was untenable. 'All disease is disorder of function,' F. G. Crookshank wrote in 1928. 'If there is no functional disorder there is no disease, and the so-called organic changes we find in some cases are just as much the effect as the cause.' Accurate diagnosis was all very well, but for many diseases there was in fact no effective treatment. 'Organic disease is what we say we cure, but don't; functional disease is what the quacks cure and we wish to goodness we could.'

Three years later Crookshank returned to the assault. The concentration of medical research on organic symptoms, he complained, had led to blind indifference to their functional origins. He had even begun to wonder why 'some hard-boiled and orthodox clinician' had not thought of categorizing emotional weeping as a new disease, calling it 'paroxysmal lachrymation', prescribing a salt-free diet, with locally applied drying agents, and 'proceeding in the event of failure to early removal of the tear glands'. Ludicrous though this might sound, Crookshank claimed, 'a good deal of contemporary medicine and surgery seems to me to be on the same level.'

In 1930 two young cardiologists in the London Hospital, William Evans and Clifford Hoyle, became worried by the ineffectiveness of some of the drugs then in use in the treatment of angina. It occurred to them that one way to find out which of the drugs were worth prescribing was to test them against placebo pills, manufactured from bicarbonate of soda. In their report in the *Quarterly Journal of Medicine* in 1933 they described how they had found that the placebos 'gave better results than most of the actual drugs, and appeared statistically to be the better form of protection'. A few of the drugs, such as morphine, were a little more effective; but this had to be set off against the risk of addiction.

Further trials along similar lines were soon to show that placebo-effect, as it came to be called, was surprisingly consistent, particularly in the treatment of pain of many different kinds. A third, sometimes as many as a half, of patients put on a course of placebos responded as well to them as to the standard pain-killers. This was a startling vindication of Coué's theory. Clearly the explanation must lie in auto-suggestion, patients' expectations being responsible for the beneficial effects.

To admit this, however, would have been embarrassing. Angina was assumed to be organic. It would be difficult to send patients away from hospitals and consulting rooms on the ground that if it responded to auto-suggestion, it must be functional. Placebo-effect was taken up by the profession, but only in its role as a handy technique for testing drugs. The evidence which it provided for the therapeutic powers of the subliminal mind was tacitly ignored.

The absurdity of dogmatic organicism was to be underlined by Sir Walter Langdon-Brown, Emeritus Professor of Physics at Cambridge, in *Thus We Are Men* (1938). From his long experience he had come to the conclusion that the incidence of organic disease was much lower than was assumed, largely because hospitals gave an erroneous impression – most hospital cases had been selected precisely because they were taken to be organic. In general practice it was a very different story. He had asked a number of GPs what proportion of their patients they thought were suffering from functional, rather than organic, disorders; 'not one of them placed it at less than 40 per cent, while some put it as high as 75 per cent.'

For a GP to use hypnotism to treat these patients would have been regarded as, at best, eccentric; by the 1930s auto-suggestion was also recalled chiefly as just another weird craze of the 1920s, like mah-jong. And shortly before the outbreak of the Second World War the advent of the sulfa drugs, soon to be reinforced by penicillin and the antibiotics,

relieved GPs of any need to reconsider whether the rejection of hypnotherapy had really been justified. It even became possible for patients
to believe that in the not too distant future, there would be 'a pill for
every ill'.

SHELL-SHOCK

Fugue

One trance condition managed to gain a measure of orthodox acceptance in this period – though, again, only as a pathological symptom:
'hysterical fugue'. Describing fugues as 'ambulatory automatism' in
his 1907 Harvard lectures, Janet claimed that they were 'one of the
most wonderful phenomena of hysteria'; but such was the contempt
into which hysteria had again fallen that they aroused no interest until
they were reported in disturbing numbers from the trenches in the
First World War.

That this would happen had been predicted a few months before
the war broke out by Silas Weir Mitchell, America's elder statesman
psychologist. Half a century before, serving as a neurologist in the
Civil War, he had become interested in the subject of fugue; and in a
paper he read just before his death in 1914 he expressed regret that
so little attention had been paid to 'an interesting psychic malady,
making men hysterical, and incurable except by discharge'. Should
war break out again, he forecast, the problem would recur, but this
time, victims would be besieged with questions about the condition of
their unconscious minds.

Mitchell was being sarcastic – he thought Freud's influence pernicious – but his forecast was proved correct. Prolonged trench warfare
imposed a strain on soldiers of a kind that had never been known
before, and breakdowns became a common occurrence. Sometimes
they took the form of a paralysis so complete that it resulted in total
immobility; sometimes the victims suddenly walked away behind the
lines, where they would be found wandering. At first this rendered
them likely to be court-martialled and shot; but it soon became
apparent that they were not malingering. Often they were officers or
'Tommies' who were recognized as among the bravest men in the line.
Serving as a medical psychologist, McDougall found that many of

those who came under his care were men of fine type, intellectually and morally. It was as if some fuse in their minds had blown under overwhelming stress, leaving them either physically helpless, or in the grip of a form of somnambulism.

When such men escaped court martial, and were sent to base hospitals for diagnosis, the more enlightened doctors realized that they were dealing with hysterical fugue. They also realized that it would not serve as a diagnosis, because of the prejudice against hysteria. They fell back on a ruse; the men must be suffering from 'shell-shock'. Some of them were; the bursting of a shell could cause actual brain damage. As it could not always be detected whether the damage was organic, presumed victims of fugue could be slipped into that category – much to the annoyance of those doctors who remained convinced that they were cowards: McDougall heard one medical officer, a general, 'declare emotionally that every case of shell-shock should be shot forthwith as a malingerer'.

The man who did most to establish that shell-shock was a trance condition, to explore ways of treating it, and later to put it into its evolutionary context, was Halse Rivers, who early in the war took up an appointment as medical psychologist in the British army, and quickly established himself as the leading authority on the subject. Rivers had qualified as a doctor, and begun to research in physiology; but in 1898 he was invited, along with McDougall, to join an anthropological expedition to the Torres Straits, where they were able to observe tribal communities and wild animal life at first hand. The outcome was unexpected. 'They went as physiologists; they returned as psychologists,' Sir Walter Langdon-Brown recalled. 'This was in effect the beginning of the new psychology in England.'

Shell-shock, Rivers felt justified in admitting publicly after the war ended, had been an unfortunate and misleading diagnosis; 'the great majority of the functional disorders of warfare are not "traumatic" in the strict sense' – the sense in which, 'in accordance with the general materialistic tendency of medicine', an attempt was being made to confine trauma to organic injury. Rivers preferred the Freudian version of trauma, acknowledging that he could not have understood the genesis of shell-shock, let alone be able to treat it, if he had not – unlike most of his contemporaries – studied Freud. Freud's great merit, he had found, was the provision both of a theory of repressions to account for the mechanism which produced the symptoms, and of a method by which the repressed material could be brought to light.

Freud, however, had not concerned himself with fugues. Rivers felt that they needed to be examined from a different angle, in the light of a theory put forward by the neurologist Hughlings Jackson, to account for mental development. There were three levels, Jackson had suggested, reflex, sensory-motor and psychological, each reflecting a stage in the evolution of the mind. When the mind was disordered, it was the most recent psychological stage which was first affected, with resulting loss of mental control. Rivers agreed, but contended that there were different levels within the third stage which Jackson had not considered: conscious and unconscious. And although the symptoms of loss of mental control might appear to be pathological, as in shell-shock, they could in fact indicate that a valuable protective mechanism, acquired earlier in evolution, was being revived, temporarily, to replace consciousness.

The condition of total collapse which was characteristic of one of the common forms of shell-shock, Rivers argued, was not an indication of 'giving in'. It was the exploitation of the immobility which forms one of the instinctive reactions to danger in many animals, either to conceal them from predators or – as apparently in the case of 'playing 'possum' – to deceive the predators into thinking the animal is dead. For such immobility to be of any use, it was absolutely essential that it should be total. 'If an animal capable of feeling pain or fear, in however crude a form, were to have these experiences while reacting to danger by means of immobility, the success of the reaction would certainly be impaired and would probably fail completely.' Both fear and pain had to be entirely suppressed. Any graduation of the process, 'any attempt to discriminate differences in external conditions, and to adjust the degree of suppression accordingly, would be fatal.'

Trance, in which the victim became oblivious to his surroundings and deprived of the use of his senses, was the device, Rivers believed, by which the unconscious mind, realizing that it was at the end of its tether, could deprive consciousness of the ability to interfere as it would ordinarily do by raising moral objections to, say, a refusal to obey an order to get up and go 'over the top'. Fugue was the way in which the sufferer 'regains happiness and comfort, if not health, by the recurrence of symptoms which enable him to escape from the conflict in place of facing it'.

Rivers's contribution was more important than he, or anybody else, realized at the time – except, perhaps, a few of his patients. 'Though there were twenty years between us, he talked as if I were his mental equal, which was very far from being the case,' Siegfried Sassoon recalled in *Sherston's Progress* (1936), describing his experience at Craiglockhart Hospital where 'that great and good man gave me his friendship and guidance'. Its importance lay in the revelation that trance, in at least one of its forms, was in the evolutionary perspective a protective device, and was still fulfilling that role, though in circumstances which could make the fulfilment hazardous. After the Armistice, however, the type of fugue which had been labelled shell-shock was rarely encountered; and as the families of soldiers who had been invalided out on the strength of that diagnosis were unlikely to probe behind it, and find that it had been a mask for a form of hysteria, the reality was quickly forgotten.

This did not necessarily mean that hysterical fugue would disappear; as it represented an evolutionary device, the development of ways to adapt to danger, Rivers expected to encounter it in some other disguise, when he returned to civilian life. He duly found that mimesis – as he called it, following Paget – was indeed common, in the form of the variety of symptoms which were described as functional or neurasthenic. Fugue in peacetime, Rivers realized, was a less easily recognizable condition. It could take the extreme form of total paralysis, but this was unusual, because there was less occasion for it than there had been on the Western Front, and also because it offered less advantage. The commoner symptoms could, however, be regarded 'as partial manifestations of a process which, if it were complete, would produce insensibility of the whole body'. Total insensibility was unnecessary, provided the successful mimicry of less extreme symptoms would suffice to release people from obligations, and even gain sympathy.

Nevertheless the process, Rivers argued, was the same. Hysterical mimesis represented the atavistic way in which the unconscious had learned how to exploit its powers to escape from unwelcome situations without loss of face. In peace, as in war, the symptoms arise when there is a conflict 'between a higher and more recently developed set of motives, which may be summed up under the heading of duty, and a lower and earlier set of motives provided by instinctive tendencies'. For the hysteric, the solution was provided by the shutting off of the higher set.

In *Instinct and the Unconscious* (1920), Rivers discussed the relationship of fugue to other forms of trance. Clearly it had close links with somnambulism. A sleep-walker is capable of 'carrying out a series of activities, often of the most varied and complicated kind, which are wholly independent of the activities of his normal life' – just as somebody in a fugue might do; 'there is, in fact, no difference between a fugue and a somnambulistic attack except that one occurs in sleep and the other in the waking state.'

There must also be a close link, Rivers thought, between fugue and cases of dual personality. He had met and talked to patients who were in the fugue state, without his realizing it – even when he was looking out for it; only later had he realized that there had been signs of very minor changes of personality. 'All gradations may be met, between a change so slight as that which I failed to recognize in my patient and the pronounced cases of double or multiple personality' – they had been featuring in psychological literature – 'reaching their climax in the classical case of Miss Beauchamp.' In ordinary fugues, however, there was not the element of co-consciousness, by which 'Sally' tapped Miss Beauchamp's thoughts.

Perhaps the most original, and not the least important, of Rivers's contributions to the understanding of trance came in his comments about the role of the unconscious in sport. They were related to his discovery about fugue that in cases where the condition was not total, the trance component could come and go, or fuse with normality to the point where he would only realize later that it had been there, meshing with normal consciousness. The same process, he pointed out, could be observed in the action of a billiards player, a golfer, or a footballer, representing 'a highly complex and delicately balanced adjustment between controlling and controlled processes' – between the conscious, which has determined the aim, and the unconscious, which has to be geared to carrying it out.

The mistiming of a stroke or a kick, Rivers suggested, was an indication that the balance between conscious and unconscious had been upset – and not necessarily because of a lack of co-ordination. The unconscious might be momentarily unco-operative; it was as if there was a 'guardian who allows or encourages the occurrence of the false stroke, in order to cover and disguise some more discomforting experience'.

'Guardian' was as near as Rivers came to Myers's concept of the subliminal self playing an active part with, as it were, a mind of its own. He was thinking in this context, though, of a 'spoiler' – the sporting equivalent of a blush, after a gaffe. The 'delicately balanced adjustment' which a stroke required could be disrupted by the intrusion of some nagging unconscious worry which happened to interrupt at the most inconvenient moment.

There were other indications in *Instinct and the Unconscious* that Rivers was moving towards Myers's theory of mind. Although a hysteric's fantasies, if allowed to burgeon out of control, could slide into schizophrenia, they could also, Rivers believed, generate creativity: 'many lines of evidence are converging to show that all great accomplishment in human endeavour depends on processes which go on outside those regions of the mind of the activity of which we are clearly conscious,' he claimed. 'There is reason to believe that the processes which underlie all great work in art, literature or music take place unconsciously or at least instinctively.'

Rivers, however, was formulating a more pragmatic version of the subliminal; derived partly from Freud, partly from his wartime experience, partly from his realization that the trance component which produced the varied symptoms of hysteria was present not only in many disorders which were rarely labelled or even recognized as hysteric, but also in everyday life – as in sport. In everyday life, he believed, as in illness, it would be essential to take this into account, in order to secure the desired balance between the designs of consciousness, and the needs of the unconscious.

Whether Rivers would have been able to persuade his fellow psychologists to accept his views, and to return to the study of spontaneous and induced trance, was not to be tested. In the early 1920s he became involved in a busy round of activities designed to improve the academic status of the discipline. It was largely through his influence that psychology was at last admitted in its own right to the deliberations of the British Association for the Advancement of Science. There had been psychotherapists before him, Sir Walter Langdon-Brown was to recall, 'but the orthodox profession were inclined to regard them as cranks. Rivers' position as an academic scientist was unassailable, and his adhesion to this new branch of medicine commanded respect for it.'

Unluckily Rivers became involved in the early 1920s not only in the internal wrangles of academic psychology, but also in politics. Dissatisfaction with the social conditions he found in the course of his work prompted him to join the Labour Party; and he might have found himself in Parliament – in all probability, such was his reputation, as a minister in the first Labour government – if he had lived. But he had taken on too much; he died in 1922, when he was still in his fifties, and when his influence was at its height. That psychology in Britain was never so dominated by behaviourism as it was in the United States was partly due to that influence; but this 'very wise man', as Langdon-Brown described him, left no successor capable of carrying on his campaign to restore the study of trance, spontaneous and induced, to a leading role.

Mass hysteria

One other form of hysteria attracted some attention at this period. In *The Crowd* (1896), Gustave Le Bon had presented a theory to account for the way in which people in crowds or mobs behaved in ways in which, as individuals, few of them would have been likely to behave, and his theme was to become the starting-point for theorizing about mass hysteria.

'Men the most unlike in the matter of their intelligence possess instincts, passions and feelings that are very similar,' Le Bon observed. 'From the intellectual point of view an abyss may exist between a great mathematician and his bookmaker, but from the point of view of character the difference is most often slight or non-existent.' In crowds, intellectual control was weakened; instincts, passions and feelings strengthened. 'The heterogeneous is swamped by the homogeneous, and the unconscious qualities obtain the upper hand.'

Yet observations showed that the behaviour of crowds is not dictated simply by a kind of averaging out of its members' feelings. A crowd creates new characteristics. Partly this is because, by virtue of numbers, a feeling of power is generated; partly because an individual in a crowd, being relatively anonymous, sheds the sense of responsibility which caution or convention ordinarily instil. But another element has to be considered: contagion.

On this issue Le Bon felt the need for caution. Its presence was easy to establish, but it was not easy to explain. It must, he thought, 'be classed among those phenomena of a hysteric order'. Individual subjects under hypnosis readily obey suggestions from a hypnotist which makes them behave in ways which are out of character. An individual immersed in a crowd in action, too, 'soon finds himself – either in consequence of a magnetic influence given out by the crowd, or from some other cause of which we are ignorant – in a special state, which much resembles the state of fascination in which the hypnotized individual finds himself in the hands of the hypnotist.'

In *Instinct of the Herd* (1916), Wilfred Trotter complained that psychologists had made hardly any attempt to follow up Le Bon's initiative. Trotter himself was concerned less with crowds than with herd instinct in a more general sense; the kind that promotes conformity and often stultifies thought and behaviour. Christianity bore some responsibility, he thought, because of its emphasis on the family as the initial unit, stemming from Adam and Eve. Darwin had finally exploded that myth, and psychologists should have been looking for the real origins of human behaviour (which they had hardly begun to do) in the behaviour of animals. To understand man in his gregarious capacity, they should be studying ants and bees.

A few earlier writers had the same idea. Mass hysteria was a throwback to ant behaviour, Frances Power Cobbe had suggested in 1872. But Trotter was chiefly curious about how the behaviour – whether of bees or humans – was regulated. In the hive, he pointed out, specialization in the form of markedly different roles is accompanied by co-ordination so rigorously enforced 'that each individual is actually absorbed into the community, expends all its activities therein, and when excluded from it is almost as helpless as a part of the naked flesh of an animal detached from its body.' A hive 'without any very undue stretch of fantasy, could be described as an animal of which all the individual cells have retained the power of locomotion'. How, he wanted to know, was this accomplished?

Trotter did not commit himself to a theory about the ways in which the herd instinct works; his aim was simply to impress on his readers, and psychologists in particular, that it is the biggest single influence on our lives. It could endow a man with courage and endurance in noble causes, but it could also 'make him acquiesce in his own punishment and embrace his executioner, submit to poverty, bow to tyranny, and sink without complaint under starvation'. The form it took which most irritated Trotter was the bias it instilled in favour of conformity. 'If we examine the mental furniture of the average man, we shall find it made up of a vast number of judgments of a very precise mind upon subjects of very great variety, complexity and difficulty,' he observed. All of us tend to have decided views on subjects ranging from whether there is life after death to whether the selectors have been right or wrong in their choice of players for the coming international. Yet the only judgement we are really fitted to make is that our judgement needs to be suspended, because we are not qualified to make it.

Far from adopting this attitude, Trotter pointed out, we regard our beliefs as rational, and defend them as such, 'while the position of one who holds contrary views is held to be obviously unreasonable'. It was of cardinal importance to recognize that however ingenious the rationalizations in support of any belief of this nature, they are merely a manifestation of the strength of the ingrained belief – in other words, of a habit of mind engendered by the herd instinct.

McDougall shared Trotter's view that the herd instinct was extremely important, but thought it unfortunate that so much emphasis had been placed by commentators on the subject on the way in which group life dragged individuals down. Group activity, he believed, could provide an ennobling influence, if the ways in which intercommunication worked were better understood. And valuable though Le Bon's contribution had been, he argued in *The Group Mind* (1920), it had not gone far enough. Crowd behaviour reflected the existence of a more binding form of contagion than hypnotic suggestion would supply. There must be direct induction of emotion, through some as yet undiscovered channel.

Might the solution be found in telepathy? In *Les Sociétés Animales* (1878), Alfred Espinas had drawn attention to the mysterious way in which some primitive organisms had the capacity either to act as if they were a single living entity, or to split up into individuals capable of existing on their own. There was an element of collective consciousness, he argued, in all social groups, including humans.

Sixteen years later Charles Riley, Entomologist to the Federal Department of Agriculture in Washington, bluntly stated that there could be no doubt that many insects 'possess the power of communication at a distance' in a manner of which 'we can form some conception by what is known as telepathy in man'. But it was Edmund Selous, one of the leading ornithologists of his time, who first put the case for extra-sensory intercommunication as the explanation of behaviour in flocks, in *Thought-Transference or What? in Birds* (1931), his thesis being that the standard assumption, the equivalent of what was to become known as 'formation flying' by airmen, simply did not fit the observed facts. A collective agency, Selous decided, must be in operation; in effect, a flock 'brain' controlling the movements.

If some form of telepathic intercommunication was the most plausible explanation that had been put forward for the behaviour of termites, or starlings in flocks, the less said and written on the subject, orthodox biologists felt, the better. For this conspiracy of silence they were castigated by the American zoologist Henry Morton Wheeler in a lecture he gave in 1910. Biology would be found wanting, he told them, so long as group behaviour of the kind flocks or termites displayed was not studied because of 'fear of the psychological and the metaphysical'. Materialists might wince, but there must be some form of 'superorganism' at work. It ought to be investigated.

Influential though Wheeler was, his plea went unheeded. 'Super-organism' came into use for a time, but simply as a label. The field was left to those who were ready to speculate, notably Halse Rivers. 'If animals are to act together as a body, it is essential that they shall possess some kind of instinct which makes them especially responsive to the influence of one another, one which will lead to the rapid adoption of any line of conduct which a prominent member of the group may take,' he argued. 'In emergency each member of the group wholly subordinates his appetites to the group's immediate needs.' Animals possessing this group cohesion would have an advantage in the struggle for existence. 'If, as there can be little doubt, Man in the earlier stages of his cultural development was such an animal, we have an ample motive for his suggestibility.' On this assumption, mass hysteria could be explained as a resurgence to this type of reaction in threatening situations.

Rivers, though, was reluctant to commit himself to any theory of how the group cohesion operated. Studying termitaries in South Africa, Eugene Marais was forced to the conclusion – as the title of his account of his research, *The Soul of the White Ant* (1937), indicated – that there must be some form of group control, capable of design as well as construction and action. Termites, though physically separate, appeared to be as much under central control as blood corpuscles in a human body; thereby constituting 'the strongest possible proof that it may be possible for the psychological influence to have effect on an organism at a distance' – as mysterious a process, he thought, 'as telepathy, or other functions of the human mind which border on the supernatural'.

The physicist Whately Carington, who on the strength of some personal observations during the First World War had decided to devote his career to psychical research, came to the same conclusion about human behaviour under the influence of mass hysteria. Going to Germany in 1938 to rescue the woman he was to marry from the clutches of the Gestapo, he decided that the Nazis at their rallies were exploiting the same force that binds birds together in flocks. 'In their own perverted way,' he surmised, 'they have builded better than they knew.' They had found how to tap the psychic component which is responsible for action and communication at a distance.

Ectoplasm

Invalided out of the Royal Flying Corps in the First World War, as a result of injuries sustained in a forced landing, Whately Smith (he changed his name to Carington later) had become involved in psychical research through a meeting with the leading British mental medium Mrs Osborne Leonard, and through an investigation of a physical medium, Kathleen Goligher, in Belfast. It was still possible, in the 1920s, for scientists to investigate mediums without feeling too embarrassed. In the early years of the century many of the most eminent of them continued their investigations: James in the United States; Lodge, Crookes and Barrett in Britain; Flammarion, Richet, Bergson and Marie Curie in France; Lombroso, Enrico Morselli and Filipo Bottazzi in Italy; Flournoy in Switzerland; Hans Driesch and Baron Albert von Schrenck-Notzing in Germany. All of them, along with many others as well-known at the time, participated in carefully controlled trials, and all were convinced of the reality of the phenomena.

Already, however, there was a growing tendency to regard any scientist who admitted to undertaking psychical research *as* a psychical researcher, the implication being that his status as a scientist was becoming suspect. A few individuals managed to overcome this handicap, even though they had to put up with some derision: Richet won his Nobel Prize for his work in physiology in 1913, though he had been a leading investigator of trance mediums for more than a quarter of a century; and Lodge continued to be held in esteem as a physicist, in spite of his dedication to spiritualism, in the inter-war years. But they had established their reputations as scientists before the turn of the century. It was becoming increasingly difficult for a young scientist to involve himself in research into trance conditions of any kind: to be involved in research with trance mediums was coming to be regarded as eccentric, or worse.

Nevertheless it was in this period that some of the most striking results were obtained, both with mental and with physical mediums. In the last report that William James made about psychical research, an essay which appeared in *The American Magazine* in 1909, a few months before he died, he admitted he was theoretically no 'further' after a quarter of a century of investigation than he had been when he started – in fact he was 'tempted to believe that the Creator has eternally intended this department of nature to remain *baffling*'; nevertheless from his, Hodgson's and other collaborators' work with Mrs Piper, and from the reports of researchers in Europe, he insisted that the fact that he was baffled was not to be taken as suggesting that he was in any doubt about the reality of psychic phenomena. They were not rare: '*I wish to go on record for the commonness*'; and 'the next thing I wish to go on record for is *the presence*, in the midst of all the humbug, *of really supernormal knowledge.*'

Opinions about the *source* of Mrs Piper's information, he pointed out, might differ. It had converted Hodgson from scepticism to spiritism; but there were other possibilities, and James himself had been left uncertain. But whatever the source, her knowledge could not be accounted for except by admitting the existence of some faculty which, in orthodox scientific eyes, was *not* normal.

The only 'normal' explanation offered other than fraud had been hyperacuity of the senses, enabling her to pick up, unconsciously, information from sitters. Some of the trials with Mrs Osborne Leonard set up by the SPR in London during and after the First World War were designed to preclude this possibility. The sitters were proxies, who did not know whether the information which she was providing through her 'control' was correct until it had been shown to the people they were proxies for. Her record in these trials was sufficiently impressive to demonstrate that the knowledge appeared to be obtained either by telepathy from the mind of the absent client, or from the spirits.

But which? This issue was to remain in dispute within the Societies. Some members were convinced by finding that a medium gave them correct information of a kind they did not themselves know until they had checked, as Lodge had found with Mrs Piper. Others, such as Flournoy, who eventually became convinced of the reality of supernormal powers, nevertheless continued to reject the spiritist interpretation. Many preferred to leave the issue open. But it is difficult for anybody who is prepared to wade through the lengthy and extremely boring records of the research with Mrs Piper, Mrs Leonard and others not to have to admit that they present a powerful case for the reality of supernormal communication emerging in their trances. The precautions taken were of a kind which leaves only one alternative: that the mediums and their investigators, James, Hodgson, Lodge, Flournoy and others, were in collaboration to perpetrate fraud.

This applied even more clearly to the research into physical mediums. They could be watched, and the effects they produced seen and sometimes photographed. Eusapia Palladino has yet to have a detailed biography, but when it appears it should show how the precautions against fraud in the tests to which she was subjected grew more and more elaborate, notably in an investigation by French scientists in Paris in 1905, and another carried out in 1909 by three members of the SPR who had won a reputation for unmasking fraudulent mediums. They knew that in her trances she cheated if she could, and they went to great lengths to ensure that she could not. 'Tables, we knew, or thought we knew, do not go into the air by themselves,' Everard Feilding wrote in his curiously moving account of the shock they experienced. 'Curtains do not bulge without some mechanical agency; and although we saw them do so, we still refused to believe that they did.' In light good enough for them to watch her every move, she eventually shattered their disbelief.

It proved to be effort wasted. On a visit to America, Palladino was investigated by, among others, Muensterberg. After she had produced – by his own account – some convincing telekinetic effects, he allowed her to free a leg, and took the opportunity to convict her of cheating in a report which implied that as she had been detected in deceit, it must account for the otherwise unaccountable manifestations which he had described.

This was unwise of him, a fellow-sceptic pointed out. What he had described could not conceivably be explained by the use of a freed leg; how, then, had she got her remarkable effects? But it was Muensterberg's 'exposure' that was remembered; and the numerous reports testifying to Palladino's telekinetic powers were soon forgotten.

Some psychical researchers, even, tended to find the evidence for telekinesis produced by trance mediums in this period an embarrassment. If the mediums had merely caused objects to move at a distance, as some of them showed they could do in carefully controlled trials, they would have been regarded as welcome allies in the fight against materialism. But others, notably Marthe Béraud, materialized human figures out of 'ectoplasm', as Richet had christened it; and the fact that

figures could often be photographed, far from lending credence to the
reports of the research, served to make the research the target of
ridicule – the figures looked so bogus, that it was all too easy to claim
that they were faked. The appearance of J. B. Rhine's *Extra-sensory
Perception* in 1934, dealing as it did with the evidence of ESP gleaned
from students who were not mediums, and who were not in trance
while they were being tested, came as a relief to those researchers who
had been ill at ease about the work with trance mediums. Henceforth,
they hoped, psychical research could be conducted on a more scientific
basis, leaving ectoplasmic materializations to the spiritualists.

Sir Oliver Lodge – he was knighted in 1902 – did his best to keep
science and psychical research from splitting apart, becoming the first
broadcaster to make a name as an expounder of scientific issues when
the British Broadcasting Company was set up in the 1920s; and he
continued to stress the importance of trance and the phenomena,
natural and paranormal, associated with it. Some people, he noted in
My Philosophy (1933), reveal a kind of duplex personality 'whereby,
although the ordinary course of life is managed by one, every now and
then another personality takes control; and in those cases
the occasional interloper *may* have greater powers of intelligence.'
But there are many grades of personality change: 'the process is
called "inspiration" in the higher stages, and sometimes "possession"
in the lower.' To the higher grades 'we owe most of the supreme
works of art which humanity treasures'; at a lower grade there is
mediumship; lower still, psychiatric conditions. 'But whatever their
grade, or whatever their value may be, they are all examples of the
interaction of a spiritual world, or rather of a psychical influence of
some kind.'

Lodge's insistence on the psychic component, though, again explains
why trance had ceased to be regarded as worthy of scientific investigation. It was impossible to read of trance conditions, whether historical or experimental, without coming up against psychic phenomena
– as Traugott Oesterreich, Professor of Psychology at the University
of Tübingen, showed in his *Possession* (1930), the most detailed survey
of the subject that had yet appeared (or has appeared since). His aim
was to show that the *facts* of possession were remarkably consistent,
throughout history; only the interpretations which were put on them
– for example, whether the possession was divine or diabolic, or simply
a form of mental disorder – varied. But among the facts reported,
again and again, were psychic phenomena, ranging from clairvoyance

to imperviousness to heat. And these were facts of a kind which few of Oesterreich's fellow-psychologists were willing to face.

Hallucination

For the same reason, hallucination ceased to be considered a safe subject for psychologists to investigate. Camille Flammarion followed up *The Unknown* with a three-volume collection, *Death and its Mystery* (1922), containing scores of accounts of hallucinations of various kinds, either sent in to him, or taken from earlier collections. His emphasis, though, was heavily on veridical hallucinations; sightings, sounds and other sensory experiences which turned out to be related to the deaths of the individuals who were 'seen', or 'heard', or in some crisis in their lives.

Eleanor Sidgwick's collection, published in the SPR's *Proceedings* in 1922, and another by Hornell and Ella Hart giving similar accounts from the United States, together with Flammarion's, presented a formidable array of testimony to the ability of the mind to slip temporarily into a form of trance in which information emerges as if through one or more of the senses, which may turn out to be related to an action, or thought, or emotion occurring at a distance. But by so doing, they tended to make the study of hallucination in its own right a risk which only psychical researchers were prepared to take. And this was the more unfortunate, as during the First World War, a time of appalling stress both for the men at the front and their loved ones at home, there had been innumerable reports of hallucinations which could have repaid investigation.

Not all of them were veridical in the strict sense the SPR used the term, implying that a person was 'seen' at, or very close to, the time when he was dying, or in grave danger. Perhaps the best-known account from this period appeared in Harold Owen's *Journey from Obscurity* – memoirs of his family published in 1963–5. As a young officer in the merchant navy, he was in Cape Town when the news of the Armistice came through, but he could not enjoy the celebrations as he was worried about his brother, serving in the army on the Western Front. A few days later, when his ship was off the Cameroons, Harold went down to his cabin to write some letters and to his astonishment found his brother sitting in the chair. 'Wilfred!' he said. 'How did you get here?' There was no reply, but his brother looked at him as if trying to make him understand something; 'when I spoke, his whole face broke into the sweetest and most endearing dark smile.' Harold was content not to press him, so pleased was he that his brother was there; he turned away for a moment, and when he looked back his brother had vanished. Wilfred, it turned out, had been one of the last soldiers to be killed; the news of his death had reached his mother, in fact, when the church bells were ringing to celebrate the news of peace.

Owen's hallucination was not veridical in strict SPR terms because he had been worried about his brother, and he had it several days after his brother's death. Nor was the hallucination Robert Graves recalled – 'I saw a ghost at Bethune' – in *Goodbye to All That* (1929). Private Challoner had been with him during their army training, and when they had gone out to the Front he had said, 'I'll meet you in France, sir.' In June 1915, Graves was having dinner in his company's billet when 'Challoner looked in at the window, and passed on. There was no mistaking him or the cap-badge he was wearing.' Graves jumped up and looked out of the window, but there was no sign of him. He had been killed in action, Graves found, the previous month.

The number and quality of such accounts, from people who had no incentive to invent them, remains impressive, rendering the common refusal to 'believe in ghosts' childish. This applies even to reports of collective hallucinations, less common but featuring in most collections. A trivial yet remarkable example was given by Sir Ernest Bennett in his *Apparitions and Haunted Houses* (1939). At a small tea and music party given by Mrs Blanche Hornsby in London in 1932, four of the guests noticed a man they did not know, and rang her up afterwards to find out who he was. No such man had been at the party, Mrs Hornsby knew. Puzzled, she rang up another of the guests, Dame Rachel Crowdy, who also remembered the man, and provided the same description of him as the other guests had. She recalled where he had sat, adding that he was reading papers all the time. She 'entirely declined to believe he was not there!'

Contacted by Bennett, Dame Rachel recalled the occasion; she had noticed the man specially, she wrote, because she wondered how he could read his papers with such concentration with the party going on around him: 'I still find it hard to believe he was not one of the guests.' Two of the other guests whom Bennett also contacted confirmed the story. One of them remembered that when she had referred to the man after the tea-party her husband, who had been with her, said he had not seen him.

Hallucinations combine two qualities, G. N. M. Tyrrell noted in *Apparitions* (1942), a careful survey of the evidence by one of the most respected psychical researchers of the time. 'They are (a) non-physical in character, yet, when at their best, they are (b) indistinguishable from the material figures, normally perceived, so far as visual and auditory senses are concerned.' They might even be indistinguishable to the other senses; Tyrrell had come across no less than 56 cases where the hallucination had been in the form of a sense of touch.

Hallucinations of smell and even of taste had also been reported. That the mind could conjure up apparitions in this way helped to explain much that had been mistakenly dismissed as delusion or superstition. Now, however, apparitions were again being demoted to the superstitious category – as were most other trance phenomena, even automatism.

During the First World War, Sir William Barrett – like Lodge, he had been knighted for his services to conventional science – conducted some simple but ingenious tests to check whether pushing or pulling, conscious or unconscious, could account for the movements of the 'traveller', as he called it, on the ouija board. With a small team in Dublin, he experimented with various devices to rule out that possibility by shuffling the letters around the board, blindfolding the sitters, or putting an opaque screen between them and the board, with note-takers to write down the letters as the 'traveller' moved to and fro between them – so fast, one of the note-takers said, that he was thankful he knew shorthand. The experiments left Barrett in no doubt that the movement could not be accounted for by conscious pressure; and occasionally it would present them with information of a kind that none of them could have known, and which turned out to be veridical.

In spite of these results, and the remarkable flow of quips, poems and novels that flowed from 'Patience Worth', playing the ouija board came to be denouced alike by the clergy, as 'dabbling in the occult', and by sceptics, who simply declined to accept that the reports could be genuine. People who had no first-hand acquaintance with automatism were again finding it hard to believe that individuals could produce coherent prose without knowing what they were writing, McDougall sadly observed in his *Outline of Abnormal Psychology* (1926)

– scepticism which he felt was wholly unjustified 'in the face of the abundance of carefully studied cases'.

Dowsing, too, came again to be derided as an old wives' tale. Barrett's survey, revised and supplemented after his death by Theodore Besterman and published as *The Divining Rod* (1926), contained numerous reports of the work of dowsers, amateur and professional, abundantly confirming the view of the dowsing process which Barrett's earlier research had led him to adopt a quarter of a century before – that it 'undoubtedly operates through the dowser's superconsciousness' – hence the desirability of entering a state of light trance; that the information reached the dowser through clairvoyance; and that the movements of the divining rod served the purpose of conveying the clairvoyant information 'precisely as does, in similar cases, the planchette'.

Had Barrett's research presented him with an explanation which would fit materialistic preconceptions, he might have won a Nobel Prize. He went part of the way to mollify his fellow-physicists by reiterating his conviction that the rod was moved by unconscious muscular contractions on the part of the dowser, rather than through external telekinetic influence; but this was not enough. If dowsing could be accounted for only by invoking extra-sensory perception, then dowsing was not accounted for. It must be returned to the category of occult superstitions.

An Experiment with Time

In the course of the nineteenth century several books appeared whose authors were trying to make sense of dreams; but none had aroused more than passing interest until Freud's *The Interpretation of Dreams* was published in 1899. By general consensus it was his major work, Ernest Jones thought, 'the one by which his name will probably be longest remembered'. It was the product not of prolonged cogitation, but of serendipity; the discovery about dreams which formed the book's theme 'was made quite incidentally – one might almost say accidentally – when Freud was engaged in exploring the meaning of the psychoneuroses'.

Freud's book proved to be influential not, as Jones thought, because it was original – it had many echoes, as Freud realized, of the *Oneirocritica*, written by Artemidorus of Daldus in the second century

AD – but because it established dream interpretation in the public mind as a rational activity. This took time. Only 600 copies of the book were printed, and it took eight years to sell them all. But in some mysterious way the message spread, even to people who had never thought to read the book, that dreams provided clues to the nature of material in the unconscious in the form of symbols, so that a snake or a stick might represent the penis; a tunnel, the vagina. Freud's assumptions have since come in for searching criticism; if *The Interpretation of Dreams* still enjoys a reputation, it is less in its own right than as his launching pad.

Dreams were also to play a decisive part in the development of Jung's theories. It was by observing them that, in 1909, he was led to assume the existence of a collective unconscious, and dreams remained for him the chief route which its messages took to reach the human mind. It could almost be claimed, he was to tell Mircea Eliade in the course of an interview, that every dream carries a message which could either warn that something is amiss, or could offer a solution to a problem – 'for the collective unconscious which sends you these dreams already possesses the solution; nothing has been lost from the whole immemorial experience of humanity, every imaginable situation and every solution seems to have been foreseen.'

Jung's theories took longer to percolate through to the public than Freud's; it was not until after the Second World War that the superiority of his interpretative methods came gradually to be recognized. Between the wars, the book about dreams which attracted the largest readership was J. W. Dunne's *An Experiment with Time* (1927). In simple yet convincing language Dunne described a succession of his dreams which appeared to be linked with future events. A few were dramatic, but most were of trivial incidents. In one, for example, he saw a folded umbrella standing unsupported with its handle on the pavement outside the Piccadilly Hotel. The next day, going along Piccadilly in a bus, he saw an old lady walking along the pavement; she was carrying an umbrella as if it were a walking stick, by the ferrule end, 'and was pounding along towards the hotel with *the handle on the pavement*'.

Dunne was careful to deny that he had any occult leanings. His belief was that dreaming the future could be rationally explained by his theory of time. Few people have professed to be able to fathom its complexity, and those who have agree that it is untenable; but it remains difficult, reading the book, which is still in print, to reject the actual accounts he gave as coincidental – the more so as his suggestion, that anybody interested should put pad and pencil beside the bed and write down any remembered dream in full, first thing on waking, and then wait to find if upside-down umbrellas or anything else is repeated in waking hours, has often borne fruit.

Years later, J. B. Priestley, who had known Dunne and vouched for his integrity, asked BBC television viewers for accounts of occasions when for them the conventional idea of Time as 'an ever-rolling stream' was upset. Cases of precognitive dreams provided the majority of the hundreds of letters which flowed in; some of them left him in no doubt of the extent of Dunne's influence. Priestley rejected Dunne's theories, and regretted the time and energy Dunne had spent defending them; 'but his experiments with dreams and his analysis of the dreaming self seem to me to be worth more than anything produced by the combined efforts of all other people in this field.'

6

THE POST-WAR SCENE

PSYCHOLOGISTS

Materialism enthroned

When peace returned in 1945, trance all but disappeared from science's domain. A few academic researchers continued to investigate hypnosis; but their aim, for the most part, was to strip it of any pretensions to being an identifiable state of mind, distinguishable from the normal state. And the 'normal' state was claimed by materialists as theirs. Science was 'dominated in the Western and Communist worlds alike by the belief that man and his behaviour, along with everything else, can be fully accounted for in terms that are strictly material without resorting to any kind of non-physical force or agent', the neuro-physiologist Roger Sperry has recalled about those years in *Science and Moral Priority* (1982). The possibility that mind, spirit, thoughts, hopes and ideals have a causal role of a kind that science should concern itself with was ignored; 'one risked derision by even mentioning words such as "conscious" or "mental" at a serious scientific gathering.'

It was at this time that I began to become aware of the influence of materialism. I had taken largely for granted, at home and at school, that scientists and doctors – doctors, especially – were to be trusted, unlike priests and politicians. It took time before the effects of this conditioning wore off. When I wrote a feature for the *Irish Times* in 1946 to mark the centenary of the discovery of anaesthetics, giving the discoverers the credit for the conquest of pain in surgery, it was without a thought for the mesmerists. I even joined my doctor friends going to the round room at the Mansion House, in order to heckle the speaker at an anti-vivisection meeting; to parody Percy French's

'Mountains of Mourne', 'I jeered, God forgive me, I jeered with the rest'. But gradually the rigorous organicism of the medical profession, powerfully reinforced at this time by the introduction of the antibiotics, cortisone and other drugs began to jar with my own experience.

Each of the reporters on the *Irish Times* had 'his' illness. It might be asthma, or backache, or headaches, or some gastric complaint. In my time as a junior reporter, I had been called upon as a stand-in when any of the others did not come in to the office. Their absences, I soon began to realize, often coincided with work coming up which they did not want to do. Sometimes it was as if they felt they had earned a break. Yet they were not malingering. The bronchitis of the oldest of them was so obtrusive that if he came in, he would have to be sent home. I no more suspected them of deliberate deception than I suspected that the office alcoholics were consciously timing their benders to give them the excuse of their hangovers not to have to come in. We all 'covered' for them, when necessary, without feeling put-upon.

I had no conception, then, of the earlier role of hysteria in medicine; but in 1947, Flanders Dunbar's *Mind and Body* was published in New York, reviving Tuke's ideas about psychosomatic medicine. As she presented it, 'psychosomatic' implied recognition of interaction between mind and body in the disease process. We are all likely to be predisposed, she argued, to certain types of illness. Heredity, constitution, upbringing, and emotional conflict share responsibility, though the precipitant of the symptoms, when they emerge, may be a germ or some other pathogen. The reaction of the professional establishment, however, to her emphasis on the crucial part the mind could play was a compound of irritation and derision. Any theory which attributed disease to abnormal states of mind, Britain's leading cardiologist Sir George Pickering protested in the *Lancet* in 1950, was 'unworthy of serious consideration by scientific medicine'. And neither Dunbar nor those who took up the psychosomatic cause could persuade the public that psychosomatic did *not* mean the mind, alone, was responsible for coughs and colds and 'flu, still less that such symptoms were 'all in the mind'; that the sufferer was not *really* ill.

I had many friends in the medical profession in Dublin, most of whom were orthodox in their views, which led to arguments on the issue. This compelled me to look for evidence to support the psychosomatic case. It was rarely to be found in medical journals, or indeed anywhere else at the time; but in the process I began to examine what was happening in psychology.

Behaviourism Mark 2

At Oxford, before the war, I had read Freud on the interpretation of dreams, and formed the vague impression that his work had transformed psychology in ways acknowledged even by those who had been appalled by his insistence on sexual trauma as the cause of repressions. In a sense, this was correct; his influence has remained pervasive, in spite of the gradual realization, among his followers, that many of his assumptions are untenable. But in university departments of psychology, particularly in the United States, behaviourism had firmly established itself. In some it was presented as the new orthodoxy.

Its new guru was Burrhus F. Skinner, whose 'box' experiments made his name. The box was empty, except for a lever. A hungry rat, put into it, would eventually depress the lever by accident, and would find itself rewarded by a pellet of food. Soon, it would learn to depress the lever to obtain food. 'Operant conditioning' on this model, Skinner claimed, was the clue to human behaviour, too.

Skinner was not quite as simplistic as Watson. Watson's tactics, he claimed, had been naïve, calculated to give unnecessary offence to the 'mentalists' – people who still believed in 'mind'. Behaviourism, Skinner insisted, did not deride the idea of events taking place in our private worlds. 'It does not deny the possibility of self-observation or self-knowledge or its possible usefulness.' What it did was to question the nature of what is felt or observed. Introspection, in other words, was legitimized; but we must not delude ourselves that it can influence our behaviour.

'A scientific analysis of behavior must, I believe, assume that a person's behavior is controlled by his genetic and environmental histories rather than by the person himself as an initiating, creative agent', Skinner argued. No feature of behaviourism, he realized, had raised such violent objections; 'we cannot prove, of course, that human behavior as a whole is fully determined, but the proposition becomes more plausible as facts accumulate.'

The accumulating 'facts' were derived almost exclusively from laboratory experiments with rats and pigeons, of which it could be said that either they do not have trances, or that they are in a trance condition all their lives. Skinner had no hesitation in making the same point about humans. Crucial to his theory was the repudiation of any division into conscious and unconscious. Psychoanalysts often said that behaviourism could not deal with the unconscious; 'the fact is that, to begin with, it deals with nothing else.' Consciousness enables people to become aware of the agencies responsible for our behaviour; but it is not itself an agent. Nor, for that matter, is the unconscious. The only causal agents are those provided by 'reinforcements' – the human equivalents of food pellets – and 'negative reinforcements' – the human equivalent of the withholding of the pellets. Thinking is merely a form of behaviour indulged in because it is reinforcing. Artistic creation 'is controlled entirely by the contingencies of reinforcement'.

That behaviourism had not caught on in Britain could be attributed partly to the influence of Halse Rivers, who before his death had set psychology on a different course; partly to C. D. Broad, who was to become Knightsbridge Professor of Moral Philosophy at Cambridge University. Broad had trained as a scientist, winning a First in the Natural Science Tripos; then had turned to philosophy, winning a First in that, too; and – much as William James had done – he had then managed to fuse the two with psychology, which became his main interest. In the Tarner Lectures, which he delivered in Cambridge in 1923, he had mocked Watson's behaviourism as typical of certain theories 'which may be self-consistent but which must be described as "silly"'; by this, he explained, he meant any theory 'which may be held at the time when one is talking or writing professionally, but which only an inmate of a lunatic asylum would think of carrying into daily life'. It must not be thought, though, that the people who believed in such theories were silly. On the contrary, 'only very acute and learned men could have thought of anything so preposterous against the continual protests of common sense'.

Doubtless the fact that psychology took longer to establish itself in British universities than it had in the United States helped to ward off behaviourism; and to Broad and others it was to remain silly in Skinner's version. Yet its influence began to be felt, particularly in the mid-1960s when it was at its height in the United States, with polls taken of the views of psychology students showing that Skinner was easily the most influential figure in their discipline. So it came about that 'in the protected duchies of academic philosophy', as Sir John Eccles has described them, it had become possible to 'think up the notion that there are no thoughts, come to believe that there are no beliefs, and feel strongly that there are no feelings'.

The most bizarre feature of behaviourism, though, was that 'nobody really believed he was not conscious', Julian Jaynes has recalled. It simply provided an excuse not to face the problems which 'mind' posed. 'There was a very real hypocrisy involved, too'; those interested in mind and its problems 'were forcibly excluded from academic psychology, as text after text tried to smother the unwanted problem from student view'.

For a time Jaynes had himself been caught up in behaviourism; and he put in a defence. It was a method, rather than the theory it purported to be, 'and as a method, it exorcized old ghosts', giving psychology a 'thorough house cleaning'. But it was not *old* ghosts that behaviourism swept away. It was the last remnants of what had been the new and vital psychology of James and Myers. Scientists had fallen into the trap of scien*tism*; of inventing dogmas to legitimize their practices, much as churches had done. Behaviourism was one of a number of faiths, 'clusters of scientific ideas which come together and almost surprise themselves into creeds of belief,' Jaynes lamented. 'Like the entrails of animals or the flights of birds, such scientific superstitions become the preserved ritualized places where we may read out the past and future of man, and hear the answers that can authorize our actions.'

Hypnosis

One of the effects of scientism, I was to find, was that hypnotism was held in contempt by psychologists, and hypnotherapy by the medical profession. My interest had initially been kindled by the visit of a professional hypnotist to Dublin. He came round to the *Irish Times*, where he tried to hypnotize some of the reporters – without success, but I was left in no doubt that some of the people he hypnotized in his stage act were genuinely in a trance. When I read some of the books on the subject, though – *Trilby* among them – there was little up-to-date information about research.

Then, in 1952, the story was widely reported of the use of hypnosis to treat a boy suffering from congenital ichthyosis, a condition which in his case had led to parts of his body being covered with malodorous warty scales. As a last resort, other forms of treatment having failed, he had been sent to the Queen Victoria Hospital at East Grinstead, where during the war the celebrated Archibald McIndoe and his team had used skin-grafting from other parts of the body to replace burnt tissues on face and hands. The same technique was tried on the boy, but it, too, failed.

At this point A. A. Mason, a senior registrar at the hospital, offered to try hypnosis, beginning with the suggestion that the boy's left arm would clear up. Within a week the scales had fallen, revealing fairly normal skin; the procedure was repeated; and it was not long before the skin all over his body was sufficiently free from them to allow him to begin a normal life which had been denied to him earlier.

The high hopes raised by this cure were quickly dashed; the method did not work for other sufferers from congenital ichthyosis. As the researchers of the 1880s had found, individuals responded unpredictably to hypnotherapy. A confident, competent hypnotist such as Liébeault, in good rapport with patients, could get reasonably consistent results; but he was treating simple, everyday disorders. A better understanding was needed, Mason realized, of the way hypnotherapy works in complex cases.

Nevertheless the case had shown what hypnotherapy could do; and it might have been expected to arouse psychiatrists and psychologists to the need to investigate hypnosis – a need which Hans Eysenck underlined in his *Sense and Nonsense in Psychology* (1957) in a section on hypnosis and suggestibility. This was surprising, as Eysenck was a hard-line behaviourist, who might have been expected to pass trance by. His campaign on behalf of behaviourism, however, was aimed mainly to establish it as a rival form of therapy to psychoanalysis, particularly the Freudian variety. He mentioned the 'box', but refrained from following Skinner down the course which has taken behaviourism to its logical, absurd conclusion; and although he had little to say about the research into hypnosis of the 1880s, apart from the work of Liébeault and Bernheim in promoting suggestion under hypnosis as a form of therapy, he raised and discussed some of the issues that the nineteenth-century mesmerists and hypnotists had considered, and which had continued to intrigue the public, but which his fellow-psychologists had tended to avoid.

A question still often asked, for example, has been 'what is the proportion of people who are hypnotizable?' It remains impossible to say with any certainty, because when somebody apparently cannot be hypnotized, it may simply be that the hypnotist went the wrong way about it, or gave up too soon. Eysenck cited 'one of the best-known hypnotists' reporting that with one of his subjects, it had taken him '300 hours of systematic labour' before a trance could be induced. Another hypnotist, exasperated at his subject's lack of response, had lost his temper and shouted 'For ——'s sake, go to sleep, you ——!'; the subject had immediately fallen into a deep trance.

Eysenck also offered shrewd answers to other questions which had provoked disagreement among the investigators of the 1880s. Can subjects be hypnotized against their will? And if so, could they be persuaded to commit crimes?

The answer, Eysenck argued, depends partly on the subjects themselves, partly on how the hypnotist sets about persuading them. He cited the reaction of a girl, one of Charcot's subjects, to the suggestion that she should take off her clothes; she had come out of a deep trance and slapped the hypnotist's face. A craftier hypnotist, though, might have achieved seduction; first by inducing the hallucination that he was a *woman* friend of the girl; then, saying it was getting late; and finally suggesting that as they had to get up early, they should take off their clothes and go to bed. The experiment had not, so far as Eysenck knew, been done; but 'there was little doubt that, under these conditions, there would be no difficulty at all in producing the desired result.'

The following year, however, the prospect of psychologists going back to the 1880s to reassess the evidence about hypnosis was shattered by what amounted to a manifesto from Theodore Xenophon Barber, from the Laboratory of Social Relations at Harvard University. Hypnosis, he asserted in 1958, is not a state of consciousness; it '*is not a state of any kind*'. The term was simply '*a descriptive abstraction*'.

Discussions of hypnosis, Barber complained, were still 'encumbered with static and mentalistic concepts' – in other words, with the belief in mind, and its division into conscious and unconscious. It should not be considered an example of unconscious awareness; it would 'retain the status of an "unexplained" phenomenon as long as it is conceptualized in this manner'. All it is, he argued, is a process of relative detachment from the environment, 'often conceptualized as a mysterious entity called "trance". There is no objection to using the term trance to describe this process if we remember it is not an "entity" and that it is not unusual. It is, in fact, a not too uncommon aspect of our daily life.'

Up to a point, Barber was simply comfirming the verdict of the researchers in the 1880s, that trance should not be regarded as in any way strange. But to fall into line with the prevailing behaviourism it was necessary to go further, and reject the subliminal component. There was no real difference, he argued, between hypnosis and reverie, which also was not a 'state'. Sleep presented him with more of a problem; but he insisted that it, too, is not a 'state', but 'an organismic process'.

It was a futile argument, because Barber did not define what he meant by 'state'. We may say somebody is 'in a state', after all, if he is angry or harassed or miserable. But the point Barber was trying to make in any case could not be sustained, except by fudging. There had been ample proof that under hypnosis a subliminal self comes into action – as, indeed, Ernest Hilgard was soon again to show in experiments at Stanford University, where he was Professor of Psychology. Subjects immersed their hands in icy water: under hypnosis they claimed to feel no pain, but when Hilgard asked the 'hidden observer', as he called the subliminal self, what it felt, it reported almost as much pain as the controls – subjects who had not been hypnotized – were feeling.

Experiments of this kind have made the stock behaviourist rejection of the subliminal untenable, as Barber was himself later to recognize. Not so some of his disciples, who have continued to try to justify their contention that hypnosis is not a 'state' by falling back on an argument very similar to the one which had been used to deny the reality of the mesmeric trance. It has recently been expounded by Graham F. Wagstaff, a lecturer in psychology at Liverpool University, in a paper 'Hypnosis as compliance and belief; a socio-cognitive view' (1987). He puts terms such as 'hypnosis' or 'hypnotizable' into inverted commas: 'They do not imply the existence of, or susceptibility to, a special sort of "trance".' Behaviour under 'hypnosis' is accounted for by 'compliance' – 'overt behaviour that becomes like the behaviour that a group or person wishes an individual to show'. People report that they have felt hypnotized not because they have actually been in a trance, 'but because they sincerely believe that their experiences were concordant with their expectations of "being hypnotized", even though such experiences may be readily explicable in terms of ordinary psychological processes'. When subjects are confronted by a suggestion or a set of suggestions, Wagstaff explains, they

1. decide what the hypnotist 'really' wants;
2. attempt to employ cognitive strategies to produce congruent actions and experiences;
3. if (2) fails, resort to behavioural compliance.

Subjects who perform as the hypnotist tells them to perform, in other words, are so ready to obey that they will persuade themselves that he has hypnotized them, and act accordingly. Failing that, they comply anyway.

How, then, does Wagstaff account for the mass of evidence, accumulating over two centuries, which makes 'compliance' untenable? Is he seriously suggesting that patients who have undergone surgery while mesmerized or hypnotized have only been pretending to feel no pain? Wagstaff in fact mentions James Esdaile, but wisely does not care to insist that the Bengali coolies Esdaile operated on, knowing what he wanted of them, employed 'cognitive strategies' to produce the appropriate 'congruent actions' – the immobility he required for surgery – and then 'experienced' the belief that they felt no pain.

The weakness of the 'compliance' hypothesis is unwittingly exposed by Peter L. W. Naish in *What is Hypnosis?* (1986), which he edited, and which includes Wagstaff's paper. One of the stock ploys of stage hypnotists is to call for a volunteer, hypnotize him, and tell him he is a wooden plank. He can then be laid across between two chairs, with his neck on one and his ankles on another; and he will remain rigid to the point of having people jump up and down on him. The audience assumes, Naish comments, that the feat 'could not have been performed without the aid of hypnosis'. But it *can* be performed, he explains. If somebody stretches out as stiffly as possible, he can be lifted by two assistants, one supporting the neck and the other the ankles, and he 'will not find it too hard to remain effectively stretched straight for a short while'.

The 'short while' is the give-away. Under hypnosis, the short while can be a remarkably long while, *because* the volunteer is in a trance. He does not have to try to stay stiff, he *is* stiff. In other words, he *is* in a condition significantly different from his normal one. But this does not mean that he could not, without benefit of hypnotism, transcend his normal ability to stiffen. There are countless stories of the way in which people have performed feats of agility or strength in crises – when chased by a bull, or rescuing somebody from a fire – which they subsequently realize they could not hope to emulate if they try to repeat them. They might, though, be able to emulate them under hypnosis, particularly if the suggestion is put in some vivid form – 'your house is on fire, quick!' As Albert Moll put it nearly a century before, 'hypnosis, or at least many hypnotic phenomena, is merely a means of easily and safely producing symptoms which, under other circumstances, are not easy to produce because all the necessary favourable conditions do not concur.'

So little is this understood that the entry in the *Encyclopedia Americana* (1970), after giving a few examples of what is considered to be trance, claims that the term is 'less correctly used when applied to the condition of a subject under hypnosis' – a view which can only be sustained because psychologists shy away from conducting research along the lines familiar a century ago, such as the experiments which Janet, Richet, Myers and Ochorowicz carried out with 'Léonie' at Le Havre. Although Janet had backed away from any further research which might carry an occult taint, he had admitted that 'such phenomena merited being reproduced and studied'. But this, as Jule Eisenbud has since complained, 'is precisely what was *not* done'. The line of research 'was abandoned so completely that one might have thought it to have been merely one more unrewarding blind alley in the history of the occult'.

To this abandonment there has been one striking exception: experiments carried out in Russia in the 1930s, at a time when the prestige of Vladimir Bekhterev, whose research with dogs had convinced him that they responded to 'mental suggestion' even when they could not see their master, was still powerful enough to allow hypnosis to be investigated at the otherwise orthodox Institute of Brain Research in Leningrad. The researcher, Professor Leonid Vasiliev, conducted a series of controlled trials which revealed that subjects could be hypnotized at a distance of up to 1700 kilometres, with 90 per cent accuracy in the timing of the start and the termination of the trance.

Vasiliev realized that the memory of Bekhterev, who had died in 1927, would not save him from the wrath of those scientists who adhered to the Party line that telepathy was 'an anti-social, idealist fiction', as the 1956 edition of the *Soviet Encyclopedia* described it. His results were not published. But under Khrushchev there was a temporary thaw, during which it became possible to investigate extra-sensory perception and telekinesis, and to publish the findings; and in 1962, Vasiliev's *Experiments in Distant Influence* described his work in detail, revealing how much more carefully planned and carried out it had been than the Le Havre tests. Yet the translation into English the following year aroused interest only among psychical researchers.

Eisenbud confessed to having been as guilty as anybody else of this indifference, as in an informal trial with patients who were coming to him for psychotherapy he had succeeded beyond his own expectations in hypnotizing them into, say, ringing him up at hours when, knowing that they ought not to be disturbing him, they felt compelled to produce 'obviously trumped-up pretexts' for making their calls. It was difficult, however, to rule out the possibility of coincidence; and when one of his subjects complained he could not get Eisenbud out of his mind, he had not persevered.

Hypnotherapy

Hypnotherapy has also suffered from the fact that occasionally, as in the case of the cure of the boy with congenital ichthyosis, its effects are so at odds with orthodox assumptions that they are brushed aside as anomalous. A typical example has been the reaction, or lack of it, to the findings of Dr Dabney Ewin, an associate professor of surgery at Tulane University in New Orleans. He has confirmed that suggestion under hypnosis can be extremely effective in preventing skin damage after burns; but it has to be induced as soon as possible – not as a last resort. It is as if there is a brief time-lag, he explained in a television interview in 1982, between the burn and the setting-up of the inflammation that ordinarily follows. If he can get to the patients within an hour or two of the accident he can hope to 'have them react as though they had not been burned'.

Research has revealed other ways in which suggestion under hypnosis can produce desired physiological changes. Hearing that some hypnotists outside the medical profession were claiming that they could help women to enlarge their breasts, R. D. Willard of the American Institute of Behaviour and Mind Sciences invited one in 1974 to submit to a controlled trial of his technique. Twenty-two volunteers aged between 19 and 54 were put into light trances and given suggestions which, the hypnotist had found, had given satisfactory results. They turned out to be even more satisfactory than he had expected. By the time the trial ended, a quarter of the participants had already stopped attending because their breasts had reached the size they wanted, and all but three of them had some enlargement – the average being 1.37 inches.

Thinking that a variable might have been missed – perhaps the increase in size might be related to the menstrual cycle – two Houston psychologists repeated the experiment. The cycle, they found, did not affect the results, which confirmed Willard's. They also found that the gain in size had been maintained three months later; and in every case, there had also been a reduction in waist measurements. 'The implications of these experiments are extraordinary,' Gordon Rattray Taylor commented in *The Natural History of the Mind* (1979). 'If one can increase the size of one organ,' he mused, 'why not that of another?' Ruefully he had to admit that 'men are notoriously sensitive on such matters.'

In spite of such findings, there has been little sign that the medical profession is willing to do more than accept that hypnotherapy can be of value, but is of limited usefulness. A few doctors and dentists use it, but there has been no attempt to make it an integral part of medical training. 'Hypnotism now stands ready for full clinical and scientific success,' Peter Brook, a regular contributor to the *Guardian*'s 'Society Tomorrow' page, claimed in 1983. It still stands ready; but it is still waiting.

The public, too, still tends to find hypnosis disturbing. Hypnotists are often regarded as potential Svengalis, and hypnotherapy as quackery. When in 1988 the *Lancet* reported the results of a controlled trial in which hypnotherapy was successfully used as an adjunct in the treatment of duodenal ulcers, it was reported in the press as if alternative medicine should be given the credit.

The prevailing ignorance of what hypnosis can usefully do has been illustrated recently in a British Home Office document setting out guidelines for Chief Constables about the use of hypnosis in trying to solve crimes. The advice followed lengthy research and consultation with medical and psychiatric groups – hardly the most reliable sources of information. The general conclusion, as summed up by a Home Office spokesman, is 'there is no real proof that you can obtain information by hypnosis that could not be obtained in other ways'; and the verdict: 'we do not think it is a practical weapon for the police to use against crime.'

The spokesman received his come-uppance a few weeks later when the newspapers reported that Victor Miller, sentenced to life imprisonment for a murder after he had pleaded guilty to several cases of kidnapping, attempted kidnapping, and indecent assault, had been caught when one of his intended victims, a newspaper delivery boy, 'relived his ordeal under hypnosis and gave police details of his car'. Under hypnosis, the boy had been able to give so accurate a description of the car Miller had been driving that the police were able to trace it; and an unusual tread on the tyres matched a set found where the murder was committed. The spokesman's comment, 'you could not cross-examine someone on something they had said under hypnosis', is consequently irrelevant. In such cases there is no need for any such cross-examination.

Worse, the spokesman actually trotted out a hoary old accusation, levelled against mesmerists as well as hypnotists: 'You could not guarantee that a person who has been hypnotized was not going to suffer psychiatric problems later in life.' You cannot guarantee that *anybody* is not going to suffer psychiatric problems later in life; but there is no shred of evidence to suggest that hypnosis leaves people more at risk.

A few psychologists have refused to allow the contemptuous attitude of their colleagues to deter them from conducting serious research into hypnosis, notably Stephen Black in Britain, and Ernest Hilgard and Charles Tart in the United States. The form of 'altered state of consciousness' that most impressed Charles Tart early in his career as a researcher was hypnosis, and he found he could produce hallucinations, freedom from pain, and some trivial but startling effects, such as telling a subject he had lost his sense of smell and then asking him to sniff a bottle of ammonia. Not only is it a strong smell, it gives 'an extremely painful sensation as if your nostrils were on fire'. A suitable hypnotic subject could take a deep sniff, while Tart winced: 'No reaction. No tears would form in his eyes.' But research of the kind that might establish the reality of the higher phenomena has been left to parapsychologists; and although they have conducted several trials to find whether hypnosis facilitates ESP, on balance with positive results, there has been no sign of a readiness to undertake systematic research of the kind that so absorbed psychologists a century ago.

One consequence has been that there is still confusion about what hypnotists can do. It was illustrated in 1988 in a court case in Wales, where Michael Gill, a self-styled hypnotherapist, used a black box with flashing orange lights to hypnotize women and then rape them. The three women in question were all over thirty, which brought up the issue whether 'rape' was the appropriate description. Eventually the rape charge was dropped, when Gill pleaded guilty to the less serious charges of indecent assault and unlawfully procuring sexual intercourse. The prosecution accepted the pleas, saying that it was bearing in mind legal technicalities based on difficulties about the question of consent to sexual intercourse under hypnosis; and the judge, directing the jury to return a verdict of guilty on the procurement charge, commented 'the public interest would not be served by further continuing with this trial.'

From time to time the subject of hypnotism is raised in Parliament, usually with the request that the government of the day should introduce legislation to make the practice illegal unless conducted by a member of the medical profession. Yet the position is the same as it was a century ago, when William James ridiculed the idea; few members of the profession, and indeed few psychiatrists, could claim to be qualified to practise hypnotism safely.

Conventional psychologists, though they now realize that their discipline made a fool of itself over behaviourism, do not yet dare to break loose from restraints and return to the exploratory ways of James, Myers, Janet and their contemporaries. Behaviourism has yielded ground mainly to cognitive psychology, whose practitioners deal in what they describe as 'information processing' – examining how information 'is sampled, synthesized and stored'. If a cognitive psychologist were asked to decide how best a new supermarket could serve its customers, he would recommend which goods should be near the entry, and which near the exit: how high, and how low, the shelves should be; the type of lighting – and so on. The quality of the goods, he would explain, would not be his concern.

The cognitive psychologist likes to handle the subject of, say, memory, without the need to confront problems of the kind which intrigued Hartmann, James and Myers – as Ulric Neisser of Cornell University in effect admitted in his *Cognitive Psychology* (1967). When we stop trying to recall a name, and leave it to the unconscious to find the right page for us in memory's book, who, he asked, 'does the turning?' Could it be that there is 'a little man in the head, a homunculus?' He hastened to give reassurance: of course not! But he felt compelled to admit that the study of cognition, by evading such issues, 'is only one fraction of psychology, and it cannot stand alone'.

For many academic psychologists, it stands alone as their bulwark against having to come to terms with subliminal intelligence. But a few have confronted this important aspect of the problem, and in the process largely vindicated Emile Coué – though this is rarely conceded.

Coué revisited

By the 1960s, Couéism was a faint memory – a discarded craze. Accounts of the powers of auto-suggestion had fallen into the category of old wives' tales. Medical students were still being taught, as dogma, that although the autonomic nervous system, controlling respiration, temperature and blood pressure, could be temporarily affected by events, as when a scare makes the heart beat faster, there was no way in which the human mind could learn to regulate the system's workings.

In 1965, however, a treatise appeared reviving the theory and practices of Coué's contemporary Johannes Schultz, who had taught his patients that they could exercise a measure of control over their autonomic nervous systems which they could observe and measure for themselves. Using techniques of meditation, they had found they could warm their hands by generating heat internally. Experimenting half a century later, Wolfgang Luthe of Montreal found that 'autogenic training', as he called it, could give people a surprising degree of control over functions which had been presumed to be outside the mind's capabilities; and he wrote a book about it, crediting Schultz as co-author.

All of a sudden it became apparent that some psychologists, dissatisfied with the aridity of Skinner's behaviourism, were ready to welcome this discovery. A few were already exploring its possibilities with the help of 'bio-feedback', a term which for a time was to enjoy a vogue. Bio-feedback is, in fact, something which all of us use every time we look into a mirror to check whether we are presentable. What was new were various ways of exploiting it in the practice of auto-suggestion: for example, by attaching miniature thermometers to the fingertips, and finding how to repeat Schultz's hand-warming.

As Coué had claimed, this was found to be a matter of imagination, not of will. People who used autogenic training with the help of bio-feedback found that the method worked best if they could put themselves into a frame of mind in which self-consciousness, in the sense of thinking about everyday ideas and worries, could be set aside, leaving the imagination free to roam until it came up with the answers – higher temperature, or lower blood pressure.

This happened to be of particular significance because, largely as a result of investigations conducted in Framingham, Massachusetts, it was coming to be realized that heart attacks, the commonest cause of sudden death among the middle-aged, were intimately related to life-style – to unbalanced diet, smoking and high blood-pressure. And high blood-pressure, the medical profession was reluctantly coming to accept, could be psychosomatic – a 'stress disorder', as it was by this time known. But as it was in the charge of the autonomic nervous system, the assumption had been that it could be reduced, and kept down, only by drugs.

Among the researchers into the potential of bio-feedback were a number of behaviourists who were experimenting with animals, notably Neal E. Miller, Professor of Psychology at the Rockefeller University of New York. Employing techniques derived originally from Pavlov, he obtained astonishing results in the late 1960s with rats; using the by this time established laboratory technique of 're-inforcement', in the form of pellets of food whenever they displayed the abilities he was looking for, he found that they could learn to increase or to decrease heart-rate, blood-pressure and temperature at their extremities. Incredibly, one rat actually learned how to 'blush' in one ear, and not in the other.

Herbert Benson, an associate professor of medicine at Harvard, was conducting similar experiments with baboons when he was asked by some student disciples of the Maharishi Mahesh Yogi whether he would like to test them instead. At first he refused, but eventually he gave way. Each of them had a mantra which was employed in their meditation in much the same way as Coué's 'every day, in every way, I get better and better' incantation. This did not, Benson found, lower their blood-pressure – but only because their blood pressure was low anyway. When he experimented with volunteers from outside the ranks of the Maharishi's following, the transcendental meditation technique enabled them to bring down their blood-pressure and keep it down. And other researchers, notably Elmer and Alyce Green at the Menninger Foundation in Kansas, were by this time obtaining some even more impressive results, exploiting auto-suggestion.

'A few years ago it would have been considered "paranormal" to claim control over blood pressure,' Robert Ornstein observed in *The Psychology of Consciousness* (1972). 'Now a freshman in a psychological experiment can expect to learn some measure of blood pressure control in half an hour.' The common factor in this, as in all the developments of this kind over the past few years, has been the exploitation of self-induced light trance states. Controlled trials on a quite extensive scale in a London hospital have shown that the ordinary run of patients can learn to reduce high blood-pressure effectively with the help of a technique of meditation. But the great majority of patients are still prescribed drug treatment, in spite of its higher cost and sometimes destructive side-effects. It is as if organicist assumptions are so ingrained that the medical profession cannot face the unpalatable evidence which has been accumulating to show that they are fallacious. And this refusal to recognize that a long-held dogma has been discredited can be seen at its most obstinate in connection with psychiatrists' attitudes to hysteria.

PSYCHIATRISTS

'A disguise for ignorance'

If 'psychosomatic' – in the sense of mind interacting with pathogens to promote physical symptoms – was unacceptable, 'hysteria' – in the sense of mind actually being responsible for physical symptoms – was inevitably regarded with even deeper suspicion. And hysteria did not arouse clinical interest during the Second World War, as shell-shock had in the First; largely because there was no repetition of the prolonged trench warfare on the Western Front, but also because there was a greater readiness to allow for individual frailty, in cases where it was hard to decide between nervous breakdown and malingering, by diagnosing 'combat fatigue' or 'battle neurosis', and recommending discharge from the forces – albeit sometimes an ignominious one. As a result there was little incentive for clinical psychologists and psychiatrists to re-examine what Rivers, McDougall and others had to say on the subject of fugue, or hysteria in general.

Since the war, hysteria has been largely rendered superfluous as a diagnosis by the medical profession's new maid-of-all-work, 'a virus'. Viruses cannot always be identified; general practitioners have consequently felt safe to blame them, rather than 'neurasthenia' or other evasions, for any disorder they cannot diagnose; and patients have felt reassured that their disorder cannot be dismissed as neurotic or hysterical. As a result the extent to which mimetic symptoms have been attributed to a virus cannot even be guessed at. Ironically, they are most often recognized only when they disappear, as when somebody who has been regarded as organically blind or deaf suddenly recovers sight or hearing. Then, hysteria is retrospectively diagnosed.

Where emotional symptoms have been too strident to be ignored, patients have sometimes been referred with a note – 'hysteria?' – to a psychiatrist. But psychiatrists have themselves become reluctant to confirm such a diagnosis. A paper read at the meeting of the American Psychiatric Association in 1959 described how a follow-up of 100 consecutive patients who had been diagnosed at the Johns Hopkins University Hospital as having 'conversion reactions' revealed that almost all the 'reactions' had been severe physical symptoms, for which no organic cause could be found, which appeared to be 'psychologically or emotionally derived', and which had been 'moulded by unconscious simulation of disease entities', occasionally of a remarkably sophisticated kind. There could hardly have been a more clear-cut description of the symptoms of hysterical mimesis; yet it had never been given as the diagnosis.

The reason it had never been given can be gauged from an outburst by Eliot Slater, delivering the Shorvon Lecture to a medical audience in 1965. 'The diagnosis of "hysteria",' he asserted, 'is a disguise for ignorance and a fertile source of clinical error. It is in fact not only a delusion but also a snare.'

Slater was no maverick; he was one of the most eminent of British psychiatrists, co-author of a standard textbook on psychiatry. He was simply reflecting the frustration felt by orthodox psychiatrists, arising from the prevailing organicist assumptions within the medical profession. Not that he objected to them; he shared them. His belief was that research into mental disorders, schizophrenia in particular, would eventually provide psychiatrists with sufficient information about the genetic background and the chemical foreground to bring schizophrenia firmly into the organic category; perhaps manic-depression, too. Hysteria showed no signs of qualifying as a candidate for this promotion to clinical respectability, which was why he resented it.

Worse, it was not a clinical entity. When a GP referred patients to a psychiatrist with the diagnosis 'hysteria?' it meant, nine times out of ten, that they had serious-seeming disorders which could not be traced to any organic cause, and were not responding to placebo-type treatment or going into remission spontaneously, as simple functional ailments usually did. For a doctor who as a medical student had been taught that positive diagnosis is of primary importance, to have to fall back on negative diagnosis – to decide, in effect, that as every other possibility had been excluded, it must be hysteria – was embarrassing. For consultant psychiatrists to have to admit that they knew of no better way to identify hysteria, and of no way at all to treat it, was humiliating.

The profession's irritation with hysteria was to affect the treatment of patients suffering from fugues – or, as they came more often to be described, amnesias. In 1979 a clinical psychiatrist who had been conducting research into hysterical amnesia reported in a newspaper interview that, in her experience, the victims had genuinely lost their memory 'when they wanted to do something their conscience would not let them do' – confirming Rivers's opinion. But as it is not believed that they really cannot remember, they tend to be given 'a very hard time' in hospital, with nurses trying to catch them out, and other patients goading them.

The prejudice against hysteria as a classical entity even extends to rejecting it as the explanation of cases where individuals suddenly lose all control of their movements, locked in panic.

Among pilots being taught to fly difficult aircraft in the First World War, this form of trance came briefly into prominence in the form of what came to be known as 'freezing on the joystick'. The joystick, so-called because it came up between the pilot's legs, was the control column; it could be moved forward to lose height, backward to gain height, and sideways to 'bank' into the turns which were made with the help of the rudder bar worked by the pilot's feet. If the aircraft fell below a certain speed, it would stall and go into a slow spin. For aerodynamic reasons, easier to demonstrate than to describe, using the rudder to try to counteract the direction of the spin did not work. An inexperienced pilot, realizing the aircraft was sinking, would pull the control column back into his chest – but that did not work, either. What he needed to do was, contrary to instinct, to push the control column forward. The aircraft could then respond by gaining flying speed on its more rapid descent, allowing the rudder to become operative again. But all too often inexperienced pilots 'froze' (post-war films sometimes showed instructors, in the cockpit behind, leaning over and knocking the trainee pilot out with a spanner, to get him to release his grip).

One of the people I have asked what mind's eye picture of trance is conjured up has cited this type, because it happened for him to have been a dramatic experience. The author and broadcaster Frank Delaney was interviewing an officer by the roadside in Ulster when the man suddenly froze in mid-sentence, as if struck dumb. Surprised, Delaney after a few moments turned round, and found they were looking into the barrel of a gun. As it turned out, a practical joker was behind it; but this was an interesting example of primitive instinct breaking through in sufficient strength to paralyse thought and inhibit rational reaction to danger.

Hysterical immobility is probably much commoner, on account of the general reluctance to take hysteria seriously, than is generally realized. Many a motorist must have experienced momentary panic when he has pressed down the brake pedal, and nothing has happened, or when a foot has slipped off the brake on to the accelerator. On such occasions there is often a brief 'freeze'; it is as if the conscious mind wants to take over, but is at a loss because learned habit has relieved it of the need to intervene in the process of braking. In such circumstances a driver may be in much the same position as I am if I am asked where, say, on the keyboard the letter 'K' is found. I have to go through the motions of typing, in order to remember.

Cases are occasionally described as having occurred in circumstances which make hysterical 'freezing' the most obvious explanation. At an inquest in Winchester in 1987 the court heard how a 21-year-old woman making her first parachute jump on behalf of a charity had been killed when she drifted down into the path of a helicopter; spectators claimed she could be seen to go rigid, as if unable to pull the cord which would have taken her out of danger. But hysteria as a cause of death is rarely, if ever, formally admitted.

It was the obvious, but evaded, explanation of the Moorgate underground crash in London in 1975. Analysts searching for the psychological or chemical cause could find nothing the matter with the driver, who appeared to have been healthy. But so anxious were the investigators to find something, anything, rather than hysteria, which could be offered as a possible cause, that much was made of the fact the driver appeared not to have eaten since the evening before – though early-shift workers commonly postpone breakfast until they have a break from duty – and that he had a very small quantity of alcohol in his system – presumably left from a drink he had enjoyed the previous day.

Accounts from people who were on the train suggested that the driver had been irritable, impatient, as if he had something on his mind. Witnesses who had been on the platform at Moorgate when the train came in described how he could be seen to be sitting completely still, staring straight in front of him, his hands on the controls. He had slowed the train down before entering the station, but had then accelerated again. The most plausible explanation was that putting on the accelerator by mistake while in a state of abstraction, he 'froze'. That possibility was not even considered at the inquiry.

Creative malady

From time to time, however, voices have been raised to question the prevailing assumptions about hysteria. One of the pleas came unexpectedly in 1981 from Lord Taylor of Harlow, a former minister in the post-war Labour government, who had left politics to practise neuropsychiatry and write about psychiatric subjects. Hysteria, he pointed out in *World Medicine*, 'can be a blessing or a curse'. 'A tincture of hysterical behaviour finds a proper outlet on the stage, at the Bar, in Parliament, in the lecture theatre and the operating room'; and it can help an individual 'to achieve near miracles in the arts, in business and in administration'.

If it was unexpected that Lord Taylor, with his conventional medical background, should express such an opinion, the contents of Sir George Pickering's *Creative Malady* (1974) provided an even greater surprise. It consisted of biographical sketches of Charles Darwin, Florence Nightingale, Mary Baker Eddy, Elizabeth Barrett Browning, Sigmund Freud and Marcel Proust, showing how each of them had been invalids who had unconsciously exploited their illnesses to enable them to fulfil their various destinies.

I was asked by the *Guardian* to interview Sir George at the time of publication; and I thought I might have some quiet fun by reminding him of his assertion in his 1950 *Lancet* article that to attribute disease to abnormal states of mind was 'unworthy of serious consideration by scientific medicine'. The maladies he now described in his book were clearly created by the unconscious desire to have them, in order to exploit them. He turned the tables on me by simply handing me the article, having guessed I would bring it up. His target in 1950, he claimed, had not been psychosomatic theory as such, but the arrogance of some 'psychosomaticians', as he described them, in blandly appropriating certain types of illness – asthma, in particular – as their own territory.

Still, he was not denying that he had modified his earlier organicist views. His conversion, he recalled, had been gradual. It had begun when for the first time he had felt compelled to recognize that one of his heart patients, though unquestionably ill, was not suffering from any organic disorder. He had been courageous enough – foolhardy enough, his colleagues must have thought – to send her to the Maudsley Hospital, where she had been successfully relieved of her symptoms by a psychiatrist. Then he happened to come across an article contending that Darwin's invalidism was not, as had been assumed, the consequence of a bite from some tropical bug, but was a neurosis designed to provide him with what he most needed – the excuse to stay out of public life, so as to get on with his private life's work on evolution.

The other people whose careers and maladies Sir George had included in the book had similarly exploited their maladies purposefully, though not consciously: it was as if their maladies had shrewdly exploited *them*, enabling them to do what they could not otherwise have done, because of the demands on their time and patience. He was not sure that Elizabeth Barrett Browning quite came in this category; she might have written as well in any circumstances. For the rest, though, he felt sure that all needed their crutches.

Sir George's conversion had been completed when he realized that he himself had unconsciously been exploiting an illness as a form of protection. His 'crutches', paradoxically, had been his arthritic hips. They had been 'an absolute godsend', sparing him from attending functions which bored or irritated him. It had taken him most of his life to realize this; now, when he was on the brink of retirement, he recognized their message when they passed it to him, and he took the appropriate remedy – 'in bed, I cannot attend committees'.

Sir George diagnosed 'psychoneurosis', in the Freudian mode – except in the case of Mary Baker Eddy, a hysteric; but he left no doubt that the others, too, represented what Freud himself had initially regarded as hysteria. They also helped to explain why so many earlier researchers had placed so much emphasis on the links between hysteria and hypnosis – even to the point of confusing them, as Charcot had done. The symptoms of hysteria reflect the ability of the subliminal self to dictate its requirements directly to mind, or body, or both, without the need for anything which we would recognize as a trance condition as an intermediary.

Sometimes trance is needed in the early stages, as it was in Mary Baker Eddy's case. She did not learn how to transform her hysteria from making her a nuisance to providing her with a crutch until she had been treated by the hypnotherapist Phineas Quimby. In other cases, it is as if the nagging of the subliminal self – saying, in effect, 'you have better things to do with your life than waste it in whingeing, or committees, or company' – eventually overcomes the resistance put up by conscience. The same effect may be achieved by a hallucination of the kind that transformed Saint Paul's life, or by some insight gained in hypnotherapy. The subliminal self has to take whatever opportunity presents itself. 'Of all maladies, hysteria is unquestionably the most intelligent,' as Stefan Zweig remarked in his essay on Mary Baker Eddy; 'the one most intimately expressive of individual impulse, the one which alike in the offensive and the defensive most plainly reveals the sufferer's secret wishes.' She had learned in childhood how to get her own way; without that lesson, she could never have created the International Church of Christ, Scientist, which remains her monument.

The only living beneficiary of the creative malady that Sir George felt free to cite was himself; he knew of others, he told me, but was aware that they might be deeply offended if he had named them. Evelyn Waugh, however, actually used to admit he exploited a form of hysteria; though he, too, did not use the term. His deafness, he had decided, was psychosomatic. It became much worse when he was bored.

Cure by laughter

Two years after the publication of *Creative Malady*, a second impressive vindication of hysteria appeared in the *New England Journal of Medicine*, widely regarded as without peer among medical journals, and more ready than any of them to admit off-beat material.

The writer was Norman Cousins, who for many years had been the editor of the *Saturday Review*. He described how in 1964, following his return from a conference in Moscow, he had begun to feel ill, and soon was in great pain, unable to walk or even to turn his head. Hospital tests revealed the reason, though not the cause; his bloodstream was silting up. Realizing that his condition was rapidly deteriorating, he asked to be told if his life was in danger. His physician, an old friend, admitted that it was. One of the specialists who had been called in said he had never seen anybody recover from the symptoms Cousins was by this time displaying.

As it was apparent that the treatment he was receiving was not working, Cousins decided he must prescribe for himself. 'Auto-immunity' had not yet become a familiar term, but in effect his diagnosis was that his had failed him. Something had happened to upset his endocrine system – perhaps, he surmised, an evening of intense frustration, his last in Moscow, when the government driver who was to take him to an important reception out of Moscow drove him by mistake more than a hundred kilometres in the opposite direction. The long flight back to New York the next day had not helped; and it had been the following morning he had started to feel ill.

Ten years earlier, Cousins had read Hans Selye's *The Stress of Life*, in which Selye had shown that the adrenal glands could be adversely affected by frustration. If negative emotions had a destructive effect on the body's chemistry, Cousins surmised, might not positive emotions produce positive chemical changes? Reviewing the emotions which during his life he had found positive, he thought of 'love, hope, faith, laughter, confidence and the will to live'. He had the will to live all right, but there was only one of the others, he realized, that could be induced. His physician agreed to collaborate with him in a research programme investigating 'the full exercise of the affirmative elements as a factor in enhancing body chemistry'. It was to consist of a course of induced hysterical convulsions – belly-laughter.

Cousins's friend Alan Funt, producer of the *Candid Camera* television series, lent him a projector and some of the programmes, which he watched. The treatment was a resounding success: 'I made the joyous discovery that ten minutes of genuine belly-laughter had an anaesthetic effect, and would give me at least two hours of pain-free sleep.' Might this have been coincidence? No: as part of the research programme, his blood sedimentation rate was being tested before and after each session; and although the amount that it fell after each session was small, it proved to be cumulative. The only snag was that his hilarity disturbed other patients; but this was soon remedied, as he grew well enough to move out into a hotel. Within six months he was on his feet; soon, he was back at his desk at the *Saturday Review*; and although it took time for his joints, muscles and tissues to recover, they eventually did. When his account was published twelve years later, he felt none the worse for his experience.

Only the most impervious of organicists – a species gradually becoming extinct, but taking an unconscionable time about it – could deny that laughter was responsible for at least part of the cure (Cousins also took vitamins). But was it the emotional release, or the fact that he was convulsed by what he watched, that was decisive? Or both?

On this issue, Rivers had had to admit he was baffled. Hysterical immobility he could understand, as an atavistic reaction to danger; but what evolutionary purpose could convulsive seizures serve? In view of his fascination with evolutionary development of trance it is odd that the obvious explanation did not occur to him. If total immobility fails to protect and flight is impossible, many species will turn and fight as best they can. The reaction of a fly in a spider's web, or a hooked trout, is a frenzy of activity. For animals, convulsions are a standard reaction to frustration. It is tempting, in fact, to speculate that distemper in young puppies may be related to the frustrations they have to put up with during house-training; its symptoms, though the sole responsibility for them is ordinarily credited to a virus, are sometimes very similar to those traditionally described as hysteria in humans.

Even more surprising, in view of Rivers's early first-hand experiences as an anthropologist, is that he did not think to relate hysterical convulsions to their human roots in shamanism. Many observers of tribal rites in which shamans enter their trance in order to communicate with the spirits have likened the symptoms to hysteria or epilepsy. Some had assumed that they must actually *be* the symptoms of hysteria or epilepsy. Such convulsions appear to be linked to the transition from consciousness to trance – an association that was taken for granted until Puységur established that it was possible to induce a mesmeric trance without them.

Convulsions have continued to occur, though, in connection with spontaneous trances. They are a commonplace at revivalist meetings in many religions, from Voodoo to Charismatic Christianity, the assumption being that they herald possession by the spirits – or the Holy Spirit, as Wesley believed. Spiritualist mediums, too, often have mild convulsions entering trance, as Mrs Piper did; and they are occasionally felt by people attending seances. In a footnote to his description of an evening with D. D. Home in 1868, Lord Adare noted that sitters' hands were often 'taken possession of and agitated'. In his own case, his hand had actually been shaken 'sometimes violently, sometimes gently, without any act of volition on my part'.

   The poet W. B. Yeats, too, had a violent reaction at the first seance he attended. First his shoulders and hands began to twitch – 'I could easily have stopped them, but I had never heard of such a thing and was curious.' When the movements became more violent, he stopped them; 'I sat motionless for a while and then my whole body moved like a suddenly unrolled watch-spring and I was thrown backward on the wall.' When the group held hands, his right hand banged the knuckles of the woman next to him; 'I was now struggling violently with this force which compelled me to movements I had not willed, and my movements became so violent that the table was broken.' For years afterwards he would not go to a seance. 'Was it part of myself – something always to be a danger, perhaps?' he asked in his 'Reveries over childhood and youth'; or had it come 'from without, as it seemed?'

   At first glance, the convulsions of laughter seem harder to account for in evolutionary terms. Speculating upon why babies laugh when tickled, Darwin surmised that they may be learning to distinguish between friendly and threatening approaches; but the assumption since has tended to be that laughter simply reflects temporary loss of self-control. When somebody tells us 'it was hysterical', after all, we take for granted that whatever 'it' refers to was funny; and to give way to hysterics, even if the effect can be exhilarating, used to meet with disapproval. 'A laugh which cannot be checked, but continues until tears flow or the limbs become convulsed', the entry in Quain's *Dictionary of Medicine* (1883) stated, 'is a typical example of such suspension of control.' For Herbert Spencer muscular convulsions accompanying laughter 'are distinguished from most others by this, that they are purposeless', a view which has been echoed since – even, surprisingly, by Arthur Koestler. Laughter is 'unique in that it serves no apparent biological purpose,' he wrote in *The Act of Creation* (1964). 'Its only utilitarian function, as far as one can see, is to provide temporary relief from utilitarian pressures.'

   But it is precisely this function, surely, for which laughter is needed. It provides a simple relief mechanism, a way of shrugging off cares physically as well as mentally – as Dr Van Helsing in his broken English claimed in Bram Stoker's *Dracula*; his hysterical laughter, following a burial he had attended, came unbidden and uncontrollable: 'We men and women are like ropes drawn tight with strain,' he explained to Dr Seward. When tears come, like rain falling on ropes, the strain becomes too great; 'but King Laugh he come like the sunshine, and he ease off the strain again.'

Confirmation of the notion that convulsive laughter can have a therapeutic function has come from an experiment undertaken recently by researchers sponsored by the United Nations Children's Fund in the Philippines. One in five of the children under six at the villages where they were working, they found, was disabled. Lacking the resources to try more sophisticated forms of treatment, they fell back on the provision of vitamin A, as it was cheap, and on teaching the mothers a form of massage which included tickling. 'Four months ago Josefine, a ten-month-old baby girl, was a human cabbage. She lay bonelessly in her mother's arms, unable to lift her head, never responding to a voice or a smile,' a Sunday *Observer* correspondent reported in 1981. Then her mother was taught where and how to tickle the baby. 'Now she plays enthusiastically, and is as responsive as any normal child of her age.'

Hysterical laughter makes even clearer evolutionary sense when it is linked with other convulsive forms of emotional release; notably orgasm, which Wilhelm Reich tried to establish as therapeutic, as well as delightful. We talk, too, of somebody 'trembling', or 'shaking', or being 'beside himself' with rage, as if subliminal pressure has burst through consciousness's restraints – sometimes to forestall apoplexy. The eighteenth-century surgeon John Hunter said he feared that his life was at the mercy of any fool who might put him in a passion. He would have been nearer the truth if he had said that passion would be destructive if he could not release it, as was to happen in his case; he collapsed and died at a hospital board meeting.

The convulsions associated with grief, too, appear to provide a release for the body as well as for the emotions. It has often been suggested that the Western convention by which mourners restrain themselves to weeping – sometimes not even to tears – is ill-advised; we would be all the better for it if we were allowed to follow the Eastern example and give way to uncontrollable grief, an idea put forward by the physician and mystical philosopher Van Helmont in a treatise in 1692 on the importance of the emotions in health. 'Laughter and weeping are proper to mankind,' he claimed. Should we suffer some deep sorrow, such as follows the death of a friend, we should weep freely, as 'our sorrow by this means is alleviated.' People who did not weep freely when they felt sorrow, experience has shown, often fell ill as a result.

Laughter and tears, then, suggest that hysterical convulsions have a therapeutic potential. Up to a point this has been recognized in orthodox psychiatry, in the form of electroconvulsive therapy – though the use of muscle relaxants means that the actual convulsive flailing movements are curbed. Unquestionably some patients, usually those who are suffering from depression, react satisfactorily. Psychiatrists agree, however, that the method works well only if patients are carefully selected; and no objective selection method has been found.

The main weakness of ECT, as it has commonly been employed, is that it has been impersonal, prescribed for the symptoms rather than for the individual patient. Often it has been carried out by inadequately trained hospital staff, with no supervision. In one extraordinary case, in a British mental hospital, it was found after several months of the use of an ECT machine that it had not been properly connected; all that the patient had received were, in effect, placebo shocks. Cousins's experience suggests that ECT should be used on a more personal basis, with induced laughter, if patients feel like trying it. But it is not easy to visualize such a therapy commending itself to some psychiatrists. They might feel they were being laughed *at*.

There is one other form of hysteria which is recognized by the medical profession, but imperfectly understood. It sometimes happens that a patient with symptoms which can be accepted as organic displays them in so exaggerated a form that an attached emotional element becomes obvious. Then it may be attributed to 'hysterical overlay'. The tendency is to regard it as a complication – a nuisance, rather than an integral component of the malady.

Hysteria the slayer

The danger of thinking in these terms was exposed in the 1950s by a Glasgow physician, David Kissen, who specialized in diseases of the chest. Many of his patients had tuberculosis, a disease which Koch had shown to be organic by his discovery of the tubercle bacillus, and which since then had been assumed to be infectious. But was it infectious, Kissen wondered, in the sense of being transmitted from person to person on the breath, as was assumed? Sometimes it spread through a family; more often it was oddly selective. And why should its incidence have been slowly but steadily declining for a hundred years, in spite of the fact that no reliable remedy had been found?

Kissen concluded that improvements in living conditions, better housing and hygiene, must be largely responsible for the general improvement. How, then, to account for the way in which the disease often singled out well-off individuals, usually young people, to attack? The bacillus was ubiquitous; everybody was, or could be, infected. The need was to find why some individuals remained unaffected, while others succumbed. 'Consumption', as TB had earlier been called, had often been linked in the nineteenth century with hearts broken or bruised by unfulfilled love affairs. Was it possible, Kissen wondered – he had studied the literature of psychosomatic medicine – that emotional deprivation of some kind might have a responsibility for letting the tubercle off the leash?

One of the problems confronting the pioneers of psychosomatic medicine was the difficulty of mounting controlled trials. Although simple questionnaires, distributed to TB patients, might have elicited some interesting information, it would have been dismissed as anecdotal. Kissen, however, realized that he had controls ready to hand. New patients over the age of fifteen who came to the diagnostic clinic where he was working were given a questionnaire designed to discover, among other things, if they had recently suffered from bereavement, divorce, separation, or an unhappy love affair. Diagnosis followed; and this meant that the replies could be put into two categories, those patients who had TB and those who did not. Comparison of the two showed a far higher proportion of 'broken love links', as Kissen described them, among the patients who had TB.

Kissen made three investigations using this method, the last of them being designed to explore whether personality traits might play a part; and this produced the most striking of all the statistics. The outstanding personality trait common to all the TB cases studied showed an 'inordinate need for affection', he noted in his conclusions. This occurred in 100 per cent of the tuberculous cases, compared with 16 per cent of the controls.

Before the tubercle bacillus was discovered, TB of the kind that could be put down to broken love links had been regarded as a form of hysteria; a diagnosis confirmed by such case histories as Elizabeth Barrett's, with her startling recovery when Robert Browning came into her life. Kissen's research strongly suggested that the hysterical component in TB cannot be dismissed as 'overlay'; it can be one of the factors responsible, either in preparing the terrain, or in precipitating the symptoms, or both. Ironically, though, Kissen could carry the research no further along the lines he had taken it, because the introduction of a drug which dealt effectively with the bacillus meant that the long decline in the incidence of TB was speeded up, and new cases became unusual.

Kissen, however, switched his attention to cancèr, following up research which had been conducted in New York by Laurence LeShan. Here, too, controlled trials revealed that broken love links were significantly often associated with the onset of the disease; and repression of feelings was significantly often an underlying personality trait. But though individual doctors began to realize their attitude needed to be modified, in the light of the growing proof of the subliminal at work even in infectious disorders, organicism is so ingrained that it has proved impossible to break down.

Charms

A typical example of the medical profession's inability to face uncomfortable facts has been provided by its refusal to pay serious attention to the highly significant results of research into a relatively insignificant branch of dermatology: the treatment of warts. In folklore warts can be 'charmed' away, with magic spells. In Ireland, when I was growing up there, warts were 'bought' for sixpence, the buyer promising they would disappear, as often they did. But warts are classified as epidermal tumours. More than that, they have been traced to a virus which, to quote Macmillan's recent medical encyclopedia, 'invades the skin cells and causes them to multiply rapidly'. And warts are infectious, 'spread by touch or by contact with the shed skin of a wart'. In short, they are by definition organic. It has consequently been impossible for orthodoxy to accept that they can be treated except by approved physical methods such as applications of a paint which in effect burns them out. 'There are many folk remedies for removing warts,' the encyclopedia comments, 'but no evidence to show that they work.'

This is only one of many examples of the way in which orthodox medical teaching blandly ignores evidence which does not fit its dogmas. There has, in fact, been ample proof that auto-suggestion and hypnosis are highly effective wart-removers. In *Uses and Abuses of Psychology* (1955), Eysenck described a controlled experiment in which two groups of children were the subjects, one group receiving conventional treatment, and the other being told they could lose their warts by drawing a picture of their hands, 'with the wart on it, and then, with a certain amount of hocus-pocus, drawing circles round the wart and reducing the size on the picture day by day until the wart had completely disappeared in the picture'. The hocus-pocus turned out to be far more effective than the orthodox treatment – a finding which has since been confirmed in further trials.

The implications, as Lewis Thomas realized, are startling. 'You can't sit there under hypnosis, taking suggestions in and having them acted upon with such accuracy, without assuming the existence of something very like a controller,' he commented in his essay on warts in *The Medusa and the Snail* (1980). 'Some intelligence or other knows how to get rid of warts, and this is a disquieting thought.' It is also, he added, 'a wonderful problem in need of solving'; because if we had an idea how warts are hypnotized away, 'we would be finding out about a kind of superintelligence that exists in each of us, infinitely smarter and possessed of actual know-how far beyond our present understanding.'

This prescription, an echo of Myers, has found few takers in the medical profession. It is not necessary for a dermatologist to learn to hypnotize patients, or to teach them auto-hypnosis. It is not unusual, I have found, for dermatologists to be among the most dedicated critics of psychosomatic theory and practice. In any case, they have no formal training in the use of hypnosis or auto-suggestion, and may find themselves unable to make effective use of them – let alone of hocus-pocus – when they try.

This has had depressing consequences in connection with a malady much more widespread and serious than warts: pain. It is hard to credit, but pain was not recognized as a disease condition by the medical profession until the 1980s. It was, of course, accepted that pain could occur as a consequence of illness: but not that it was an illness in its own right.

It was not recognized chiefly because it could not be explained in organicist terms. It could not be measured except by the subjective impressions of the individual feeling it, and its intensity could not be predicted with any certainty. If somebody was pinched or pricked in the course of a test it would usually be safe enough to forecast a yelp or a scream related to the amount of force used. But what happened in test conditions could not account for the wealth of stories of people who had suffered severe injuries yet felt no pain so long as they were absorbed in whatever they were doing, from playing in a football game to leading a bayonet charge.

That trance, in some form, must have the ability to relieve or remove pain could hardly be disputed, in view of the mass of evidence from the mesmerists and their hypnotist successors. But this idea was so unwelcome that the medical profession continued to rely on the argument that had been used when anaesthetics were first brought into use: they were easier to use. As Myers complained, this left out one important aspect: chloroform, the anaesthetic then in most general use, is a poison, which hypnosis is not. 'In a word, the hypnotic subject is *above* instead of *below* pain.'

This inconvenient fact might be ignored, but in 1971 James Reston, of the *New York Times*, was on a visit to China when he had appendicitis; and although his appendix was removed while he was under an anaesthetic, he was subsequently given acupuncture to relieve his post-operative pain. His report that it had worked came as a shock. Acupuncture had been the object of derision by orthodox medical practitioners: it had featured among the list of 'lunacies' in a chapter on 'Superstition and Ignorance' in Louis Lasagna's *The Doctors' Dilemmas*. When further investigation demonstrated that it was indeed an effective pain-killer, there had to be a hasty reassessment, prompting research to find a neurochemical explanation, which might with luck keep pain within the organicist camp.

Sure enough, neurotransmitters were found, enkephalins and endorphins, the body's self-manufactured opiates; and for a while there was a dazzling prospect of refining and marketing them as pain-killers. But by 1980 a conference on the neurophysiology of pain reminded Geoff Watts, reporting on it for *World Medicine*, of the mediaeval disputation on the number of angels that might dance on the head of a pin: 'almost everything about pain is uncertain, or equivocal, or complicated, or all three – and the accretion of knowledge appears, at present, to be adding to the complexity without noticeably reducing the uncertainties and equivocations.'

Still, the discovery that the opiates were being manufactured in the human body had come as a relief. 'Neurologists are dedicated to the proposition that mind *is* matter – cerebral matter, to be precise,' David Bowsher of the neurobiology laboratory at Liverpool University claimed in 1979; the phenomenon of pain suppression in the case of people suffering martyrdom could consequently be shown 'in some cases to have a neurohormonal basis'. Two years later the *British Medical Journal* felt able to claim in an editorial: 'Chronic pain is now recognized as a disease state, and its treatment and management are receiving increasing attention.' So they were, but the attention was largely concentrated, at least so far as well-funded research was concerned, on the neurological aspects, trying to map the channels through which pain is transmitted. This has been providing some understanding of the channels, but not about the 'controller' which decides whether pain is to be felt, and if so, on its intensity.

An obvious starting-point would be to conduct experiments with people who have learned to control pain by auto-suggestion, in some form. Some have learned as children, as the Irish travel writer Dervla Murphy did. In her case, it was part of a protracted battle with one of the nuns who taught at her primary school, and used to beat her. 'During my "war" with Sister Andrew, I discovered that it was possible to triumph over pain,' Dervla Murphy recalls. 'I find it hard to explain, but I managed to send a message down to the painful part and control it.' She practised with self-inflicted pain, 'such as standing in boiling water', to improve her technique: 'I could detach myself totally from the pain and, to an extent, I can still do that today.'

A few individuals have been able to display astonishing pain resistance, notably Jack Schwartz, investigated by Elmer Green at the Menninger Clinic. Not only could Schwartz freely skewer himself, pushing needles into his arms; he was able to stop the flow of blood, whenever he decided to; the punctures would heal rapidly, leaving no scar, and there was never a trace of infection, though no attempt was made to keep the needles clean.

If the subliminal has such powers, why should it not be able, say, to cure cancer? It can remove tumours, Matthew Manning, a leading exponent in Britain of auto-hypnosis, has found; but only if the patient's imagination is sufficiently roused. And there is now a body of evidence to show it can be roused through techniques such as those introduced by the Simontons in the United States and by Ainslie Meares in Australia.

For Meares, the explanation for the way his method worked lay in what he described as 'atavistic regression' – a return to the natural state of man before the development of self-consciousness, when instinct was the guide. He did not claim miracle cures; indeed, his chief claim was that his patients, almost all of whom had been told by their doctors that there was nothing more that could be done for them, learned how to approach death peacefully. But in some cases, as many as one in ten, the tumours disappeared.

That Meares, an eminent psychiatrist, should have become hooked on the study and practice of trance induction surprised his colleagues. That Bernie Siegel, Assistant Clinical Professor of Surgery at Yale Medical School, should have taken the same course must have been even more startling to those who had known him before, in 1978, he attended a seminar given by the Simontons. 'Here I was, an MD, a "Medical Deity", and I didn't know what went on in the head at all,' he recalls. 'The literature on mind–body interaction was separate, and therefore unknown to specialists in other areas.' He began to apply the lessons he learned at and after the seminar, and the outcome has been his *Love, Medicine and Miracles*, the most heartening account that has yet appeared of the use of trance – in the widest sense – to conserve and restore health.

Divided lives

Another of the issues which fascinated psychologists and psychiatrists a century ago, but which their successors tended to regard as a rather freakish curiosity, has recently forced itself back into their attention as a more widespread and complex problem than they had realised: dual, or multiple, personality.

My first introduction to a dual personality came in the 1950s, in the course of a holiday spent in the company of, among others, a married man whose wife was away with her parents for a few weeks, and who was determined to make the most of the opportunities her absence offered. By day he was civilized, intelligent and good company. Come the evening and a few drinks, he became restless, on the look-out for 'talent' as he described it – for any woman who might be accommodating. The rest of us in the party were at first mildly amused, and a little envious of the skill with which he managed to make his conquests. But if his technique failed, he would return to us to get drunk, and at a certain point he would cease to be civilized or good company, and become boorish, offensive, deliberately rude not only to us but to anybody who might attract his attention.

I had known alcoholics before; drink was, and remains, notoriously journalism's occupational hazard. And some of them had been obnoxious when drunk. But this man's change of character was startling – Jekyll into Hyde; and it would occur within seconds. The explanation began to dawn on me when I read *The Three Faces of Eve* (1957), in which two psychiatrists, Corbett Thigpen and Hervey Cleckley, described a remarkable case which they had investigated. 'Eve White' was 'a neat colourless young woman', being treated for headaches and other symptoms, who eventually admitted to her doctor she 'heard voices' – she had not cared to mention them before, for fear of being admitted to a lunatic asylum. Then, suddenly, the 'voice' she had described broke through. Before his eyes, as well as in his ears, 'Eve White' metamorphosed into 'Eve Black', a brash, sexy layabout who bore a quite remarkable resemblance to Morton Prince's 'Sally', in particular the ability to read the thoughts of the personality whose body and brain she shared. 'Black' knew 'White' intimately, despised her, and enjoyed leaving her in embarrassing situations.

The story of the two Eves – succeeded by a third personality, Jane, and eventually transmuted into a fourth – was to become widely known thanks to the Hollywood film, which was reasonably faithful to the reality. But it was assumed to be a freak case, of a kind so rare that psychologists and psychiatrists would hardly need to take it into consideration. People who showed indications of secondary personalities continued to be diagnosed and treated as psychotic.

Eventually, however, the introduction of more sophisticated methods of monitoring electrical or chemical changes in the brain led to research to find whether changes of personality manifested in psychosis could be monitored; and in 1970 psychiatrists at the National Institute of Mental Health in Washington found that there were neurophysiological ways of distinguishing 'multiple personality disorder'; different personalities produced consistently different wave patterns.

The most likely explanation for MPD, it was submitted, is that in childhood, fantasy selves often arise out of imaginative daydreaming. Ordinarily they are eventually forgotten, or incorporated into the everyday self; but in some cases, Dr Frank Putnam suggested on the basis of the research, particularly following some traumatic experience, a split-off self may remain, emerging later as MPD.

Although it was now recognized, MPD attracted little attention until later in the 1970s it forced itself upon psychiatrists' attention in connection with veterans of the war in Vietnam. The frequency and violence of their mental breakdowns led by 1980 to the introduction of a polite identification-tag: Post-Traumatic Stress Disorder.

PTSD victims frequently described themselves as split personalities. Most of them had come back from Vietnam relieved to be out of it, delighted to return to a civilized job, a home, wife, kids. And often they achieved that ambition – but were unable to settle down. The combat self, Bruce Goderez of the Veterans Administration Center in Northampton, Massachusetts, explained, lurked below the surface. Alert, fierce, primed for instant reaction, it was apt to break out violently – particularly in those cases, perhaps more common in Vietnam than in any comparable war, where uneasiness about the United States' role, and about occasional atrocities, had led to guilt feelings, even among those who had not been involved, but had realized what was happening and not attempted to intervene.

At first, PTSD was categorized an 'anxiety disorder'. When it became increasingly obvious that many of the victims actually *were* split personalities, it began to give way to 'dissociation'. And after all the years of neglect, hypnotherapy was tried, and came briefly into its own again. PTSD victims were found to be more readily hypnotizable than patients with other types of neurosis, or psychosis; and it was sometimes possible to trace the source of their divided selves, and instil some harmony, by much the same technique as Breuer employed with 'Anna O.', more than a century ago.

Morton Prince's 'co-consciousness' has also been brought back into the public eye in *The Minds of Billy Milligan* (1981), in which Daniel Keyes described how Milligan, the first person in the United States to be acquitted of criminal charges on the ground of multiple personality disorder, had no less than 23 egos. Yet still, psychologists and psychiatrists display a marked reluctance to explore this territory – and also another obvious area to examine for clues: autism.

Autism

Early in the present century the Swiss psychiatrist Eugen Bleuler, director of the hospital where Jung first practised psychiatry, proposed the term 'autistic thinking' for thought which is divorced from logic. He recognized the link with schizophrenia, but pointed out that other trance conditions also produce autistic thinking. From time to time psychologists and psychiatrists considered the subject, discussing where the dividing line lay between logical and autistic thought;

McDougall came to the conclusion that no such line could be drawn. But the importance of recognizing autistic thinking in children, and learning how to handle them, was not set out until Leo Kanner published his findings from studying them – and their parents – in 1949.

The autistic child behaves, Kanner explained, as if withdrawn from ordinary reality: as if in a trance. It does not react normally – for example, if picked up it does not adjust its posture to fit in with the hold. Withdrawal of this kind is also characteristic of psychosis; in its extreme form, catatonia, the limbs retain any position in which they are placed. But whereas psychotics lose contact with reality, autistic children retain awareness of what is happening; they simply reject it. Though ordinarily quiet, they can on occasion display a remarkable command of language, revealing that they have a high degree of intelligence which has remained unimpaired, even if it is not ordinarily in evidence.

A few psychologists grasped the importance of these findings. There is a need to keep in mind that there are these two types of thought, Peter McKellar pointed out in *Imagination and Thinking* (1957): 'R-thinking' (reality adjusted) and 'A-thinking' (autistic). 'Autistic' characterizes dreams and trances; 'it is dependent upon mere association of ideas rather than upon logical connection and testing against reality', and liable to the intrusion of fantasy. But psychiatrists, although they accepted 'early childhood autism' as a convenient description for a certain type of behaviour, in general failed to grasp Kanner's main point, and continued to make more specific diagnoses according to their preconceptions. A report published in 1971, surveying 448 cases, revealed that the children had been variously diagnosed (apart from autistic) as brain damaged, emotionally disturbed, deaf, psychotic, retarded or schizophrenic. When the children were submitted individually for second opinions, the same range of diagnosis resulted, but it bore no relationship whatsoever to the first set. The labels might have been pinned on at random.

This diversity of diagnosis was by no means the only example of orthodox psychiatry's confusion. In a paper delivered to a World Psychiatric Symposium in 1969, Arthur Koestler, the only outsider invited – presumably, he thought, 'to represent that infernal nuisance in the psychiatrist's life, the patient' – unkindly drew his hosts' attention to reports of the results of trials designed to compare diagnoses made on the basis of elaborate case histories, sometimes re-

inforced with videotapes. The findings revealed ludicrous differences
between British and American psychiatrists. Manic depression was
diagnosed twenty times more often in Britain; 'on the other hand,'
Koestler remarked, 'if I were to go off my head in America, I would
stand a ten-times-higher chance of being classified as a case of cerebral
arterio-sclerosis than in England, and a thirty-three per cent higher
chance of being classified as a schizo.'

In the case of autistic children, opinions also differed over the
presumed cause of the symptoms. The prevailing organicism ensured
that most 'experts' attributed them either to a genetic defect or
to brain damage, often reassuring parents by saying they were certainly in no way responsible – gratifying for parents, but leaving a
bleak outlook for the autistic children. The minority who accepted
that the cause must be sought in the children's environmental
background were divided among themselves over such issues as
whether it should be looked for in the child's mind – perhaps the
result of an experience which it had found traumatic – or in some
failure of communication with the child on the part of the parent.
Autistic children were consequently being prescribed a variety
of treatments reflecting the different preconceptions of the psychiatrists, and there was nothing to suggest that the recovery rate was
any better than if the treatment, as well as the diagnosis, had been
randomized.

There could hardly have been a more devastating exposure of
the fallibility of psychiatric diagnostic procedures – and, for that
matter, of the dangers inherent in the emphasis, in medical schools, on
reaching a diagnosis. But there was more to it, as Niko Tinbergen
pointed out in the lecture he gave when he received his Nobel Prize
in 1973.

Tinbergen had won his award for his studies of animal behaviour,
which helped to re-establish ethology as a scientific discipline; and he
and his wife had adopted a similar method, observant but unobtrusive,
with autistic children. The 'unobtrusive' element was essential, he
knew, because children, like animals, behave differently when they
are aware they are being observed. A diagnostic system by which
symptoms are looked for and discussed is calculated to make autistic
children withdraw from reality – the method they adopt to shield
themselves from the need to behave in accordance with parental
expectations.

It is quite normal for children to display autistic symptoms when

strangers call, reflecting 'a conflict between two incompatible moti-
vations', curiosity and fear. The first essential, Tinbergen had
found, is to allay the fear while gently encouraging the curiosity by not
reacting in any of the ways the child would associate with the
mother's expectations, and with its mother's reactions to mis-
behaviour.

The method Tinbergen and his wife Elizabeth had adopted was to
enter into collusion with the autistic child with the help of a kind of
'grandmother's steps' in reverse, encouraging the child to indulge its
curiosity without the risk of 'grandmother' looking round to see
whether the child is observing her, or moving up closer to her, until
confidence, and then rapport, can be established.

What is the cause of autism in children? Kanner had established
that almost all the parents of the children he studied were successful
in their careers, but suffered from what he described as 'a mechani-
zation of human relationships'. They were undemonstrative, lacking
emotional warmth. Only one of the mothers who had brought an
autistic child to him had cuddled it. As for the fathers, they 'hardly
knew their autistic children'. They 'rarely step down from the pedestal
of sombre adulthood to indulge in childish play'. The resulting 'mech-
anization' of relationships, though it did not cause autism, prepared
the ground for it.

The Tinbergens came to a similar conclusion: early childhood
autism arises environmentally. There are many indications 'firstly,
that many autists are potentially normal children, whose affiliation
and subsequent socialization processes have gone wrong in one way
or another', and secondly, that this can often be traced back to the
parents, particularly the mothers. Tinbergen was careful to insist he
was not blaming the mothers. To judge from the frequency with which
autistic children were first-borns, inexperience must often contribute,
or the mother might be over-apprehensive, or over-intrusive, or herself
under some stress. 'The parents deserve as much compassion, and
may be as much in need of help, as the autists themselves.' But in
practice they could expect little understanding. 'We are alarmed
because we found this corner of psychiatry in a state of disarray,' he
commented, 'and because we discovered that many of the established
experts – doctors, teachers and therapists – are so little open to new
ideas and even facts.' He was quickly proved right; his presentation
of the evidence, prestigious though the occasion was, made little
discernible impression on psychiatrists. Tinbergen, after all, was a

'mere animal watcher', as he put it himself. What did he know about psychiatry?

The wrong course, still too often followed, is to treat autistic symptoms simply as something to be 'cured'. As Bleuler pointed out, autism can promote great art, and has provided mathematicians with solutions to problems that have baffled them; it may not be logical, but it can open up horizons beyond the reach of logic. Autistic thinking is 'unstructured, non-logical (but not necessarily illogical), whimsical thinking, that is the key to creativity,' Joseph Chilton Pearce claimed in *The Crack in the Cosmic Egg*, published in 1973 (the year that Tinbergen gave his Nobel lecture on the subject); it is the product of the subliminal self. It can be indulged in, as in reveries; or it can break through, without loss of consciousness. It has no value judgements because 'trance by-passes the ordinary criteria for data selection.' Nevertheless it is 'a pearl of great price. It is the way by which potential unfolds.'

'Prodigies' illustrate Pearce's point. With them, too, conventional psychiatric methods can be inappropriate, as Oliver Sacks has illustrated in his account of 'the twins' (1985). When he met them, he recalls, they were 26, 'a sort of grotesque Tweedledum and Tweedledee', identical in mind and personality, unable to do simple mathematical problems, yet given any date in the past or the next 40,000 years, they could tell almost instantly what day of the week it would be or had been. Even more striking, they could tell him what date Easter would be in any year he chose to name. Asked how they did it, they said simply 'we see it.'

Eventually an explanation – that the twins used algorithms – was presented, to the relief of psychologists who no longer had to contemplate the unwelcome possibility of clairvoyance. The fact that it explained nothing, and was in fact of quite startling irrelevance, made no difference; it was acceptable. As there was no further need to investigate the twins it was decided they should be separated 'for their own good'.

Psychopaths

Another manifestation of dual personality presents society with problems which we have hardly begun to consider, let alone to solve. The psychopath is often to all appearances a normal integrated personality.

But as Hervey Cleckley argued in *The Mask of Sanity* – first published in 1951, but considerably expanded later – the normality is a 'front'. It is almost as if it is a trance condition, which for convenience he slips into in his dealings with other people. 'We are dealing here not with a complete man at all, but with something that suggests a subtle reflex machine which can mimic the human personality to perfection.'

The psychopath, Cleckley emphasized, is in full possession of his faculties. But the man behind the mask lacks any sense of morality. It is as if he has stuck in that stage of childhood when the instinct is to grab what we want, whether it is a packet of sweets from a shop counter or another child's toy, without thought for the feelings of others, or for the possible consequences in the form of parental retribution. The psychopath has no use for 'Mrs Doasyouwouldbedoneby'. Otherwise, though, his mental processes are unimpaired.

Jung classified pathological lying as a trance condition, and probably the most frequently encountered psychopaths are fantasists. All of us indulge in fantasy; we may even, Walter Mitty fashion, allow ourselves to be taken over in our trance condition to the point where we become temporarily oblivious to our surroundings. But there are men and women whose fantasies become so real to them that they blot out reality, by a similar process to that with which from time to time we make improvements to a good story until eventually we cannot distinguish the embellishments from the facts.

A form it has often taken makes headlines when the man – it is usually a man – is detected working as a doctor in a hospital when he has had no medical training. Such is the power of the fantasy, it often carries such total conviction that doctors, nurses and staff suspect nothing until something or somebody gives him away.

I had first-hand experience of such a fantasist while working on the *Irish Times* after the war. A press relations officer in Aer Lingus invited me to meet a pilot who had been seconded from British Overseas Airways Corporation to help train Irish pilots to fly Constellations on the new Atlantic service. He was a congenial character, well-informed, with an engaging ability to make fun of his accomplishments; he had once, he told us, held the record for the fastest trans-Atlantic flight – but only for a few minutes: the increasing tail-wind soon brought another airliner in even faster. I wrote a piece about him, which appeared the following day. The Aer Lingus management promptly rang up to complain. They had not, they insisted, brought over anybody from BOAC to train their pilots. The man was arrested and brought to court on a charge of obtaining money on false pretences; he had taken a camera 'on trial' and pawned it. But those of us who had met him before he was unmasked – including the embarrassed Aer Lingus PRO, who had been so impressed with his talk he had not bothered to check with the management – knew he was not a confidence trickster. He was simply living out a fantasy, entranced by the power of his imagination.

The psychopath cannot resist temptation, and is little influenced by fear of detection – one of the reasons why the death penalty is so ineffective as a deterrent. Because he seems eminently sane, he is likely to be sentenced to go to prison rather than to mental hospital when caught. But one form of psychopathic behaviour is recognized as a form of mental disorder: kleptomania.

It was first analysed in *Popular Errors on the Subject of Insanity Examined and Exposed* (1853) by James Foulis – he was later to become President of the Royal College of Physicians of Ireland – as an example of what the medical profession had come to look on as a form of insanity, but the legal profession continued to insist was criminal. He defined kleptomania (which he spelt with a 'c') as a tendency to steal, differing from the ordinary criminal type in that 'it is not prompted by the wants of the individual, neither is it practised with any view to the subsequent use in any way of the article that has been stolen.' Sometimes it was prompted by a desire to elude the vigilance of the owners; sometimes by 'a passion to accumulate all sorts of things without the least regard to their subsequent utility'. It could never be easy, he admitted, to be absolutely certain when kleptomania was responsible for thefts; 'but a careful investigation into the offender's past history, and into his conduct at the time of committing the act, will almost to a certainty set the matter at rest.'

This has proved unduly optimistic; shoplifting by individuals who are rich enough not to need to steal has become so common, and so much of a nuisance, that a defendant's plea he could not stop himself would be unlikely to impress a jury. Still, kleptomania is recognized as a disorder, at least in theory. The assumption is that it is a type of fugue, in which a psychopathic personality takes over.

NEUROLOGISTS

Epidemic hysteria

If hysteria was so unpopular with psychiatrists, epidemic hysteria could be expected to be even more of an irritation; but they were spared having to deal with it, thanks to the prevailing organicism. After the Second World War, there was an unwelcome and inexplicable increase in reports of outbreaks in institutions – schools and hospitals. The symptoms varied, but in the main followed the traditional pattern; they were listed by Frieda L. Gehlen of the University of New Mexico, in a review of the published material on 'hysterical contagion' in 1977: 'nausea, stomach cramps, uncontrollable trembling or twitching, dryness of mouth or throat, fainting, mild convulsions or even paralysis'. But when such outbreaks occurred they were rarely immediately identified as mass hysteria. The initial assumption was that some physical agent must be responsible; a virus, food poisoning, or a gas leak. The doctors called would treat the symptoms as best they could, and arrange for investigation to find the cause. Psychiatrists were seldom consulted; hysteria was rarely even mentioned, partly because the doctors would look foolish if a physical cause were to be found, partly because of the wrath the diagnosis would provoke with the patients, their relations and friends.

An exception, however, was reported by the *New Yorker*'s medical pundit, Berton Roueché, in 1978; largely based on the recollection of Dr Joel L. Nitzkin, chief of the Office of Consumer Protection in Dale County, Florida. Called to investigate 'a leak of poison gas' at an elementary school, he found when he arrived that seven children had been taken to hospital; about twenty-five had been collected and taken home by their parents; and forty were being treated in the 'cafetorium' – café at mealtimes, auditorium for meetings – for headache, dizziness, chills, abdominal pain, and shortness of breath. Most of the victims were girls.

These were not symptoms of the kind that a poison gas would have been likely to produce; and although there was a curious smell, which had helped to lend credibility to the rumour, it turned out to come from the harmless adhesive used to fix a new carpet a couple of weeks before. The epidemic had started with an eleven-year-old girl leaving a rehearsal in the cafetorium, and falling unconscious onto a couch;

the other children had begun to collapse when she was being taken
out on a stretcher – too short an incubation time, Nitzkin decided, for
a virus to be held responsible. When he saw that a couple of the
victims were gasping for breath, the explanation, he told Roueché,
'finally hit me'; it was mass hysteria.

Nitzkin knew enough about epidemics of this kind to realize that
the most effective way to deal with it would be to tell the assembled
teachers, nurses, parents, reporters and photographers what it was,
and to suggest that they all went straight back to their classrooms
or their other jobs, in order to let the canteen staff get on with
making the place ready for lunch. But he also knew he would be
sticking his neck out; if the epidemic turned out not to be of hysteria,
he would be in trouble. And his diagnosis would certainly be unpopular. 'You should have seen their faces,' he recalled. 'The
parents of the sick children looked horrified, insulted – I was telling
them their children were crazy.' It was unlikely, though, that any
of them would be tempted to offer him violence – he was six foot
nine. All he had to put up with was some very angry telephone calls,
later.

In this case, as in many others which have been reported, the girl
who had slipped away from the rehearsal actually was ill, Nitzkin
thought. Seeing her being carried away on the stretcher was the trigger
for the hysteria of the others. The epidemic could consequently
be attributed to unconscious imitation. There have been other
cases, though, which could not be accounted for so readily.
Sometimes epidemics have broken out simultaneously in different
parts of a school, sometimes in more than one school at the same
time.

In 1975, for example, doctors in the Division of Communicable
Diseases in Pennsylvania were called upon to investigate simultaneous
outbreaks of itching and rashes in two schools ninety miles apart.
Tests failed to track down any virus or allergy which might have been
responsible. The investigators noted that most of the victims had been
girls, and that they had suffered from a curiously similar type of
rash. They had considered the possibility that the outbreak might be
'psychosomatic', as they discreetly described it. But this, they admitted, would not explain why the same symptoms should have appeared
so far apart. They had apparently discounted the possibility that
hysterical contagion may not be bound by the geographical limitations
imposed on contagious disorders of other kinds.

Even if extra-sensory communication is discounted, hysteria could still be responsible for spreading symptoms through a community by telephone, radio or television. Otherwise, how to account for the epidemic which started in 1960 with a number of patients being admitted to hospital in Rotterdam suffering from a mysterious rash and other symptoms, soon followed by others in different parts of the Netherlands, so that within three days the epidemic was being featured in newspapers the world over?

At first it was thought to be caused by a virus, but then the rumour spread that the culprit was Planta margarine, a Unilever product. Most of those who were ill claimed to have consumed Planta; and though only about a quarter of its consumers had any symptoms, the manufacturers felt bound to withdraw it from the market. The most likely explanation, it was agreed, was the new emulsifier in the margarine. It had been tested on animals, but not on humans. The manufacturers accepted responsibility, and offered substantial compensation to the victims.

When doubts were eventually raised whether Planta should be held responsible, it was widely assumed that Unilever must be using its massive resources to try to sidle out of its responsibilities. But the doubts increased when extensive tests on humans failed to pin the responsibility on the new emulsifier. If it really was responsible, why did so many Planta eaters suffer no ill-effects? Why, too, did a few people who had not eaten Planta also suffer? And why, when the new emulsifier was introduced in Germany, were no adverse reactions reported? In 1964 the case against Planta collapsed when the planned prosecution of the company was withdrawn.

Reliable information about these epidemics is hard to come by. Institutions which are affected understandably try to keep the news out of the papers – or if it gets around, to claim that a virus or food poisoning is suspected, hoping that by the time the tests have failed to disclose them, the story will no longer be considered newsworthy. Many outbreaks reported in local papers, too, are not thought worthy of attention by the national newspapers, or are given no more than a sentence or two. 'A mysterious illness has caused 24 pupils at a primary school at Tywardreath, Cornwall, to roll on the floor and hold their heads', the *Sunday Telegraph* noted in 1977. Seven had been taken to hospital; 'no explanation has yet been found.' That was all.

'Royal Free Disease'

An outbreak in 1955, however, started a controversy which has
grumbled on in the medical journals ever since. Three hundred people
at the Royal Free Hospital Group in London fell ill, during that
summer and autumn, with various forms of malaise. Most had nothing
worse than aches, dizziness and nausea; a few suffered from muscle
spasms, or weakness, and from uncontrollable weeping. Every possible
source of the infection, as it was assumed to be, was considered. The
water, the catering, the bedclothes were all subjected to tests; all had
to be exonerated. No germ, virus or toxin could be traced. Surveying
the evidence ten years later the *British Medical Journal* suggested
that it must have been Benign Myalgic Encephalomyelitis – a bland
label.

One possibility, however, was evaded by those involved in the
search for the cause. Out of the three hundred victims only twelve
were hospital *patients*. The rest were doctors, medical students, nurses,
and other staff members, and the great majority were women. Reviewing the evidence in the *British Medical Journal* in 1970, Colin McEvedy
and A. W. Beard pointed out that this made it unlikely that there
could be any organic cause. They noted, too, in the published report
of the Royal Free Hospital's investigation, that sometimes 'a peculiar
jerking could be observed in a limb'; when McEvedy and Beard
studied the actual case histories, they found that ten out of the fifteen
most serious cases had suffered convulsions, including one lasting
about twenty minutes, 'consisting of throwing limbs about, foaming
at the mouth, staring eyes'. Epidemic hysteria, they concluded, was
the most likely explanation.

The staff of the Royal Free were outraged. Schoolgirls might be
hysteria victims, or teenagers at pop concerts, but nurses – no! As for
doctors, the idea was inconceivable. A barrage of objections descended,
most of them merely indicating that the medical profession's conception of hysteria was derived from organicism at its most primitive. It
was even contended that the epidemic could not have been of hysteria
because it produced some physical symptoms – as if hysteria had not
been notorious for that throughout history. And in 1978 a symposium
was held at the Royal Society of Medicine with, as one of its aims, the
wiping away of the hysteria stigma.

McEvedy and Beard were not invited. Of the papers read, not one
dealt with the possibility of hysteria. It was mentioned only once, by

a speaker who suggested the possibility in some cases of hysterical 'overlay'. In his concluding remarks, the chairman felt justified in claiming, about the outbreak, 'there seems to be a practically unanimous belief that it was organic in origin.'

This was hardly surprising, as nobody had cared to suggest the obvious alternative. Nevertheless the meeting ended in some confusion. The symposium had been given the title of 'Epidemic Neuromyasthenia 1954–7: current approaches'. Why, some of those attending wanted to know, had there been the switch from the established Benign Myalgic Encephalomyelitis? The reason, they were told, was that neuromyasthenia had become the preferred version in the United States.

The explanation failed to satisfy many of the British members of the audience. Myasthenia implied little more than muscle weakness and fatiguability; the British version specifically indicated inflammation of the brain and the spinal column. As one speaker protested, myasthenia 'in no way embraces the manifestations we encountered at the Royal Free'; a view which won majority support.

Could it be, the leading American expert who was present, Professor A. Sholokov, asked, that they had in fact been talking about two different diseases? This was the conclusion he himself had been forced to reach. He went on to argue that the evidence they had heard did not suggest a single cause; the symptoms might turn out to have been 'only the expression of a common final pathway' of causes – a proposition which cruelly undermined the case the British had been building up in favour of an as yet unidentified virus. It was time, the chairman decided, to turn to another topic.

The American uneasiness about accepting Benign Myalgic Encephalomyelitis was understandable. Dorland's medical dictionary defines it as a disease, 'usually occurring in epidemics', characterized by headache, fever, myalgia (muscle pains), muscular weakness and – most embarrassing of all – 'emotional lability'. This was too close to hysteria for comfort. The British version, inflammation of the brain and the spinal cord, avoided this problem in the traditional fashion: so long as a syndrome can be given a sufficiently resonant name ending in '-itis', it can be smuggled into the organic category.

'The most heinous offence a scientist can commit', Sir Peter Medawar asserted in his 'Essay on Science', 'is to declare to be true that which is not so'; science 'can only proceed on a basis of confidence'. Medicine is not a science, but its practitioners, if they wish to retain the community's confidence, need to accept that principle. Yet here were members of a medical speciality, some of them eminent, engaged on an exercise in self-deception. They did not care – they did not dare – to allow the case for mass hysteria to be put because they knew it to be powerful. This is not the same as saying that it was necessarily the *correct* explanation for 'Royal Free Disease', as it came to be known. But in view of the fact that nobody at the meeting was able to present a more plausible explanation, the case should at least have been heard.

The reaction of the *British Medical Journal* was regrettably typical. Its editorial chose to ignore the problem that Sholokov had posed; the existence of two different interpretations of what had been assumed to be the same set of symptoms. It actually claimed that agreement had prevailed that Myalgic Encephalomyelitis was a clinical entity, whose organic basis was also clear. 'Some authors have attempted to dismiss this disease as hysterical', it recalled (it was left to the source references to disclose that the authors were McEvedy and Beard, and that their paper had been in the *British Medical Journal*); 'the evidence now makes such a tenet unacceptable.' Admittedly no cause had been found for the outbreak, or others of the kind; they should be investigated 'by a collaborative team of neurologists, epidemiologists, virologists and immunologists'. Unless a maverick epidemiologist happened to be one of the team, the possibility of hysteria was clearly not going to be considered.

The absurdity of ignoring hysteria, as it happened, had already been underlined by reports of other epidemics, in particular one at the Great Ormond Street Children's Hospital in London in the winter of 1970. Again, it was the staff who suffered; almost all the victims were women nurses. 'Symptomatology was protean' – the symptoms being those which are traditionally associated with mass hysteria: malaise, fatigue, depression, aches, sore throats, rashes and so on. And, as the report actually noted, they were 'almost identical with those found during the Royal Free outbreak'. Mass hysteria was discounted, however, on the ground that it is known to take a short intensive course, and the Great Ormond Street epidemic spread over months.

This fallacy has been perpetuated because, with children, outbreaks usually *are* short and intensive. With adults they may spread over months, even years. But it provided the investigators with the opportunity to deliver their verdict, Epidemic Neuromyasthenia. Since this diagnosis raised objections at the Royal Free symposium, however, it has been replaced by Myalgic Encephalomyelitis. Following the tradition of neurasthenia, the fact that the symptoms traditionally associated with hysteria were given an impressive-sounding name and organic respectability has led scores of doctors to take advantage of 'ME', as it came to be called, and thousands of ME patients who had originally been told by their GPs there was nothing the matter with them were able to seek justice by banding together in an ME association. In 1987, thanks to its energetic lobbying, the Department of Health granted ME official recognition as a viral disorder; it even provided the Association with a grant.

Meanwhile, however, a research team at the Charing Cross Hospital had been investigating; and in the summer of 1988, its report insisted that ME is *not* a viral disorder. It is a type of extreme nervous exhaustion, akin to wartime battle fatigue. In other words, it is neurasthenia – by extension, hysteria – revived. Significantly, the report does not suggest that the patients were weak-minded – unconscious malingerers – which was the implication so many of them had originally been left with by their GPs, before ME won formal recognition. On the contrary, 'they have above average intelligence, high levels of drive, lots of enthusiasm,' Stuart Rosen, a research fellow at the hospital, insisted (echoing, without realizing it, Skey, Paget and Breuer). 'All the ones we have seen here have four-star abilities.' The trouble usually was that they also had 'five-star ambitions'. The mental and emotional exhaustion which gave rise to the other symptoms had overwhelmed their auto-immune defences; fighting against the illness, rather than recognizing the need to relax and make a reappraisal of life-style, only made matters worse.

There could hardly have been a more damning indictment of the lingering influence of organicism, discredited in theory but still immensely powerful in medical practice and in the public mind. Whenever hysteria *is* diagnosed, the public's reaction is still indignation. A typical example was the outbreak in 1980 in a Nottinghamshire field where a brass band competition was being held. More than 250 people collapsed with dizziness, fainting, aches, vomiting, shaking, and other such symptoms. At first food poisoning was blamed (it was several days before the ice-cream vendors dared to try to sell their cornets locally). Then, the rumour got around that a crop-spraying aircraft had been at work nearby. One had, in fact, done some spraying – but that had been fourteen years before. No virus could account for the sudden collapse of so many people. Eventually the official version was – mass hysteria.

This caused outrage locally, not surprisingly, considering the *Daily Telegraph*'s comment that the cause was 'nothing more serious than mass hysteria'. For those who suffered, the dizziness, aches and the other symptoms were no less alarming or painful than if they *had* been caused by food poisoning, or a crop spray. The *Telegraph*'s implication was that the symptoms spread by imitation, that only the weaker-minded were affected, and that in a sense they had only themselves to blame. But the hospital records showed that among the casualties were young babies, who could hardly be accused of imitating the symptoms of their elders.

One of the arguments used by the objectors to try to prove that hysteria could not have been responsible was that some of the victims had not made a prompt recovery, but were ill for days – the point which had also been made in connection with the hospital outbreaks, whose effects, in a few cases, had been even more protracted. Again, this misconception revealed the grip which organicism still has on the public – the assumption that as hysteria is 'all in the mind', it cannot leave lasting physical disabilities. But if the resistance of somebody caught in an outbreak happens to be low his recovery might be delayed, particularly as feeling misunderstood can make matters worse. At the Royal Free, medical students who suffered from the symptoms did their best to hide them. 'Of course, we could have gone to the physicians,' Jane Eden wrote in 1977, 'but as clinical students, we racked our memories, looked up textbooks and confirmed that the symptoms just did not fit any known disease' – except one; and 'nobody wants to be labelled an hysteric, and slung out within a spitting distance of Finals.' At schools, most children 'let go'. It may well be that the reason adult victims can take a long time to recover is that they fight the diagnosis, rather than letting the symptoms take their course.

It is usually outbreaks in schools or other institutions which are investigated and reported in the medical journals; but they also appear to be more common than is generally realized in factories and workshops. Investigating cases in the 1970s where no cause had been found, Richard Colligan, a research psychologist at the American National Institute for Occupational Safety and Health, came to the conclusion that the only way to account for them was 'assembly line hysteria', usually a by-product of job boredom, often exacerbated by poor labour relations.

It only required one worker to show symptoms – say, a rash – for others to develop it; and the immediate reaction was to look for a scapegoat. By the time all the possible culprits – the canteen food, the air-conditioning plant, and so on – had been eliminated, the outbreak was usually a memory; and neither the workers nor the management were likely to put the blame on hysteria. As a result, Colligan suspected, the incidence of such outbreaks must have been gravely underestimated. A search through the journals where such reports were most likely to be found had uncovered only two which dealt with earlier cases in American plants. But when Colligan was invited to give a paper at a meeting of the American Footwear Manufacturers Association in 1976, and he inquired whether any of his audience had known of similar cases, almost half of them held up their hands.

The form of mass hysteria which has had most publicity, and is clearly on the increase, is deliberately self-induced. In the 1960s teenagers, mostly girls, began to enjoy going into hysterics at pop concerts, screaming and relaxing physical as well as emotional control. This alarmed their parents, and from time to time there were calls for legislation to impose stricter controls. Gradually, though, it became clear that little harm was being done – except to the seats and carpets of theatres, when they were used, which would stink of urine.

By the early 1980s a more sinister form of induced hysteria was emerging, as Lord Taylor warned in his *World Medicine* commentary in 1981. When he returned to England in the 1970s, he recalled, after spending some years in Canada, it seemed to him that violence was the most immediate problem facing society; and as he studied it, he had come to realize that it was 'neither more nor less than our old friend hysteria, or the madness of crowds, taking on a new shape'. As a medical diagnosis of individual disorders, hysteria was no longer in evidence; in its contagious form, he feared, it had become all too common.

It took time for the authorities to grasp that what had become the most familiar form of crowd madness, in and around football stadiums on Saturday afternoons, was often being carefully planned and nurtured by small groups. Their members were exploring ways to coax or goad football fans in general into violence in the form either of pitched battles with rival fans, or of cutting a swathe through a district, vandalizing and assaulting anybody who happened to be in the way.

In Britain this form of hooliganism has recently taken a new turn. 'Yuppie mobs run riot', a newspaper headline announced in the summer of 1988. 'The countryside is being blighted by an alarming growth in drunken brawls as affluent youths who hold down respectable jobs during the day run riot at night,' the Chief Constable of Surrey, Brian Hayes, was lamenting. 'Most are quite respectable when they are on their own, but turn on the police and public when they get together. Their characters completely change.'

For Hayes, alcohol bears the chief responsibility. But alcohol is merely the lubricant, it helps the Jekylls prepare themselves for their planned switch to being a Hyde conglomerate. Why do they do it? Sociologists have been unable to offer any plausible explanations. 'There has been, frankly, very little work done on the subject,' Professor Howard Newby of Essex University, a leading authority on life in rural Britain, has had to admit. Although a few sociologists have performed a useful function by exposing some of the inhibitions of psychologists when confronted by anomalous phenomena – Harry Collins and T. J. Pinch in Britain; James McClenon in the United States – sociologists in general have themselves been reluctant to explore an area of human activity which is hard to account for, except by assuming that it is some form of contagion which orthodox science still finds unacceptable.

ANTHROPOLOGISTS

The mind possessed

Of all the branches of science, the one which ought to have been best-placed to study actual trance has been anthropology. The problems, admittedly, have been much greater in the twentieth century than they were before the influence of explorers, missionaries, traders, settlers and colonial officials eroded tribal beliefs and customs. By 1945 trance shamanism in its pristine form had become a rarity, and in many parts of the world had virtually disappeared. The shamans usually remained conscious, doing their divination with the help of aids – the equivalent of a clairvoyant's cards.

Nevertheless trance shamans were still to be found, and investigated. The problem was that the value of trance sessions could be estimated only if the shaman's pronouncements while in the trance, or his recollections when he came out of it, could be assessed. In so far as they simply represented advice of a general nature – Margaret Field was quite impressed with it on this level, from her experience – this was not too difficult; but it required subjective judgement of a kind which was not in favour in the anthropology establishment. And where a shaman professed to have, say, clairvoyant abilities, and made specific pronouncements which could be checked, anthropological field workers rarely had the hardihood to investigate, knowing that even to test for clairvoyance would be regarded by their superiors as silly, and could blight career prospects.

'It might seem to be the business of anthropology, the science of man,' Andrew Lang had suggested in *Science and Religion* (1898), 'to examine, amongst other things, the evidence for the actual existence of those alleged and supernormal phenomena.' But to James Frazer, there was no evidence, except what superstition and gullibility provided; and it is Frazer's view which in general has prevailed, relieving field workers of the need to take trance pronouncements seriously. 'Anthropologists insist that they are not concerned with validating the beliefs or claims of the ostensibly paranormal experiences,' Patrick Giesler has confirmed in a survey of their attitudes in 1884. They content themselves with recording what the natives believe; how they interpret their experiences; and what influence their beliefs and interpretations have on tribal life. Whether the beliefs are soundly based, or the interpretations of any value, are not regarded as relevant.

A few researchers, however, have followed Edward Tylor's advice that 'we ought always to look for practical and intelligible motives for the habits and opinions we find existing in this world', chief among them Mircea Eliade, whose *Shamanism* (1951) was the first attempt to collate the mass of information which had accumulated on the subject. It was conventional enough in its presentation of the evidence; but in *Myths, Dreams and Mysteries* (1957), Eliade clearly felt released from earlier inhibitions. 'The question of the *reality* of the extra-sensory capacities and paranormal powers ascribed to the shamans and medicine men', he argued, was of the greatest importance. Although research was still at an early stage, 'a fairly large number of ethnographic documents has already put the authenticity of such phenomena beyond doubt.' He cited case histories from various parts of the world confirming his view that the 'magic' could be real.

Shamanism, Eliade believed, must have called certain faculties and powers into being which had not existed before. In other words, evolution was improvising. In particular, he cited 'magical heat' and 'mastery of fire' as instructive, because the evidence for their existence came from so many cultural levels, 'from the most archaic to the most highly developed', and because it was so well attested. Magical heat had to be generated internally, as in the form which Alexandra David-Neel watched and tried out in Tibet; young men aspiring to be lamas would sit out freezing nights to demonstrate that with their body-heat alone, they could dry a succession of towels which had been dipped in icy water. Mastery of fire was usually demonstrated in the fire-walk, with bare feet over white-hot coals. For Eliade, the accounts of these procedures left no doubt that they demonstrated how the shaman, in trance, 'has surpassed the human condition', reaching a higher evolutionary stage.

Sceptics, Eliade realized, would need more specific proof; but he did not consider it to be his business to provide it – that was the task confronting parapsychology. From his point of view, what was important was 'to underline the perfect continuity of paranormal *experience* from the primitive right up to the most highly evolved religions'. All of them had taken for granted the reality of magical powers; the differences lay only in attitudes to the powers. Buddhism, classical Yoga and Catholicism shared the view that they are side-effects experienced on the path to enlightenment, not to be exploited. For the shaman, they were there to be exploited – but only on behalf of the tribe.

The point which Eliade was making has sometimes been contested on the ground that beliefs have often been held for centuries by intelligent men and women which have eventually turned out to be fallacious, such as that the sun goes round the earth. True; but Eliade's concern was not with *belief*, which has been shown to be wrong: that the sun rises in the morning and sets in the evening is an *experience* which remains unchallenged. That the trance experiences which have been reported in connection with shamans and their successors should be similar everywhere they have been found, in all ages, makes it particularly eccentric, Eliade felt, to dismiss them all as the products of delusion and fraud.

Eliade's qualifications as a scholar were impeccable and his erudition formidable. Academic anthropologists, having for so long dismissed even the possibility that shaman magic could be genuine, were in no position to rebut his theories, section by section. Luck was with them; when Eliade left the Sorbonne for the United States it was to become head of the department of the History of Religions at the University of Chicago. In that academic siding, he could pose little threat to their peace of mind. In any case, Levi-Strauss's structuralism was to come to their aid. The function of anthropology, it laid down, should be to look for points of similarity or divergence in tribal behaviour. They could devote their entire attention to comparing the ways in which shamans performed, without bothering about whether shaman magic actually worked.

Eliade chiefly used source material taken from reports by anthropologists and travellers. The psychiatrist William Sargant, of St Thomas's Hospital in London, studied trance at first hand. His interest in the subject was initially aroused while using ECT and drug therapy on members of the forces suffering from battle neurosis. The reactions he witnessed reminded him of the sudden striking conversions which had still occasionally occurred in the Methodist circle in which he had grown up; and in *Battle for the Mind* (1957) he linked the two, along with brain-washing and other related manifestations. The success of the book, coupled with invitations to lecture, enabled him to observe trance ceremonies in different parts of the world: Africa, North and South America, and Haiti.

Observing, photographing and filming rituals in which trance was induced to bring on spirit possession convinced Sargant of their 'tremendous importance – for a man's whole life can be so easily changed when such things happen to him'. He had encountered problems: 'too often I was straying outside my own psychiatric territory and into that of other disciplines', so that no research grants came his way. But this was fortunate, as it spared him the inhibitions of academic anthropologists. What he saw, together with what he read, enabled him to put trance into its historical and anthropological perspective in *The Mind Possessed*.

The book's chief value lay in its demonstrations of the links between so many and diverse historical strands – shamanism, hysteria, possession, convulsions, religious conversions, psychiatric beliefs and practices – with contemporary trance experiences, ranging from mystical visions to orgasm. ('Lovers in orgasm behave as if they were possessed, trembling, writhing, groaning, crying out', he noted. 'Complete orgasm often ends in a collapse phase, as in abreaction, ecstatic dancing and convulsion therapy.')

From his travels, Sargant was left in no doubt that the people who went into trance during religious ceremonies were far from being as crazy as they looked: 'I was repeatedly impressed by the dignity and the evident mental balance which many of them showed.' This applied even to Voodoo in Haiti. 'I never gained the impression that this religion was predominantly sinister and evil, but, on the contrary, that it gave to many of its practitioners increased dignity, relief from fear and something to live for which was otherwise unattainable in the ordinary circumstances of their lives.' People who had been in a state of depression, he found, would feel all the better for being put into a trance by music or drumming until they were possessed, the procedure apparently having no ill-effects – though ECT and drugs, he was careful to insist, were even more effective and more reliable.

Throughout the book, Sargant reiterated that he remained wedded to the mechanistic concept of medicine – it was sub-titled 'A Physiology of Possession, Mysticism and Faith Healing'; in the preface, he described his main work as teaching students and trying to learn how better to help patients 'mainly along the new physical and mechanistic lines'; and in the conclusions he explained that his aim had been 'to show that the same physiological processes underlie experiences of "possession" by gods or spirits or demons, the mystical experience of union with God, the gift of tongues and other phenomena' – the others including mediumistic utterance, and people's behaviour under the influence of hypnosis, drugs, or sexual excitement.

Yet the whole tenor of *The Mind Possessed*, particularly in those sections dealing with trance rituals he had himself witnessed, was anti-mechanistic, in the sense that he continually emphasized the importance of faith – in the religion, in the witch-doctor, or in the ritual. It seems never to have occurred to Sargant that this might also apply to, say, ECT. He did realize that psychiatric patients could be so suggestible 'that they produce in all sincerity the symptoms which suit their psychiatrist's theories; and if they change psychiatrists, they change symptoms'. What he did not realize was that if they changed psychiatrists, they might react very differently to the same mechanistic course of treatment.

Sargant was himself an outstanding example of the psychiatrist as shaman, or medicine man. His results, whether using drugs, ECT, or surgery, were outstanding – far better than those obtained by most of his contemporaries, using the same methods. Brain-washed as he had been during his medical training into acceptance of the mechanistic fallacy, however, Sargant could not accept that he, rather than the treatment, might be responsible.

Yet he recognized the importance of faith readily enough on his travels. 'I may have been in a suggestive state myself during all the drumming, the excitement and the "possession" I was witnessing, but I felt I was nearing a fundamental truth,' he recalled of a Macumba ceremony in Brazil. 'For successful religions – those which really grip people's hearts – are those which produce evidence of the actual existence of their gods' – as in trance possession, when the god appears to speak through the possessed person. So impressed was Sargant by the power of faith that on one occasion, at a ceremony in Barbados, he nearly allowed himself to be carried away. 'I soon realized that I was "co-operating" in their service too much!' he recalled. 'I had not come to be saved.' How fascinating it could have been, for him and for us, if he *had* co-operated, and allowed himself to be possessed! But he was there 'to examine the techniques of possession' and if you lend yourself to them, he feared, 'you can easily be influenced, and you may come to believe with a firm faith in what may be great truth or utter falsehood.'

'We need faith but must suspect it,' Sargant concluded. He had never thought of suspecting *his* faith, in mechanistic rationalism, because he had never regarded it *as* a faith. Yet that was what it was. Perhaps, after all, he was wise not to allow himself to become possessed, if it would have revealed to him that his belief in the objective value of ECT, drugs and surgery, as distinct from the subjective reaction of patients to the psychiatrists who prescribed them, had been an illusion. To have the fruits of your life's work overturned is no less a shattering experience if you yourself are responsible for upsetting them.

There was another even more widely-read writer in this field – a field worker, in fact, though his books have left many academic anthropologists grinding their teeth at the mention of his name. In 1960, Carlos Castaneda, a graduate of the University College of Los Angeles, went to Mexico to study local lore about the use of medicinal and hallucinogenic drugs; and on his return presented his findings in the form of a doctoral thesis. It described how he had taken a course of instruction from a shaman over a two-year period in which he had enjoyed remarkable, though sometimes frightening, experiences, and which had introduced him to another world of reality.

Although his supervisors were impressed, in deference to the prevailing fashion they sent Castaneda off to provide a 'structural analysis', which he did so impressively that he was duly awarded his PhD. His thesis, too, was accepted by the University of California Press, and published in 1968 as *The Teachings of Don Juan*. It is only rarely that PhD theses bring any immediate financial profit to the writer, but this proved to be the exception. It was a best-seller; and it was followed by some lucrative sequels.

Commercial success is apt to breed suspicion in academic circles, and a follow-up visit to Mexico revealed that no 'Don Juan' existed, though he might have been a composite figure. The examiners had been taken in – doubly fooled, in fact, because more critical scrutiny of the 'structural analysis' showed that it was in reality a delightful parody of structuralism at its most abysmal. So cleverly had Castaneda set up the required bogus framework, and employed the appropriate excruciating jargon, that he had aroused no suspicion.

The fact that the central character did not exist outside Castaneda's imagination, though, did not necessarily invalidate his 'teachings'. The book in fact presented a brilliantly evocative study of a shaman. It reads as if it were a personalized, dramatized account designed to complement the commentaries in *Flesh of the Gods* (1972), edited by Peter T. Furst, Professor of Anthropology at the State University of New York, and reflecting the views of some of the more enlightened academic anthropologists; and it accords well with the findings of Eliade and of the independent-minded R. Gordon Wasson, an American banker who devoted his retirement to an investigation of hallucinogenic cults in history, and their successors in the 1960s and 1970s. Not all of the contributors to *Flesh of the Gods* would have accepted the proposition that shamans enjoy magical powers of the kind Castaneda described, and his later works in the series became progressively less convincing; but 'Don Juan' provided Castaneda's readers with a better introduction to shamanism than they would have been likely to get from more conventional sources.

PARAPSYCHOLOGISTS

Hallucination

As so much of our lifetime is spent exploiting automatism, in the form of the actions which instinct, habit and improvisation enable us to perform without the need for deliberation, it might be assumed that they would still play an important part in research, as they did a century ago. Owing to the deep-rooted mechanistic antipathy to the idea of an active, useful subliminal self, however, psychologists have tended to leave the issue to psychiatrists, and psychiatrists have continued to treat many of the symptoms of sensory and motor automatism as pathological. The exploration of automatisms with a view to understanding them better, and perhaps exploiting them more effectively, has been largely left to psychical researchers.

As children we used to sing the hymn 'Now the day is over', which contained the lines

> Grant to little children
> Visions bright of thee.

If any of us had told his parents that he had seen Jesus, they would have been mildly amused; if he had persisted – 'I *really* saw him, Mummy!' – he would have been taken to the doctor, referred to a psychiatrist and doubtless prescribed a course of drugs. Broadly speaking, this still holds. Hallucinations are regarded as a symptom of mental breakdown caused, psychiatrists explain, by some mix-up in the chemistry of the brain.

My interest in hallucination was aroused in a roundabout manner. As a student before the war, I had read Dunne's *An Experiment with Time* and J. B. Priestley's *Time and the Conways*, which was partly derived from Dunne's contention that we can, and occasionally do, obtain glimpses of the future in dreams. Simply as an account of his precognitive dreams, Dunne's book was convincing, impressing even so dedicated a sceptic on the subject as H. G. Wells; and I was sufficiently impressed to try leaving pad and pencil beside the bed, as Dunne recommended, to write down dreams before they faded beyond recall. It had not worked, for me; but in 1948 I had a couple of 'Dunne dreams', as they had come to be known, and two years later read the account by John Godley, shortly to become Lord Kilbracken, of his remarkable series of dream winners of horse races.

Up to then I had tended to think of dreams along Freudian lines, as tortuous representations of repressed trauma, churning around in the unconscious; but clearly there was more to it, and I began to delve into the history of dreaming. Only then was it impressed upon me that dreams are hallucinations – the most convincing, as well as the commonest, of hallucinatory experiences, in that we are entirely satisfied that what we are seeing and doing is real. But though we are conscious of what is happening, we lack the self-consciousness – except in 'lucid' dreams, as they have come to be called – to realize that we are hallucinating; and it is this lack of conscious control that enables the imagination to run riot in ways it cannot do when we are awake.

Chaotic though they can be, dreams nevertheless can put across useful information, as hundreds of accounts throughout history have shown; and recent experiments have been providing a better understanding and appreciation of their potential. The discovery of the link between rapid eye movements and dreams enabled researchers at the Maimonides Hospital in New York in the 1960s to test for extra-sensory perception by waking subjects up when the movements occurred, getting them to relate their dreams, and comparing them with set targets – pictures, say, which the sleepers hoped to pick up. Ingenious tests in Britain and the United States have shown that the ability of the mind to solve a problem in sleep – sometimes in a dream, sometimes simply by sleeping on it – can be reproduced in experiments. And Monty Ullman, who ran the Maimonides tests, has developed a technique of group appreciation – as distinct from interpretation – of dreams which help to unravel their meaning and implications.

This ought to be improving the standing of hallucination; but old prejudice dies hard. Most people, asked if they have hallucinations, would bridle at the suggestion. But it seems certain that, apart from dreams, they are far commoner than is realized, because we are not necessarily aware we have hallucinated.

This was neatly illustrated in an experiment conducted by Gordon Rattray Taylor when he was producing the science programme *Horizon* for BBC Television in the 1960s. He was wondering if the same kind of auto-suggestion which leads to people lost in the desert seeing mirages, or shipwrecked sailors 'seeing' rescue ships, applied to the sense of smell. On the programme, it was claimed that it had been found possible to transmit a smell over the airwaves. A university professor was brought in to demonstrate how this was done, with the help of a chopped onion, coffee and some impressive-looking gadgets designed to translate the smell into electrical signals on the same principle as sight and sound. Viewers were asked to sit in front of their sets and concentrate; and if they picked up the smells, to write in to the BBC – letters to arrive by 1 April. 'Hundreds of letters arrived from people who had smelt coffee and onion'; along with a few from people who thought they had, but then had noticed the date.

Recently, too, a variety of hallucinatory states have been attracting attention which, though they had often been described before, had not been regarded as worthy of serious investigation: Out-of-the-body experiences; Near-death experiences; and experiences which suggest a regression to past lives, and are commonly regarded as evidence for reincarnation.

In an OBE, the percipient individual 'seems to perceive the world from a location outside his physical body', as Susan J. Blackmore defines them in *Beyond the Body*. She had had such an experience herself. Sleepily listening to music with some friends she heard one of them say, 'Sue, where are you?' She looked, and replied 'I'm on the ceiling' – and, watching her body on the floor down below, she saw that her mouth was opening and closing in time to the words.

In the course of her research into OBEs, Blackmore was to discover that they are much more common than is generally realized. Polls taken in a number of countries suggest that up to a third of the population have had one, or more. Her conclusion is that it is a psychological, as distinct from a psychical, experience; but many people who have had OBEs dispute this view, claiming that they have had an example of what the mesmerists described as travelling clairvoyance. They have floated away from their bodies, and on their return have been able to produce accounts of the kind Robert A. Monroe described in *Journeys Out of the Body* (1971) of what they have seen, or heard, which have subsequently proved to be veridical.

Related to OBEs are the near-death experiences of the kind made familiar to the public by Raymond Moody in *Life after Life* (1975). Moody was impressed by the consistency of the reports of 'NDEs'. Beginning as out-of-the-body experiences, the 'travel' leads – often through a tunnel, with light at the end – to a meeting with deceased relatives and loved ones who welcome the newcomer to, apparently, the border which divides life from death. 'He is overwhelmed by intense feelings of joy, love and peace'; but at some point he learns that the time is not right for him to leave his physical body, and – often very reluctantly – he returns to it.

In 1988 Sir Freddy Ayer, long the leading advocate of positivist rationalism in Britain, described in the *Sunday Telegraph* how, according to his doctors, he had 'died' for four minutes. He had not encountered any deceased friends and relations, but he knew that he had continued to live, or at least that his mind had continued to function, in that period, and this had led him to modify his earlier dogmatism.

'My recent experiences have slightly weakened my conviction that my genuine death,' he admitted, 'will be the end of me.' Later, in *The Spectator*, he was to make a partial retraction: 'My experiences have weakened, not my belief that there is no life after death, but my inflexible attitude to that belief'; and he went on to discuss the philosophical problems which arose out of this flexibility.

A hard-line rationalist would have had no problem. That the mind continues to function after the body has temporarily 'died' is well enough established; 'NDEs' are the hallucinations which happen to occur at such times. Obviously, though, they are of interest because of the possibility that they may throw light on whether there is survival in some form after bodily death; and if so, what form it may take. 'Not many philosophers of whatever persuasion believe that we are spiritual substances,' Ayer pointed out; and this left him with a choice between accepting the Christian doctrine of the resurrection of the body, which he rejected, and considering the possibility of reincarnation – which, difficult though he found it, was at least 'less radical than the speculations of mathematical physicists.'

There has been some revival of interest recently in the use of hypnosis to explore reincarnation, by regressing subjects into recollecting what are taken to be periods of their past lives. One of the most remarkable case histories has been provided in a succession of books by Arthur Guirdham, a psychiatrist who practised in Bath before his retirement. A patient of his described how as a child she had what had seemed to her to be a dream existence in which she had lived as a Cathar in the South of France, at the time the Albigensian heresy was being savagely put down by the French authorities at the behest of the Pope. Her account was so vivid that Guirdham took the trouble to have it checked by a French expert, who pronounced it accurate. There was one mistake, he pointed out – but later he wrote to Guirdham to say that fresh research had shown that it was not a mistake, after all.

I had been sceptical about accounts of reincarnation, but I had read Guirdham's perceptive *A Theory of Disease* (1957) and a review I wrote of it led to a meeting at which he told me about the case. He made it sound entirely convincing. It proved more difficult to go along with him later, when he came to explain how he had come to know no fewer than eight people who, in the twentieth century, had a previous experience as Cathars in the thirteenth century; that all of them had been born, lived or were educated in and around Bath; and that he himself had identified his earlier Cathar self. Yet, as he claimed in his introduction to *We Are One Another* (1974), he was very far from being credulous. He had had a scientific as well as a medical training; he had been sceptical by temperament; and as senior consultant psychiatrist in his clinical area he knew only too well how easily fantasy can take over. He had accordingly been careful to check and counter-check the information he received. It had convinced him that past lives can break in to present lives in the form of hallucinations, sometimes actually producing physical symptoms. Conventional medicine needed to recognize these, he argued, as for obvious reasons it was important for purposes of diagnosis.

I would have been more inclined to doubt Guirdham's findings had it not been for the publication of the painstaking research of Ian Stevenson, Professor of Psychiatry at the University of Virginia, in his *Cases of the Reincarnation Type*, as the first four volumes were called, and *Children who Remember Previous Lives* (1987). 'It may disappoint some readers to learn that this book is not about reincarnation directly,' he warns. It is about claims for reincarnation; but before they are accepted, we need to be confident that 'it offers the best explanation for these children's apparent memories'. His concern is to set out the evidence, to allow anybody who is 'interested enough to examine the case histories to decide for himself if the best is good enough.'

Stevenson's case histories, taken mainly from India and other eastern countries, show a consistency similar to that of OBEs and NDEs. A child who has the experiences, when he learns to speak, 'makes statements – rudimentary at first, and then more detailed – about the deceased person's life'. Later he begins to behave in ways that people who knew the deceased person recognize as characteristic of him. It is never easy, as Stevenson is well aware, to be absolutely certain that there is no other way the child could have picked up the information – or that the parents might not have provided it, hoping to exploit it. But the cumulative effect of the cases makes it impossible to reject reincarnation out of hand.

A child's subliminal self, in other words, can appear to have absorbed something of the personality of a deceased person. Sometimes, as in the case of Guirdham's patient, this manifests itself in trances – dreams and daydreams; sometimes the take-over appears to be all but complete, only the trance personality remaining. Hopes have been raised that the issue might be settled with the help of regression to past lives under hypnosis; but though there have been examples of regression producing fascinating material, as with Flournoy's Hélène Smith, on balance the results have been disappointing. 'Although the study of children who claim to remember previous lives has convinced me that some of them may indeed have reincarnated,' Stevenson concludes, 'it has also made me certain that we know almost nothing about reincarnation.'

Apparitions

Needless to say, reports have continued to flow in of the type of hallucination which is loosely described as 'seeing ghosts'. The confusion remains, however, which Myers and Gurney tried to get rid of by adopting 'phantasms' for use when a living person is involved; and the attempt to put across the distinction between 'ghost' and 'apparition' has not fared much better.

Still, for the sake of clarity, the distinction needs to be made. The stock tea-party question 'Do you believe in ghosts?' is hopelessly ambiguous, as Henry Habberly Price, Professor of Philosophy at Oxford and an authority on perception, pointed out in his introduction to Tyrrell's *Apparitions* (1942). For most of us, the mind's-eye picture of a ghost is of a semi-transparent wraith floating around – the earth-bound spirit, apparently, of somebody who has been stuck in a form of limbo. There are also ghosts who are rarely seen, but who make themselves felt – poltergeists. An apparition is a different species. It is a hallucination of an individual, often so lifelike that we are deceived. And to the question, 'Do you believe that people experience apparitions?' Price asserted, 'there can be only one answer: they certainly do.'

Episodes are occasionally reported when an apparition comes and goes where no recognizable link can subsequently be found to any event of the kind that might help to account for it. The main interest, however, understandably continues to centre on apparitions which turn out to be veridical; and reports of them continue to flow in to psychical researchers, as Andrew MacKenzie has shown in his carefully researched case histories. There is also reason to believe that many striking examples go unreported. In Oxford Street one morning Ben Noakes asked 200 passers-by if they, or a close friend or relative, has actually seen a ghost. One in five replied, 'yes'; and the same proportion, he found, replied 'yes' of five hundred celebrities he wrote to, putting the same question.

The title of his book in which 100 'yes's described their experiences, *I Saw a Ghost*, was presumably dictated by the publishers; many of the accounts were of psychic experiences of various kinds which had no connection with seeing ghosts. A few, however, presented convincing accounts of veridical apparitions. In one, the artist Ronald Searle recalled 'seeing' an old friend, Laura Perelman, who had died two years earlier, 'but here she was, very much alive and looking me straight in the eye'. She came straight to the point of her visit, 'Sid's dead', before disappearing; early the following morning Searle had a telephone call to tell him that Sid – S. J. Perelman – had died during the night. Colonel D. Pritchard described how he was in the pavilion bar at Lords talking to some friends when he saw Douglas Jardine standing a few yards away. They were acquainted, and raised their glasses to each other in recognition. When Pritchard went to speak to him, he was nowhere to be seen. Just before play started, there was a loudspeaker announcement; D. R. Jardine had died the day before, in Switzerland.

A few months after Noakes's book was published, Donald Trelford, editor of the *Observer*, described how he was waiting one evening, sheltering from the rain, for an old friend with whom he had arranged to see a film. He saw the man coming, dressed as usual, in the crowd of passers-by; but he, too, passed by and did not return. Irritated, Trelford boarded a bus to go home. Opening his evening paper, he read that his friend had been killed in a road accident the night before.

Was it simply that, expecting to see him, Trelford mistook somebody else for him in the crowd? 'I've been telling myself that,' Trelford remarked doubtfully, 'for nearly thirty years.' And in fact it could have been a straightforward case of coincidence; the commonest type of hallucination, after all, apart from dreaming, is the one which occurs when we are waiting impatiently for a friend or a loved one who is late, and we see her coming through the crowd, only to realize, sometimes after waving greetings, that she is a total stranger. But this cannot readily account for cases such as Searle's, where he actually 'saw' and 'heard' the apparition of Perelman's wife, and she passed on information which later proved correct.

The quantity and quality of cases where hallucinations have turned out to be veridical continue to support the theory that they are an evolutionary device for the transmission of information of relevance to the recipient, mimicking one or more of the senses so well that consciousness is for a time deceived into assuming that what we see is real. Or what we hear; but though tales of 'hearing voices' are familiar, many people still find it hard to believe that they can be indistinguishable from ordinary voices. Julian Jaynes found that they tended to say, 'after all, there is no mouth or larynx in the brain.' Nevertheless, 'it is absolutely certain that such voices do exist, and that experiencing them is just like hearing actual sound' – as anybody who has heard them will testify.

There are countless reports of 'voices' in what is even more clearly an evolutionary role: as warnings. Perhaps the most striking case in recent times was described by the Italian baritone Tito Gobbi in his autobiography. Driving too fast for safety on a narrow mountain road, he heard his brother Bruno's voice say 'Stop – instantly.' He pulled into the side; a few moments later, round the narrow bend came an articulated lorry out of control. So natural had the warning sounded that Gobbi was surprised to find that his brother was not in the car: 'the reality of Bruno's speaking to me was more intense than the reality that he had been dead several years.'

'Gilbert Pinfold'

It would be absurd, though, to dispute that hallucination frequently appears in forms not markedly different from those which are traditionally associated with mental breakdown – even with possession, as in a meticulously documented case in 1957. Although Evelyn Waugh's experiences were published as a novel, *The Ordeal of Gilbert Pinfold*, he never attempted to hide the fact that he was Pinfold. Asked by John Freeman on the BBC *Face to Face* television series whether the book described what had happened to him, his reply was that it was 'almost exact'.

In Waugh's case, the experience was triggered off by a combination of alcohol, sleeping draughts, and some new and powerful pills, unnamed, which his GP prescribed for his rheumatic pains. On a sea voyage designed to restore himself to health, Pinfold/Waugh began to hear voices which for a time he took to be real, accusing him of a variety of vices, and so effectively mocking his religious beliefs that he had to give up his prayers – 'the familiar, hallowed words provoked a storm of blasphemous parody.'

He left the ship at Port Said, and flew on to Colombo, where he hoped that he had left his tormentors behind. They soon caught up with him, and he wrote to tell his wife that he was thinking of consulting a priest who knew about diabolic possession; 'sometimes I wonder if it is not literally the devil who is mocking me.' His wife hastened to fly out and fetch him home, where his GP assured him that it sounded like a simple case of poisoning brought on by the ill-advised mixture of drugs, and that the symptoms would disappear as soon as he stopped taking them – as they did. Waugh realized, though, that it was not quite so simple. Pinfold knew 'and the others did not know – not even his wife, least of all his medical adviser – that he had endured a great ordeal and, unaided, had emerged the victor'.

The point Waugh was making was that although the drugs had been responsible for the days he had spent hallucinated, the form the hallucinations took was diabolic; a sustained attack on his beliefs to which, had he been less resolute, he might have succumbed, falling into despair and perhaps madness – the fate of some of the Loudun exorcists who had been the fiercest and the most relentless in pressing the charge of witchcraft against Urbain Grandier. They had tortured him, broken his bones, and sent him to the stake – only themselves to be possessed, and to die in hideous agonies of mind and body.

Another recent case of pathological hallucination has important implications for psychiatry. In *The Story of Ruth* (1980), Morton Schatzmann, an American psychiatrist in London, gave a fresh twist to psychotherapy by using induced hallucination to treat pathological hallucination. 'Ruth', a patient, was being plagued by the apparition of her father, who had raped her when she was a child and was displaying all the indications that he would like to rape her again. He was in fact alive, but in the United States. So far as 'Ruth' was concerned, he was in and out of her home, looking, sounding and even smelling as if he was actually there.

If 'Ruth' was conjuring up her father involuntarily, Schatzmann thought, she might be able to conjure him up deliberately; and little though she liked the idea, she allowed herself to be persuaded that if she could summon him, and he came, she might be able to banish him. And so it proved, demonstrating yet again the need to examine the possibility of treating hallucinations, when pathological, as disorders for which drugs or shock treatment may be irrelevant.

The irrelevance of conventional psychiatry in dealing with hallucination was devastatingly exposed in 1972 in an experiment conducted by David Rosenhan, a psychologist at Stanford University. He and seven friends went to twelve mental hospitals, some public, some private, in different parts of the United States. None of them had had any symptoms before of the kind that would have suggested psychiatric treatment, and they were careful not to disclose any; all they did was to pretend that occasionally they 'heard voices', saying words like 'hollow' or 'thud'. Otherwise they behaved normally.

Seven of them were diagnosed as schizophrenic, one as manic-depressive. The idea was to find how long it would be before they were rumbled, if they continued to behave normally and do whatever they were instructed to do (except take the drugs which were lavishly prescribed). Sometimes their fellow-patients realized that they were really doing research; but not the psychiatrists or nurses. When they were released after periods of between seven and fifty-two days, it was invariably because they were 'in remission'.

Mediumship

The other variety of sensory automatism which was so energetically investigated a century ago, mediumship, ceased to be of primary concern to parapsychologists in the 1930s, and has not been restored to favour. Thousands of individuals practise it in all Western countries and in some, as a religion, Spiritualism has a large following – how large, nobody has attempted to calculate; but relations between them and researchers have tended to be frosty. The members of the species who have collaborated in research have for the most part described themselves as psychics, practitioners of clairvoyance rather than inter-mediaries between the living and the spirit world; and these have rarely exploited deep trance, though many of them have entered states of abstraction to facilitate second sight.

When I joined the SPR in the early 1960s there was only one full trance medium who had established a reputation among parapsy-chologists (the term which has tended to be used by those researchers who are in the Rhine tradition). Eileen Garrett had made her name as a medium in the 1920s, and when she heard of the research beginning at Duke University she offered her services, which included tests to try to ascertain whether her results would be any different if she was in her normal mind or in a trance (she obtained similar positive results in both). She thereupon set up the Parapsychological

Foundation and devoted the last thirty years of her life to participating in, organizing, and funding research in the United States and in Europe, largely with the aim of achieving a better understanding of how mediumship works. Unlike most trance mediums she was a cool-headed business woman, and her long record as a research subject is so well-documented that sceptics have been unable to find serious flaws in it.

Mrs Garrett would go into trance which, briefly, would make her oblivious of her surroundings, before one of her 'controls', 'Uvani' or 'Abdul Latif', took over. Sitters who were present were often astonished to find how very different these 'controls' were from the traditional spiritualist 'guides'; they conversed rationally, and willingly agreed to collaborate in research. Sometimes the tests were straightforward: Rosalind Heywood used to place an object on her bedroom mantelpiece in London once a month, and Mrs Garrett would write from the United States to tell her what 'Abdul Latif' thought it was (even when he got it wrong, Mrs Heywood found, he might be describing something else which had been on her mind at the time). Or the control would produce 'communicators', in traditional spiritualist fashion, to reassure a sitter that they were very much alive in the spirit world.

Naturally Mrs Garrett's views about how her mediumship operated were sought after. Laurence LeShan, who worked with her for several years, was present on an occasion when the widow and sister of a man she had never met assured her that the 'communicator' had indisputably been the woman's deceased husband; but LeShan must not forget, Mrs Garrett warned him, that she was telepathic, and 'the stage lost a great actress in me.' She was not confessing to deception; she simply did not know, she admitted, whether her performances were the outcome of communication from the deceased, or telepathic communication with the living. 'Sometimes I think that maybe they're spirits as they claim to be,' she told him shortly before her death in 1970; but at other times 'I think they are multiple personality split-offs of my own mind.'

It would be difficult for anybody, surveying Mrs Garrett's career over half a century, to find evidence of self-deception, let alone of deceiving others. She impressed, or at least silenced, even the most sceptical of parapsychologists – and some were, and are, deeply sceptical about trance mediums. In general, however, the paths of spiritualists and parapsychologists have diverged, and research to try to find out more about survival after bodily death has been left to spiritualist organizations such as the College of Psychic Studies in London.

Their problem, not surprisingly, has been that sitters who obtain information of a kind that convinces them a 'communicator' really is alive, in the spirit world, do not care to face the possibility that the medium may be picking up the information telepathically. But in any case, as Paul Beard, the conscience of the spiritualist movement (as distinct from the Spiritualist faith) in Britain, has recently reminded sitters, they have a responsibility, when they go to a medium, to interpret what they hear. Messages purporting to come from the dead, like those from the oracles of old, need to be scrutinized. 'No authority whatever lies in a statement merely because it comes from the dead,' he asserts. 'To be blunt, if this is neglected, the result is superstition.'

Striking confirmation of the wisdom of this warning has been provided in an unusual research project conducted by Professor George Owen in Toronto. He brought a group together for table-turning sessions, but with a difference; instead of waiting, as some groups do, for a spirit to manifest itself as a 'control' or 'communicator', they invented one: 'Philip'. They provided 'Philip' with a historical identity; and soon they found they could literally conjure him up, so that he seemed to become a spirit in his own right, independent of the group, capable of communicating his whims through raps and movements of the table. It was as if contagious hysteria, generated in table-turning, may be capable of the kind of creativity so often encountered in legend. 'Philip' was an embryo djinn.

Automatic writing

In general, though, motor automatism of the type the Victorians enjoyed as a pastime is seldom reported, perhaps because the radio and television have left people unwilling to sit around a table in near darkness for long enough to conjure up the phenomena associated with table-turning. The kind of telekinesis which features most frequently in the news is in connection with poltergeist infestations; in many accounts, it is as if invisible hands are throwing crockery around, banging doors in empty rooms, spilling the contents of cupboards on the floor, creating mayhem. The most plausible explanation that has been put forward is that some form of exteriorization of the kind that Jung experienced is involved. It is as if a mischievous dual personality, deprived of recognition, makes itself felt telekinetically.

Other types of motor automatism have received less attention. Myers fondly assumed that by the end of the nineteenth century, automatic writing had at least been accepted as a fact; and in the 1920s, McDougall thought that the 'natural scepticism' which it aroused had been disposed of by 'the abundance of carefully studied cases': but to judge from letters I receive from time to time, so far as the public is concerned it is still widely regarded as pathological or paranormal, or both.

In his *Mediumship and Survival* (1983), Alan Gauld has taken the fact of automatic writing for granted, noting that two claims have been made for it. One is that in certain cases it is 'clearly the product of an intelligence', though 'the automatist does not consciously control what is written, and she may be as surprised as anyone else when she reads it' – which postulates the existence of a subliminal stream of consciousness; the other, that in some cases it appears to be the vehicle for ESP. The first of these claims, he feels, is hard to reject; the second, hard to assess, in particular the contention that ESP is facilitated by this form of automatism. The anecdotal evidence that it is, from a century ago, is strong; but little research has been done, even by parapsychologists, in recent years.

Many spiritualists, however, use automatic writing for guidance. 'Directed writing', as Paul Beard prefers to describe it, is in his view 'one of the easiest forms of mediumistic sensitivity'. Because of this, however, it is likely to contain the largest amount of erroneous material, 'if practised in undisciplined ways'. It may consist of material coming up from the subliminal regions, which can provide a useful way to bypass blockages in the conscious mind; but its messages should not be accepted, he warns, without careful scrutiny and analysis, particularly if they use flattery. People practising directed writing, Beard notes, tend to fuss too much over whether the information is coming from a 'guide', or from within themselves. For practical purposes, he suggests, the need to distinguish these sources can be regarded as not too important, 'since in the inner world we all live in a spiritual continuum where perceptions are largely shared in common, rather than merely being mine and thine'.

As a device to exploit automatism, the ouija board has remained in use, but chiefly as a sometimes scary pastime. If any scientist announced that he was preparing to investigate how the 'traveller' is propelled, let alone how it manages to produce coherent sentences and sometimes information of a kind not available to the sitters – as Barrett and his group did – he would be regarded by his colleagues as cracked. And there has been nothing comparable to the writings of 'Patience Worth' to compel the attention of doubters.

Recently, however, a few artists have credited automatism as a significant element in their work. 'I sometimes begin a drawing with no preconceived problem to solve,' Henry Moore explained, when asked how he set about working, 'with only a desire to use pencil and paper, and make lines, tones and shapes with no conscious aim.' But 'as my mind takes in what is produced, a point arrives when some idea becomes conscious and crystallizes, and then a control and ordering begins to take place.'

In his biography of Picasso, Jaume Sabartés described the trance state which Picasso entered when absorbed in a painting; 'when he creates, he is like a somnambulist, and obeys only the mysterious intuition that governs him.' Francis Bacon's paintings, according to his biographer Sir John Rothenstein, are the product of contrary procedures; the first, protracted retention in Bacon's mind of a particular image; 'the second, of automatism and chance'. He can follow the precisely formulated intention with which he always begins, in order then 'to follow blind inspiration when he becomes a sort of figurative action-painter working under the spell of the subconscious'. And his contemporary Louis le Brocquy has described how he begins by making 'gestures' with his brush, which seem to have a queer logic of their own, 'an element of accident, or discovery, or surprise', so that the picture which emerges 'is not so much made by me as imposing itself on me, accident by accident, with its own autonomous life'.

Paradoxically, it has been novelists who have hung back, as if reluctant – with a few exceptions, notably Graham Greene – to credit inspiration for their achievements. Partly this has been due to the influence, surprisingly strong in literary circles, of Freud. Creative writing was for him a substitute for analysis, through which the poet or novelist transformed repressed infantile desires into works of art. 'Psychoanalysis has to lay down its arms before the problem of the imaginative writer,' he admitted; such a writer must be able to achieve sublimation, and to enjoy a certain lack of rigidity in dealing with his repressions. This did not mean that Freud lacked appreciation of literature, Ernest Jones insisted, pointing out that he had a catholic taste ranging from Macaulay's *Essays* to Kipling's *Jungle Books*; and although it was not easy to judge Freud's critical ability, 'it must have been of a high order.' But the impression which Freud left, that literature is the by-product of psycho-neurosis, has understandably tended to irritate writers.

Bio-physics

Of the many different forms of motor automatism, only one has attracted quite extensive research in recent years: dowsing. Barrett's plea to scientists to investigate it was echoed by the discoverer of the electron, J. J. Thomson, in his autobiography (1936). 'Of all the phenomena which may be thought to be psychical,' he suggested, the divining rod was 'perhaps the one most favourable for experiment'; and from time to time since there have been tests of dowsers, in varying degrees of formality. What has emerged most clearly from them is that consciousness of being involved in a test usually leads to failure. The ability to throw off the desire to succeed appears to be an important element in obtaining positive results.

A way to get around this has been introduced in Russia – at first sight surprisingly, as dowsing was regarded there in Stalinist times as bourgeois occultism. In 1974 two researchers employed in the All-Union Scientific Research Institute of Engineering Geology, Moscow, described how they had been making mineral surveys using a variety of techniques, and had found that one of them, 'BPM', was particularly useful in uncovering valuable deposits of ore. 'BPM' stood for 'bio-physical method' – which was, in fact, dowsing. The term 'bio-physical effect' had slipped into use in the Khrushchev thaw period to provide quasi-scientific cover for dowsing research.

The most likely explanation for the success of the dowsers is that, working as they normally did in the field, they were less inhibited by laboratory-type controls of the kind that have been used in tests in the United States. Nor were they required to produce 100 per cent accurate results; their function was simply to give their findings, so that they could be compared with the results from the other techniques. A consequence of their success – and the adoption of the useful description 'bio-physical' – was that dowsing weathered the Brezhnev era. A manual, entitled *The Use of the Bio-locational Method in the Search for Ore Deposits and in Geological Mapping* (1984) and written by three professional dowsers, has since been given the *imprimatur* of an

Associate Member of the USSR Academy and other academic figures.

In the West, in spite of the evidence produced from the United States by Christopher Bird in *The Divining Hand* (1979), dowsing has still not succeeded in establishing its scientific credentials; but the outcome of one piece of research in the 1970s may eventually be crucial. An American electronics engineer, Alvin Kaufman, decided to investigate not whether dowsing works, but *how* it works. Is the movement of the hazel twig caused, as Barrett maintained, by muscular contractions responding to extra-sensory signals? Or, as Wallace thought, by telekinesis acting on the tip of the twig?

This has long been a disputed issue. Urging the need, three centuries ago, for experiments to find whether the divining rod could profitably be used in the search for minerals, Robert Boyle remarked that a man in whose hands a rod moved when he was passing over a vein of ore had told him 'that the motion of his hand did not at all contribute to the inclination of the rod, but that sometimes when he held it very fast it would bend so strongly as to break in his hand'; and many dowsers have since reported that the rod moves in spite of their attempts to stop the movements. It has always been possible, though, for a sceptic to maintain that they have only imagined that the force was external. 'If the force is external in origin,' Kaufman surmised, 'it should be possible both to be sure of it, and at the same time to measure its externality, i.e. rule out muscular action.'

This he proceeded to do by constructing metal bars, shaped like rulers, and attaching fine wires, to act as strain gauges, on either side. When these were attached to the dowser's arm, they showed that the twitch when he walked over underground water apparently did not come from his muscles, but from some external force.

It would be difficult enough to convince orthodox scientists of the validity of dowsing; to have to accept telekinesis, as well, proved altogether too much, and Kaufman's results have been ignored – by many dowsers, even, as some of them long for scientific recognition, and realize that they are not going to obtain it if telekinesis is thought to be involved. There are signs, however, that industry has been moving ahead of science, and employing dowsers – sometimes, though this is unusual, even admitting they employ them.

The rapidly expanding population involves increased demands for many minerals and, in the developing world, for water – as the World Bank recognized, inviting Bird to give a lecture. 'He's a big burly man who seldom wears a tie,' Thierry Sagnier, who covered the occasion for *The Bank's World*, reported. 'He resembles a turn-of-the-century mountain man rather than a Harvard-trained biologist.' Bird pointed out that when a senior executive of Hoffman-La Roche, employed to travel the world to dowse for water to supply the company's plants, was asked why so unscientific a method was used, his reply was, simply, 'We use methods that are profitable whether they are scientific or not.' The firms who have employed Uri Geller to dowse for them – making him a multi-millionaire in the process – do not expect him to get the answer right every time. They employ him because they have found he is cost-effective.

PHYSICISTS

Einstein transfigured

By a weird twist of Fate, it is beginning to look as if the quantum physicists are going to be the regenerators of mind, overturning matter as their deity. And in the process, they have been going some way towards rehabilitating trance.

Sitting alone or in company, Albert Einstein – his friend and biographer Antonina Vallentin recalled – would suddenly fall silent, and become 'unreachable', neither moving nor hearing what was going on around him. 'This had nothing in common with the absent-mindedness of a man wrapped up in his own thoughts,' she insisted; 'with Einstein, the eclipse was total.' His eyes would be 'dark and lustreless as the eyes of a blind man'. Then he would return to himself as abruptly as he had left. It was as if a separation took place between his mind and his body, 'not unlike the ecstasy of a saint', she recalled, 'the word "transfiguration" acquired an almost literal sense'. This helps to explain how the paper 'On the electro-dynamic of bodies in movement' which foreshadowed his theory of relativity was notable in that it contained no source references, no citations from authorities. His formulae were not derived from research or calculation, but from 'psychical entities', he told Jacques Hadamard, reaching him as 'more or less clear images'. The gift of fantasy had meant more to him, he told another friend, James Plesch, than any talent for absorbing information.

At the time Einstein was presenting his theories, so strong was the assumption that scientists achieved their results through rational, logical processes that such an account would have been rejected as malicious misrepresentation. Not until the publication in 1949 of Hadamard's *Psychology of Invention in the Mathematical Field* was it shown for the first time that not merely had it been accurate – in a letter to Hadamard, Einstein confirmed that his ideas came to him through automatism, sometimes visual, sometimes 'of a muscular type' – but that many other eminent scientists owed their fame to inspiration of the same kind. Logic, reason and midnight oil came later, when they laboured to check whether the fruits of their automatism really were inspired.

A reluctance to accept that scientists operate in this way is still commonly encountered; but it has been accepted by a few philosophers of science. 'There is no such thing as a logical method of having new ideas, or a logical reconstruction of this process,' Sir Karl Popper insisted in *The Logic of Scientific Discovery* (1959). 'My view may be expressed by saying that every discovery contains "an irrational element".' Popper, too, cited Einstein in support of this belief: there is no logical path, Einstein had claimed in an address he gave on Max Planck's sixtieth birthday in 1918, to the discovery of universal laws – 'they can be reached only by intuition, based upon something like an intellectual love of the objects of experience.' The scientist who wishes to be a pioneer, Max Planck himself claimed, must possess, in addition to accurate thinking, 'a vivid intuitive imagination for new ideas, not generated by induction, but by artistically creative imagination'.

'No more than a tiny minority of mathematical theorems have been discovered by induction,' Sir Peter Medawar, a Nobel laureate and one of the few British scientists of his generation to achieve a reputation for the sinewy elegance of his prose, asserted in *Induction and Intuition* (1969); 'most of them entered the mind by processes of the kind vaguely called "intuitive".' Deduction or logical derivation came later, 'to justify or falsify what was in the first place an "inspiration" or an intuitive belief'. But this, he realized, was seldom apparent in what mathematicians wrote, 'because mathematicians take pains to ensure that it should not be'.

As Medawar realized, this has remained an area of double-think. On the one hand scientists, including Medawar himself, have been anxious to preserve science from the intrusion of mysticism – a term still used pejoratively, in much the same sense as occultism. On the other hand, they could hardly exclude intuition or inspiration altogether, though Medawar cautiously enclosed them in inverted commas. With the downfall of behaviourism in psychology it has become impossible, except for a handful of diehards, to reject 'mind', and increasingly difficult to equate it with 'brain'.

'The more we discover about the brain,' the neurologist and Nobel prizewinner Sir John Eccles has claimed, 'the more clearly do we distinguish between the brain events and mental phenomena, and the more wonderful do both the brain events and the mental phenomena become.' This is contrary to the established neuroscientific orthodoxy, which still holds to what Popper has called 'promissory materialism': the belief that the advances in the neurosciences will eventually do away with the need for 'mentalism' by explaining everything in terms of the brain, which will be found to be not merely a computer, but a computer-programmer. For Eccles, 'promissory materialism' 'is simply a religious belief held by dogmatic materialists', with 'all the features of a messianic prophecy'.

Neuropsychologists who do not care to side with Popper and Eccles find it hard to deal with intuition, as the entry in the *Oxford Companion to the Mind* reveals. It is allowed only three short paragraphs ('Invertebrate Learning and Intelligence', which follows, has six columns). Intuition is defined, succinctly enough, as 'arriving at decisions or conclusions without explicit or conscious processes of reasoned thinking'; but the writer goes on to assert that the status of intuition has declined over the last century, 'perhaps with the increasing emphasis on formal logic and explicit data and assumptions of science'.

The writer could hardly have read Ken Wilber's *Quantum Questions*, or he would have realized how comically far from the reality his assumption was about the decline in intuition's status – at least among physicists, to judge from the passages Wilber includes from Einstein, Eddington, Planck, Schroedinger, Heisenberg and others. Arthur Koestler had earlier observed that it was becoming increasingly difficult to tell, if he did not know who had written certain passages, whether they were the work of a mathematician or a mystic. Although none of the physicists cited in *Quantum Questions* could be regarded as holding a mystical world view, from their writings it would be easy, Wilber commented, to take them for mystics.

By overturning materialism and its offspring in other scientific disciplines the new physics has been compelling a reassessment of the relationship between mind and brain. 'The qualitative, colourful and value-rich world of inner experience, long excluded from the domain of science by behaviourist–materialist doctrine, has been reinstated,' Roger Sperry, the leading advocate of mentalism in the United States, has felt justified in claiming in *The Oxford Companion to the Mind*. 'Scientific theory has become squared finally with the impressions of common experience; we do in fact use the mind to initiate and control our physical actions.'

A problem, however, remains. Sperry fears that Eccles and Popper weaken the mentalist case by accepting a distinction between mind and brain. When they 'jointly proclaim arguments and beliefs in dualism, the supernatural, and unembodied worlds of existence', he complains, 'the repercussions quickly extend beyond professional borders to influence attitudes and faith-belief systems in society at large.'

This issue has significant implications for the study of trance. Until very recently, the mechanistic hypothesis was hardly challenged. 'All the experiments of the past fifty years that I did were built on the principle that the brain generates the mind and that mind is completely dependent upon brain,' Wilder Penfield, one of the most eminent of neurophysiologists, recalled on his retirement. 'They were all built on this principle and they were all designed to prove it. All of them proved exactly the opposite.' But if the mind does not lie in the brain, where is it? Is it immaterial, lying outside the confines of space-time?

If it *is* immaterial, this would help to account for the historical links between trance and what Sperry derides as the 'supernatural'; in particular, it would make it easier for scientists to accept extra-sensory communication. Here again, quantum physics has contributed to the controversy. Einstein accepted the fact of clairvoyance, but jibbed at the evidence which suggested that telepathic communication is faster than the speed of light. He had the same objection to quantum theory, when it postulated what has since come to be called 'non-locality'. If the quantum model was correct, he pointed out, influencing the spin of a nuclear particle which is one of a pair would influence the other at vast distances apart, which on his theory was impossible. It did not prove practicable to test the idea in his lifetime, but experiments since have shown that quantum theory was correct; alter the spin of one of the pair, and the other changes too.

A few quantum physicists have strenuously maintained that this lends no support to ESP, because there is no indication that the linkage can account for the transmission of information. But psychical researchers long ago discarded the idea that information is 'transmitted' in the way it is, say, by radio. The process, Barrett argued, resembles a kind of fusion. For David Bohm, and for other eminent physicists – Henry Margenau of Yale University, the Nobel laureate Professor Brian Josephson of the Cavendish Laboratory in Cambridge – 'non-locality', though it does not in itself afford proof of the existence of ESP, at least pulls it out of the supernatural category to which Sperry consigns it. Einstein's objection has been overturned.

Non-locality, then, may turn out to be the channel through which clairvoyance and telepathy are at last brought into the arena of orthodox science. It may even permit access to telekinesis. But if some of the stranger historical evidence about trance manifestations is also to be accommodated, there will be problems.

7

TWO MYSTERIES

BEYOND THE 'BOGGLE THRESHOLD'

The burning fiery furnace

I warned in the introduction that trance is inextricably linked throughout history with phenomena whose existence orthodox science still
declines to accept; and I have included reports of some of them. But
I have kept 'boggle threshold' in mind. Most of us, to judge from
opinion polls, ignore the sceptics on the subject of, say, extra-sensory
perception; but people who accept ESP do not necessarily agree that
mind can influence matter. And some of the phenomena that have
been recorded in connection with trance seem unbelievable – yet
cannot be rejected out of hand, in view of the strength of the evidence
about them.

It is difficult enough, for example, for members of an audience who
have never seen a professional hypnotist going through his repertoire
before, to believe him when he claims that he can hold a lighted match
under the forefinger of hypnotized subjects, and not only will the
subjects feel no pain, they will show no signs of blistering afterwards.
Nevertheless hypnotists are giving such demonstrations of human
incombustibility week in, week out, wherever they have an audience
to entertain.

Trance incombustibility, as it happens, has a long history. When
somebody was observed in a trance, Iamblichus noted in his commentary on divination in the second century AD, it seemed as if 'sensation
and life had been suspended'; he has ceased to feel pain, and 'has not
felt the application of fire'. In our own century, once in his life – only
once – Joseph Chilton Pearce had the same experience. 'As a young

man I once found myself in a certain somnambulistic, trance-like state of mind,' he has recalled. 'With upwards of a dozen witnesses I held the glowing tips of cigarettes against my palms, cheeks, eyelids, grinding them out on those sensitive areas.' To his friends' astonishment there were no after-effects, and no blisters.

Accounts such as this make it easier to understand trial by ordeal, which often consisted of allowing suspects to prove their innocence by holding a red-hot bar, or plunging a hand into boiling water, for a prescribed time; they were deemed innocent if they came through the trial unscathed. It is hardly conceivable that the method would have continued in use – as it has done to this day, in some tribes – if the verdict was, invariably, 'guilty'. Even Eusebe Salverte, the first systematic explainer-away of the miraculous events recorded in history, had to admit that the men who conducted such trials were unlikely to permit such deception; and 'in the case of the red-hot iron, it is not easy to conceive fraud.'

But there are more striking accounts of incombustibility, and some of them are particularly difficult to reject, as David Hume noted in connection with the eye-witness accounts of the hysteria outbreak at the tomb of François de Paris. These included, among other reports, the testimonies to the fact that while in a trance Marie Souet, *la Salamandre*, had remained suspended in a sheet above a raging fire for over half an hour; neither she, nor the sheet, were scorched, though the flames were lapping around it. This was one of the 'miracles' of St Médard which, as Hume admitted, had been 'proved upon the spot, before judges of unquestioned integrity, attested by witnesses of credit and distinction, in a learned age'.

Can we seriously be expected to believe that trance can confer protection on cloth? Yet this has been claimed from earliest times – when Shadrach, Meshach and Abednego were let out of Nebuchadnezzar's burning fiery furnace, they were not even singed, 'nor were their coats changed' – and is still quite frequently reported by witnesses of the most familiar demonstration of incombustibility, fire-walking.

By the eighteenth century the accounts of fire-walking from classical times, describing how priests and their followers, thanks to the protection of their gods, could walk over red-hot coals without feeling pain or suffering burns, had come to be relegated to the status of legends; but the rediscovery of fire-walking by explorers and missionaries compelled positivists to offer 'natural' explanations. Of these, initially the most popular was Salverte's; in *Les Sciences Occultes* (1829) he claimed that 'a saturated solution of alum preserves any part strongly impregnated with it from the action of fire.' This did not satisfy W. B. Carpenter. He argued in 1871 that it was sweat which provided the protection: 'you can see it every day in the falling-off of drops of fluid from a heated iron, in the application of the familiar test by which the laundress judges the suitability of the temperature.' In the 1900 edition of *The Golden Bough*, James Frazer settled for a simpler explanation. 'Inured from infancy to walking barefoot, peasants can step with impunity over glowing charcoal,' he asserted; 'usage has so hardened their soles that the skin is converted into a sort of leathery or corny substance which is almost callous to heat.'

Frazer was himself breezily callous to facts, whenever they failed to fit his soon to be discredited theories. As it happened, investigators of fire-walks in the Pacific islands had found that the fire-walkers did *not* have leathery soles. Nor, for that matter, did they rub their soles with alum, or anything else; in 1898 one investigator, Dr T. M. Hocken, actually applied his tongue to their soles, to satisfy himself that there was no deception. A further possibility – that the coals, or volcanic ash, or whatever material was being used, were not really hot – also had to be abandoned, because the immunity evidently did not extend to all the walkers; a few suffered severe burns. And Carpenter's hypothesis was ruled out by the fact that it was clear, from many of the accounts, that the walkers remained on the coals too long for sweat glands to provide them with protection.

Nevertheless similar explanations have continued to appear. After experiments in Florida, Dr Mayne Reid Coe claimed in 1958 he had tested Carpenter's hypothesis, by letting drops of water fall on a heated frying pan; they did not at once turn to steam, but skipped around for a time. Anybody who has inadvertently put a hand on a hot frying pan will also have done some skipping around, but not of the kind which would lend credibility to the ludicrous theory. In 1961 two American anthropologists echoed Frazer, even stating that the epidermis on the soles of fire-walkers' feet 'is reported to us as being $1/8$ to $1/9$ inch in thickness'.

Such continuing imperviousness to fact can readily be explained. Accounts of fire-walking were not published in scientific journals, and orthodox scientists did not read or pay any attention to the journals in which they *were* published. If they had, they would have found reports which demolished their explanations. A typical sober account of fire-walking appeared in *Atlantic* in 1959, from Leonard Feinberg,

Professor of English at Iowa State College, who was spending a year as Fulbright Professor of American Literature at the University of Ceylon. As a fitting climax to a week of celebrations in honour of the Hindu god Kataragama, a pit had been dug twenty feet long and six feet wide, and filled with combustible material so hot that the crowd which had assembled to watch had to stand well away from it. Eighty people crossed the length of the pit; some skipped over it; one danced for a while in mid-crossing; most walked 'slowly and serenely' across. But twelve were sufficiently badly burned to be taken to hospital, and one of them died.

Some of the reports have noted, usually with astonishment, that protection appeared to be given to what the walkers were wearing. Basil Thomson, later to become head of the London CID, noted that anklets of tree-fern which Fiji walkers wore did not burn, though he could see the flames were licking up round their legs. V. S. Stowell of the Imperial Bank of India told Oliver Lodge that when he himself fire-walked, though the flames reached ankle level, to his surprise his white trousers were not scorched.

In the 1980s the controversy took a new twist when 'coal strolls', as they came to be called, became a popular pastime in California. Hundreds of people found they could walk barefoot over coals or other combustible materials. All that was required – or at least all they received – was a kind of conference cool-down before the walk to calm their fears and to boost their auto-suggestive powers.

This presented sceptics with a problem which they resolved by falling back on the theory offered by Carpenter, and echoed by Coe, but giving it a scientific-sounding name, the 'Leidenfrost Effect', thanks to the rediscovery of the work of the eighteenth-century physician Johann Leidenfrost, who had presented it long before Carpenter, as the explanation for the 'skipping' of droplets on smooth heated surfaces: at a certain temperature a vapour barrier builds up round the droplets. 'No special talent is required to do this stupid stunt,' Bernard Leiken of the University College of Los Angeles explained in 1985; 'the rules of physics, not one's state of mind, allow anyone to tolerate a brief barefoot walk over coals.'

But this toleration was precisely what Leidenfrost himself ruled out. By a fluke, the temperatures of coal in a pit might occasionally fall within the narrow range he postulated; but the surface of fire-walking pits is not smooth, and the sole of the human foot is not protected by droplets of sweat. It was yet another example of orthodoxy throwing at the public what might seem a plausible explanation, but which in fact was spurious.

Discussing fire-walking in his *Shamanism*, Eliade insisted that its genuineness was 'beyond doubt'. He attributed the protection provided to the ability of shamans to confer it on themselves, the members of their tribe, and even outsiders; but the popularity of coal strolls suggests that some force related to the one associated with mass hysteria must also be involved. Whatever the explanation, the way in which trance can provide insulation against the effects of even extreme heat indicates how unfortunate it is that psychologists have given the evidence so little attention.

Again, the problem is that anybody who is tempted to undertake research soon finds himself up against the equivalent of the 'higher phenomena' which the mesmerists encountered. It is not too difficult for a sceptic to delude himself that the soles of the feet are protected in a fire-walk by sweat, if he shuts his mind to any report which rules out the possibility. But no such escape route presents itself in the case of reports of people 'playing with fire'.

The ability of some entranced individuals to hold red-hot coals, juggle with them, and even impart their incombustibility to others is well-attested. Lord Adare described in 1868 how he had seen D. D. Home, in a trance, stir the embers of a fire; kneeling down beside it, 'he placed his face right among the burning coals, moving it about as though bathing in water' – an account confirmed by the barrister H. D. Jencken. The following year the author Mrs S. C. Hall wrote to Adare's father, Lord Dunraven, to report that she had been present when Home had not only carried round lumps of red-hot coal, but had placed one on her husband's head – 'I often wondered since why I was not frightened, but I was not.' Nor, apparently, was her husband, Samuel Carter Hall. Home, who was 'still in a trance', smiled, and seemed quite pleased; and 'then proceeded to draw up Mr Hall's white hair over the red coal'.

Spontaneous combustion

There is another mystery associated with fire which is hard to explain unless it, too, is tied in with trance; spontaneous human combustion. It is not common, but a year seldom goes by without a case being reported in which burning in the ordinary way, as through a fault in an electric blanket, can be ruled out. In an article in the *New Scientist* recently, the Scenes of Crimes Officer with the Gwent Police Force in Wales, John Heymer, described how within the space of a month he had had to deal with two very similar cases. In both, the torso had been almost completely consumed, the bones reduced to ash from neck to mid-thigh, while the skull and lower parts of the legs remained intact.

The fact that only parts of the body are destroyed, while the rest is hardly affected, is one of the chief characteristics of these cases; but it is not the decisive element in putting them in the spontaneous combustion category. Ordinary burning, from some external source of heat, can be ruled out because to reduce flesh and bones to ash requires such fierce heat that the rooms in which the bodies are found, and indeed the entire houses, would have gone up in smoke. Yet furniture near the bodies is often only mildly charred.

Scores of similar cases have been recorded, and a few coroners have felt compelled to recognize their existence. Dr Gavin Thurston, the Coroner for Inner West London, described them to Michael Harrison as 'preternatural combustion'. He insisted, though, that 'no such phenomenon as spontaneous combustion exists'; it is always, he assured Harrison, 'started by external fire'. But in a sense this is irrelevant. If cases such as Heymer described were started by, say, a dropped cigarette – though in fact he had satisfied himself that this could not be the explanation – it still could not account for the way in which the body burned. Even in crematoriums, bones are often not reduced to ash; and the process requires a vigorous supply of oxygen. The rooms in the Gwent cases had hardly any ventilation – which, Heymer assumed, was why the furniture did not go up in smoke.

The only suggestion I have heard which begins to make some sense of spontaneous or preternatural combustion is that it may turn out to be an inverted form of incombustibility. For some unexplained reason the body, instead of resisting heat, generates it internally, and so powerfully that flesh and bones are more effectively incinerated than they could be in all but the most powerful ovens.

From time to time reports appear confirming that not to accept the phenomenon is sheer wilful blindness, as Harrison showed in *Fire From Heaven* in 1976; and there have been several clear-cut cases since. But coroners still tend to dismiss even the possibility of spontaneous combustion as a superstition. Whatever the explanation ultimately is, this is yet another example of the unwillingness of doctors and scientists not just – as Sir Peter Medawar observed – to ask themselves questions until they can see the rudiments of an answer but, more dangerous, of their readiness to accept that embarrassing questions have been answered satisfactorily – in this case, by the assertion that an external source of fire is always present – when reports of specific cases reveal that this is simply wrong, and would be irrelevant to the main issue even if it were correct.

The nature of belief

I am often asked, do I *really* believe in . . . whatever strange phenomenon has cropped up in conversation: anything from the levitations of saints to the descent to earth of little goggle-eyed green men. I am forced to reply with what sounds like prevarication: what do you mean by 'believe in'? Just as it usually is in connection with ghosts, the term is ambiguous. If somebody stops you in the street, for example, and says 'Do you believe in Jesus?' it is unlikely that he merely wants to find whether you believe that a man of that name lived and died two millennia ago. Belief tends to imply faith; in such matters I am an unreconstructed agnostic, putting my trust only in the historical evidence, as witnessed and reported by reputable people.

On this basis the evidence for Jesus's miracles is far from reliable, put together as it was in the gospels by men who had not themselves been witnesses, and who had a motive for accepting those stories which, for them, appeared to confirm that Jesus had divine powers. But there is massive confirmation throughout history for the existence of some of the gospels' miracles; and it is one of the fundamental flaws in Hume's essay that he should have claimed: 'There is not to be found, in all history, any miracle attested by a sufficient number of men, of such unquestioned good sense, education and learning, as to secure us against all delusion in themselves'. The other major flaw is his contention that 'a firm and unalterable experience' had established the laws of nature so that a miracle, being defined as 'a violation of the laws' was out of the question. The 'laws', as they stood in his time, have proved far from unalterable.

I do not 'believe in' incombustibility. But it was witnessed at St Médard – to repeat Hume's words – 'before judges of unquestioned integrity, attested by witnesses of credit and distinction'; and the testimonies on that occasion, coupled with many others, have led me to accept that in certain hysteric states, a degree of incombustibility can occur: and the fact that in a lesser degree it can be exploited for therapeutic purposes under hypnosis, or auto-hypnosis, surely lends a measure of justification for such acceptance.

Miracles, when observed and reported as they were at St Médard and have been on countless other occasions, are in the category of facts. The beliefs associated with them are a different matter, often confusing the issue – as indeed does ingrained *disbelief*. I find it impossible to reject the vast accumulation of accounts which indicate that individuals, usually in a trance condition of some kind, can in certain circumstances transcend the powers which are regarded as normal, so that they may achieve not just what we think of as superhuman – as when in moments of extreme stress we perform feats which would be beyond our everyday capabilities – but may also find themselves doing things which transcend normality, such as levitating. The nature of the force which is responsible for levitation may elude us, but to dismiss it as contrary to natural laws is to forget that gravity-defying telekinesis can be demonstrated with the greatest of ease, simply by holding a magnet above a paper clip. To claim that all the accounts of levitations *must* be lies is rationalism at its most obtuse; the only possible alternative to accepting that they happen is some form of mass hallucination – and in that case, as it must be yet another trance manifestation, it ought to be attracting the attention of psychologists particularly those who think of themselves as Christians.

The recent attitudes of the churches, but in particular the Anglican Church, have been hypocritical: on the one hand professing belief in the divinity of Jesus, derived from the gospels which emphasize his miracle-working; on the other, shying away from acceptance of miracles of the same kind in our own time, in order not to appear unscientific.

As Thomas Mann noted through his character Serenus Zeitblom in *Doctor Faustus*, the 'accommodation theology' which has allowed science and Christianity to live in relative harmony, has led to a ludicrous compromise whereby scientists are permitted to continue to believe in the precepts derived from Jesus's teaching, while at the same time Christians have 'abandoned to scientific criticism its own most important contents: the belief in miracles, considerable portions of Christology, the bodily resurrection, and what not besides'. Nor has science come well out of the deal; for 'what sort of science is that

which stands in such a forced and precarious relation to reason,
constantly threatened by the very compromise that she makes
with it?'

TRANSCENDENCE

The experience of ecstasy

By his own account, the astronaut Edgar Mitchell had been 'as
pragmatic a test pilot, engineer and scientist as any of my colleagues'
before he took off for the moon in Apollo 14. His life was totally
dependent, he assumed, on the validity of the scientific principles he
had absorbed, and the reliability of the technology based on them.
But when he saw Planet Earth, as it appeared from the spacecraft, it
blew his mind, converting him instantly from his materialism. 'In a
peak experience, the presence of divinity became almost palpable, and
I *knew* that life in the universe was not just an accident based on
random principles.'

This knowledge, he believed, came to him directly, 'noetically'. It
was a product not of reasoning, but of private subjective awareness.
Yet it was, and remained, 'every bit as real as the objective data upon
which, say, the navigational program or the communications system
were based'. And the experience led Mitchell to set up the Institute
of Noetic Sciences in California, based on the assumption that there
are 'very large gaps in our knowledge of what is natural. We should
strive to fill those gaps.'

Ecstasy, as 'peak experiences' of this kind were described before the
word became enfeebled by casual use, has historically been closely
associated with religion. For Myers it was 'the highest form which the
various religions known to man have assumed in the past', common
to all of them; 'from the medicine-man of the lowest savages up to St
John, St Peter, St Paul, the Buddha, Mahomet and Swedenborg on
the way, we find records which, though morally and intellectually
much differing, are in psychological essence the same.'

Examining the 'mystical state', as it has also been called, for
his *Mysticism* (1963), F. C. Happold found it had certain marked
characteristics. First, it had 'the quality of *ineffability*; that is, it defies
expression in terms which are fully intelligible to one who has not

known some analogous experience.' Nevertheless the states 'have a *noetic* quality; they result in insight into depths of truth unplumbed by the discursive intellect.' They are *transient*, rarely lasting for more than a few minutes; and *passive*, in the sense that the individual feels 'as if he were grasped and held by a power not his own'. Often they give a sensation of '*the oneness of everything*'.

Throughout history there have been accounts of people who have had such experiences, and ineffability has been the most consistent characteristic. In spite of the difficulty of describing what occurs, though, the accounts are consistent. So also, interestingly, are the methods which individuals in different ages, and holding different beliefs, have adopted to try to attain ecstasy, in the belief that it is *the* transcendent experience. As James Leuba, Professor of Psychology at Bryn Mawr College, showed in *The Psychology of Religious Mysticism* (1929), whatever the religious beliefs such aspirants brought with them on account of the accident of their birth and upbringing, the objective was the same: the cultivation of trance with a view to attaining ecstasy. The terminology differed; the actual courses taken showed some variations; the vision of what ecstasy would turn out to be like was naturally not the same for Christians as, say, for Buddhists. But making such allowances, the advice given to aspiring mystics and the descriptions of what they could expect to experience were often largely interchangeable.

The starting point, according to Saint Francis of Sales – Bishop of Geneva in the early seventeenth century – in his treatise on the love of God, is meditation: encouraging the thoughts to dwell on themes of love. Selecting the most suitable of them, the meditator then moves into contemplation – the distinction being that instead of roaming, contemplation concentrates on a single set of images and ideas. The term, though, is used in a different sense from the colloquial meaning of examining something consciously. Ideally, contemplation is a 'non-analytic appreciation of an object or idea', according to Arthur J. Deikman in an article on the mystical experience in *Psychiatry* (1966); non-analytic because discursive thought is banished, and the attempt is made to empty the mind of everything 'except the perception of the object in question'. Thought is regarded as an interference with the direct contact that 'yields essential knowledge through perception alone'. The literature of mysticism in general accepts the need to banish thought in order to cultivate 'the noblest ideas of egolessness'.

At this point, the will has to step aside, Saint Francis of Sales explained, the senses are blunted, in a state of abstraction. Sometimes the trance deepens to the point where consciousness is entirely lost, in what he called 'the liquefaction of the soul in God'.

In one respect Saint Francis's instructions are different from those of other mystics: his sensuous use of words and analogies. He called the third stage 'amorous abstraction'; in it, the soul 'turns towards her most lovable and beloved bridegroom'. And after the liquefaction stage, the soul can claim, 'I have slept with my God and in the arms of the divine Presence and Providence, and I knew it not.' Sensual, and sometimes explicitly sexual, language of this kind is not uncommon in individual accounts of the attainment of unity with the divine presence; but most courses of instruction are more cautiously worded.

Although the number of stages and the effects to be looked out for vary, the eastern approaches to a cosmic consciousness have been similar – at least in the early stages. 'Through the subsidence of reasoning and ratification, and still retaining joy and happiness, the monk enters upon the second trance, which is an interior tranquillization and intentness of the thoughts, and is produced by concentration,' the Buddha explained. With the subsidence of joy and contemplative consciousness he enters on a third stage; and then, 'through the disappearance of all antecedent gladness or grief', the fourth stage begins, which 'has neither misery nor happiness, but is contemplation as refined by indifference'. In the next stage he takes off; he dwells in the infinity of space, and the infinity of consciousness, before saying to himself 'nothing exists' and dwelling in the realm of nothingness. Then again, having overpassed the realm of nothingness 'he arrives at the cessation of perception and sensation.'

Leuba cited a description of the course which a Muslim would expect to take. It 'passes through three phases: preparation, perfection, expectation of ecstasy.' In the first stage the ascetic learns the art of concentration and the avoidance of distractions, practising in public, in the streets or the bazaar. Next, he lives a solitary life, practising fasting, silence and mortifications to make him indifferent to pleasure and pain, while meditating on metaphysical issues to convince himself of the non-reality of the external world. In the third stage, peaceful expectancy, he awaits complete ecstasy in which he is 'lost as a wave in the sea of unity'.

The eventual outcome, in other words – union with the divine – shows greater variety on account of the differing views, even within a religion, about what that union will eventually be like, ranging from the total elimination of self in some eastern religions to Sydney Smith's vision of 'eating *pâté de foie gras* to the sound of trumpets'; but the general assumption, as Vivekananda put it in his *Raja Yoga* (1896), is that the mind will reach 'a higher state of existence, beyond reason, a superconscious state'. In it, the 'I' disappears, and the mind works free from desires and restlessness; 'the Truth shines in its full effulgence and we know ourselves – for *Samadhi* lies potential in us all – for what we truly are, free, immortal, omnipotent, loosed from the finite and its contrasts of good and evil altogether', and identified with 'the universal soul'.

Recently, the main interest in the 'oceanic experience', as Jung called it, has shifted away from the religious to the secular aspect, first explored by the Canadian psychiatrist R. M. Bucke. Bucke had led a conventional life until he reached his mid-thirties; then, one evening, he was relaxing in a hansom cab on his way home after an agreeable social evening when 'all at once, without warning of any kind, I found myself wrapped in a flame-coloured cloud'. For a moment he thought there must be an actual fire, close by; but when he realized it came from within he felt 'a sense of exultation, of immense joyousness accompanied or followed by an intellectual illumination impossible to describe', in which he became conscious that the foundation principle of the world, 'of all the worlds, is what we call love.'

The illumination from the inner fire lasted only a few seconds, but the memory of it, and the certainty of its reality, led him to collect such experiences for his *Cosmic Consciousness* (1900). They showed that 'there occurs an intellectual enlightenment which alone would place the individual on a new plane of existence – would make him almost a member of a new species'; and along with this he would enjoy 'an indescribable feeling of elevation, elation and joyousness, and a quickening of the moral sense, which is fully as striking, and more important, than is the enhanced intellectual power'.

Ecstasies are still occasionally reported as coming out of the blue, as it did for Bucke, and has since done for the eminent psychiatrist Alan McGlashan, author of the engaging *Gravity and Levity* (1970), in the even more mundane course of going to his consulting rooms in a London taxi, on a summer morning. He was relaxed, casually looking out of the window. Suddenly, 'I was bathed in unbelievable brilliant pure white light, and I experienced an instant certainty that all the events of my life – being a doctor, writing, flying, being married – all such things were completely irrelevant to the level of being which I was touching.' It was not that these activities were rendered meaningless, McGlashan insisted. On the contrary, 'they gained an added value.' But he knew 'beyond peradventure that all such values could only be relative to the moment of illumination', and thereafter has felt 'no need for any other religious conviction'.

Usually, however, it is possible to trace the experiences to 'triggers', as Marghanita Laski called them in *Ecstasy* (1961). She listed eleven, but left out one of the most frequent (unless she had it in mind for her 'miscellaneous' category): stress.

Perhaps the most familiar account of a stress-related ecstasy in recent years is Arthur Koestler's, in *The Invisible Writing* (1953). In a Seville gaol – under sentence of death – during the Spanish Civil War, he was whiling away the time in solitary confinement scratching mathematical formulae on the wall. One of them was Euclid's proof that the number of primes is infinite. It had always deeply satisfied him; now, he felt a wave of enchantment, leaving in its wake 'a wordless essence, a fragment of eternity, a quiver of the arrow in the blue'. He stood there 'for some minutes, entranced, with a wordless awareness that "this is perfect, perfect"', before a feeling of discomfort, nagging at him, reminded him that he was in prison and liable to execution. But his reaction was 'so what?' Then he was floating, 'in a river of peace, under bridges of silence. It came from nowhere and flowed nowhere. Then there was no river and no I. The I had ceased to exist.'

Embarrassing though it was for Koestler, who admired and practised verbal precision, to be so airy-fairy, he insisted that such experiences are not nebulous or maudlin: 'they only become so when we debase them by verbalization.' Revealing, as it did, the inadequacy of the dialectical materialism he had embraced earlier in the 1930s, the experience forced him to recognize his disillusionment with Stalinist communism. Ethical problems, which had played no part in his writings before, became his chief concern, as they were in *Darkness at Noon* (1940) – not, as has so often been assumed, intended as a political tract, though in the outcome it was one of the most influential ever written, but an exploration of the problem of Ends and Means, 'the conflict between transcendental morality and social expediency'.

Koestler's ecstasy, in short, changed the whole course of his life, as it has in other celebrated cases. Jean-Jacques Rousseau had been scratching a meagre livelihood copying music when a meeting with some of the encyclopaedists broadened his horizons; and on his way to meet Diderot, he chanced upon an announcement that the Dijon Academy was offering a prize for an essay on 'whether the progress of the sciences and the arts had tended to corrupt or improve morals'. If ever a man experienced inspiration, he was to recall, 'I did, at once a great light beamed into my mind, dazzling me with a thousand rays, and ideas crowded into it, all together, in such profusion that I was indescribably upset.' He felt as dizzy as if he were drunk; his heart beat violently; his chest heaved; and he collapsed under a tree. When he got up he found the front of his vest wet with tears, though he had not been aware he had been crying. When Diderot heard what had happened, he encouraged Rousseau to enter the competition, which he won; and although he was also to have some success as a composer, it was the 'great light' which had beamed into his mind that set him on the course to fame with the *Social Contract* and the *Confessions*.

The most celebrated example in this century of ecstasy promoting talent into genius was described by Proust in *Remembrance of Things Past*, in the scene where he tasted a spoonful of tea in which he has soaked a morsel of a *petite madeleine*: 'No sooner had the warm liquid, and the crumbs with it, touched my palate than a shudder ran through my whole body.' He had paused, riveted at the changes that were happening; 'an exquisite pleasure had invaded my senses', with no indication whence it had come, 'and at once the vicissitudes of life had become indifferent to me, its disasters innocuous, its brevity illusory – this new sensation having had on me the effect which love has of filling me with a precious essence; or rather this essence was not in me, it was myself.'

What did it signify? he asked himself. How could he seize upon and define it? As George D. Painter showed in his biography, Proust actually had the experience – though with one small detail altered; the *madeleine* had in fact been a finger of dry toast. The way he was to seize upon and define it was to begin a book which would be 'a vast unconscious memory embodying the whole of his past life', lifting him out of the ruck of gifted literary figures who abounded in France at the time.

Down to earth

Granted that Proust's experience was as ecstatic as he recalled, can it reasonably be put in the same category as the one which Bucke described, let alone those which have been achieved by the saints through contemplation? Marghanita Laski's *Ecstasy* went far to demonstrating her point that there is no essential difference between the experiences; and in her follow-up *Everyday Ecstasy* (1980), as if to reassure her fellow-rationalists that she had not been seduced away from them by her research, she played what she clearly regarded as a trump card. She would lead off, she explained, not with an ecstasy of the kind described by one of the great religious mystics, say, Saint Augustine of Hippo, or Saint Teresa of Avila, but with an experience recounted on television by Mary Wilson, wife of the former Prime Minister, and subsequently reported in *The Times*. Alarmed at the prospect of moving in to 10 Downing Street, Mrs Wilson had prayed for support. She had received it on holiday in the Scilly Islands, off Cornwall, in the form of what she felt was a mystical experience, while she was walking along a beach. It was as if she were dissolving: 'she felt at one with the past and the future, and all the anxieties of the world seemed to disappear.'

Mrs Wilson ideally illustrated Laski's point not simply because, as Harold Wilson's wife, she was a somebody, but also because at the time she was also a figure of gentle fun, hardly known to the public except through her mock 'Diary' which appeared every fortnight in *Private Eye*. If even Mrs Wilson could have a mystical experience, the implication was, there was no need to take the element of transcendence seriously, in the sense of regarding it as a mark of divine favour.

This, in fact, is also clear from the research undertaken by Sir Alister Hardy, Linacre Professor of Zoology at Oxford University. Impressed by personal experience and study of the evidence, Hardy on his retirement founded the Religious Experience Research Unit at Manchester College, asking for accounts of experiences of the kind which could loosely be called 'religious', a term which aroused less overt hostility in academic circles than 'mystical'. Replies soon flooded in to the Unit, and have continued to come to the Alister Hardy Research Centre, which took on the work after Hardy's death. They show that ecstasies, like other forms of trance, can be light or deep. Like other forms, too, they can be regarded as a form of hysteria. Sometimes they are closely linked to mental breakdown.

In *Beyond All Reason* (1964), Morag Coats recalled how one day she got up from where she was sitting and was going to another room when 'suddenly my whole being was filled with light and loveliness and with an upsurge of deeply moving feeling from within myself.'

How could she describe it? It was 'a cloudless, cerulean blue sky of the mind, shot through with shafts of exquisite, warm dazzling sunlight'. It gave her the impression that she was in touch with a reality beyond her own; that she had 'made direct contact with the secret, ultimate source of life'. But in her case it was an early symptom of the disorder which was soon to cast her into a locked ward in a mental hospital, a prey to grotesque hallucinations.

Similarly with some of the cases Hardy included in *The Spiritual Nature of Man* (1981). 'When the gloss is removed, the most remarkable feature of these accounts of religious experience is their resemblance to pathological phenomena,' Nicholas Humphrey has claimed in *Consciousness Regained* (1983); and he cites one in which the episode almost exactly paralleled Dostoevsky's accounts of what he felt when he was just about to have one of his epileptic fits, as he described them in his correspondence and also in *The Idiot*. Prince Myshkin's mind and heart on such occasions 'were flooded by a dazzling light. All his agitation, all his doubts and worries, seemed composed in a twinkling, culminating in a great calm, full of serene and harmonious joy and hope.' It seems likely, Humphrey comments, 'that many of Hardy's informants at the time of their "religious experience" were on the edge of sickness'; but as there was no one 'to *tell* them they were sick, the interpretation they put on their experience was religious'.

People who have hoped to keep ecstasy in its historical role of passport to the divine have in any case had a hard time of it since De Quincey showed, in the *Confessions of an English Opium-Eater* (1822), what laudanum – tincture of opium in alcohol – could do. That the pain he had taken it for had vanished was 'swallowed up in the immensity of the positive effects which had opened up before me in the abyss of divine enjoyment thus suddenly revealed'. This was to be followed by numerous other accounts of the similar effects of other drugs, cannabis, and later peyote. Weir Mitchell, one of the first scientists to experiment with peyote, saw 'a tall, richly furnished Gothic tower. As I gazed, every projecting angle, cornice, and even the face of the stones at their jointings were by degrees covered or hung with clusters of what seemed to be huge precious stones, but uncut, some being more like masses of transparent fruit.' All the colours he had ever seen, he felt, were dull in comparison.

Mescalin is derived from peyote; and reading a monograph on the subject prompted J. R. Smythies, Junior Registrar in Psychiatry at St George's Hospital in London, to team up with Humphrey Osmond,

Senior Registrar at the hospital, to conduct some research into its effects. There was a possibility, they thought, that it might provide clues about schizophrenia; but in any case, they felt that the hallucinations deserved study in their own right. They chose their subjects for the experiments with care; and two of them subsequently wrote books in which they described their experience: R. C. Zaehner's *Mysticism, Sacred and Profane* and Aldous Huxley's *The Doors of Perception*. Looking at his familiar bookshelves, Huxley found them unfamiliar, transformed: 'Red books like rubies; books bound in white jade; books of agate, or aquamarine, or yellow topaz; lapis lazuli books whose colours were so intense, so intrinsically meaningful, that they seemed to be on the point of leaving the shelves to thrust themselves more insistently on my attention.'

What must be disputed is 'the claim made in favour of such experiences that they have some transcendental significance, so that the knowledge vouchsafed during the experience has some special validity and importance,' Steven Rose, Professor of Biology at the Open University, argued in *The Conscious Brain* (1973). 'The obvious – almost cheap – comment is that, if it does have such significance, those who have experienced and understand it seem strangely incapable of describing the experience coherently to others.' Cheap the comment certainly was, because Rose's deduction was far from obvious; he might have paused to ask himself whether *he* could describe sight 'coherently' to a blind man, or the feelings generated by the sight and smell of a flower even to somebody familiar with them.

Rose went on to make another point which, he claimed, was more important. 'Over the last three hundred years - the most effective utilization of the human brain has been brought about by way of the organized activities of science, and the application of precisely those rational techniques of inquiry and observation concerning the universe which the "mystic experience" relegates to a secondary or inferior place.' Mystic experience does nothing of the kind. What it does is provide the illumination which precedes each new advance. It is an ally, not a rival.

'The state of ecstasy is a phenomenon of nervous super-excitability,' Brierre de Boismont observed in *Des Hallucinations* (1852). It had been witnessed in a variety of possessed people in history, from the pythonesses in oracles to the *convulsionnaires*. But it must not be mistaken for insanity; the ecstasies of the great prophets, saints and philosophers were often related to 'their extraordinary intuitions'.

Hartmann agreed. Hysterical aspects of mysticism, he argued, could arise from the frustration of having to accept the conventions and ridiculous assumptions of the time; 'so long as it keeps free from sickly and rank outgrowths, mysticism is of inestimable worth.'

The fact that ecstasy can be drug-induced, too, is not an argument for refusing to regard the experience as of value. As Huxley was careful to point out, he was not so foolish as 'to equate what happens under the influence of mescalin or any other drugs, prepared or in the future preparable, with the realization of the end and ultimate purpose of human life: Enlightenment, the Beatific Vision'. But 'to be shaken out of the rut of ordinary perception, to be shown for a few timeless hours the outer and the inner world, not as they are apprehended, directly and unconditionally by Mind at Large – this is an experience of inestimable value to everyone and especially to the intellectual.'

Mind at large

Mind at large . . . People in ecstasies have often felt their minds *were* at large, free to roam in time and space. 'Those divinely possessed and inspired,' Plotinus claimed, 'have at least the knowledge that they hold some greater thing within them, though they cannot tell what it is; from the movements that stir them, and the utterances that come from them, they perceive the power, not themselves, that moves them.' They know, too, that this is something more than can be accounted for by anything within them – 'fuller and greater, above reason, mind and feeling, conferring these powers, not to be confused with them'.

Are ecstasies pictures drawn by a poisoned brain, Smythies asked himself, or are they illustrations of Bergson's theory that the brain, in addition to producing sensations, has another role, 'that of inhibiting certain other phenomena from entering consciousness'? If a normal function of the brain is to inhibit certain mental activities, 'the inhibition in turn may be inhibited by mescalin, so that the psychedelic state may truly reveal activities in the mind not normally available to consciousness.' And these, he felt, may extend beyond the heightening of normal perception which Huxley enjoyed, to contact with the collective unconscious – a view with which Jung, when he heard it, agreed. The brain 'might be a transformer station', he suggested in a letter to Smythies, 'in which the relatively infinite tension or intensity of the psyche proper is transformed into perceptible frequencies'.

As a proselytizing rationalist, Marghanita Laski disagreed. She was anxious not merely to demonstrate that there was no cut-off point at which transcendent ecstasies can be distinguished from those which are mundane, but also to dispel any lingering doubts about their source. There were two possible explanations, she noted in *Everyday Ecstasy*, for ecstatic experiences. 'One is that they are, as many say they feel they are, from an extra-human source – supernatural, preternatural, other worldly, divine. A second explanation, and the one I believe to be true, is that these experiences are purely human, and have no external source.' But she presented no evidence for her belief. In common with many rationalists who grew up in the years between the wars, she never felt the need to examine the evidence for the 'preternatural' – the use of the old-fashioned term being itself evidence of her self-imposed remoteness from contemporary controversy.

Professor Andrew Neher, on the other hand, plunged into it, devoting half his *Psychology of Transcendence* (1980) to what he clearly believed was a dispassionate examination of the evidence about psychic and occult experiences, in order to show that they could all be explained away in terms acceptable to orthodox psychology. For his sources, though, he was unwise enough to rely upon works which had long been shown up as unreliable.

The fundamental flaw in the rationalist case was exposed by William James in his Gifford Lectures at the University of Edinburgh, revised and published as *The Varieties of Religious Experience* in 1902. James's own experience was mundane; it arose when he was fooling around with nitrous oxide, 'laughing gas'. It proved to be a turning-point in the development of his ideas, revealing to him that, as he put it, 'our normal waking consciousness, rational consciousness as we call it, is but one special type of consciousness, whilst all about it, parted from it by the flimsiest of screens, there lie potential forms of consciousness entirely different.' It was possible to go through life without suspecting their existence; 'but apply the requisite stimulus, and at a touch they are there in all their completeness, definite types of mentality.' Probably, he thought, they would all be shown to have their purpose; in any case, 'no account of the universe in its totality can be final which leaves these other forms of consciousness quite disregarded.'

For James, mystical experiences represented occasions when these other forms of consciousness broke through in ways which powerfully illuminated their immense potential. This was not in itself, he insisted, evidence for a divine component. 'Seraph and snake' emerged from

Bucke's case histories, he noted, side by side; 'non-mystics are under no obligation to acknowledge in mystical states a superiority conferred on them by their intrinsic nature.' Nevertheless 'we have in *the fact that the conscious person is continuous with a wider self through which saving experiences come*, a positive content of religious experience which, it seems to me, *is literally and objectively true as far as it goes.*'

The further limits of our being, James argued, 'plunge into an altogether other dimension of existence from the sensible and merely "understandable" world'; but this mystical region was not the less real: 'we belong to it in a more intimate sense than that in which we belong to the visible world, for we belong in the most intimate sense wherever our ideals belong.' And as mystical experience can change our lives, 'that which produces effects within another reality must be termed a reality itself.' The existence of mystical states, in fact, 'absolutely overthrows the pretension of non-mystical states to be the sole and ultimate dictators of what we may believe'. Rationalists' objections, he asserted, could have no validity because they were in no position to deny that cosmic consciousness enlarged the range of human capacity; and if they should try to deny this, he reminded them that they had similarly refused to accept the way in which hypnosis similarly enlarged that range, without even bothering to investigate it.

James took care to warn, though, that 'the mystical feeling of enlargement, union and emancipation has no specific intellectual content whatsoever of its own.' It was capable of forming alliances with very different religions and philosophies; 'We have no right, therefore, to invoke its prestige as distinctly in favour of any special belief.' But even if mystical states wielded no authority of that nature, 'the supernaturalism and optimism to which they would persuade us may, interpreted in one way or another, be after all the truest of insights into the meaning of life.'

Supporting this contention in her *Mysticism* (1910), Evelyn Underhill linked cosmic consciousness more closely to what she regarded as the most highly developed branches of the human family. 'They tend to produce – sporadically it is true, and usually in the teeth of adverse external circumstances – a curious and definite type of personality, a type which refuses to be satisfied with that which other men call experience, and is inclined, in the words of its enemies, to "deny the world in order that it may find reality".' Their experiences had provided a wealth of curiously consistent evidence 'which must be taken into account before we can add up the sum of the energies and potentialities of the human spirit, or reasonably speculate on its relations to the unknown world which lies outside the boundaries of science'.

Unluckily, as Sir Peter Medawar was to realize and deplore, scientists have since all too often failed to recognize that there are such boundaries. To this day, it is by no means unusual to hear them referring disparagingly to a notion as 'mystical' with the implication that it must be a superstition. 'It is highly probable that in due course it will be possible to explain the "mystic experience" in terms of neurobiology,' Steven Rose claimed; 'it is highly improbable that neurobiology will ever be explained in terms of "the mystic experience".' Sir Arthur Eddington demolished this type of argument over half a century ago. It is useful for us to know how science explains matters, and realize that things may not be quite what they seem, he accepted, 'but we do not pluck out our eyes because they persist in deluding us with fanciful colourings, instead of giving us the plain truth about wavelength'. It is the aim of physical science, 'to lay bare the fundamental structure underlying the world'; but if the spiritual world 'has been transmuted by a religious colour beyond anything implied in its bare external qualities' – perhaps, he suggested, by long ages of biological evolution – it is reasonable to assert this is not a misrepresentation, 'but the achievement of a divine element in man's nature'.

8
REASSESSMENT

The role of trance

To return to my starting point: what *is* trance?

The term is used in such a variety of senses that it eludes simple definition. At one extreme it is applied to what can loosely be described as possession, in which the individual's normal self seems to be displaced, leaving him rapt, or paralysed, or hysterical, or psychotic, or taken over by another personality. At the other extreme is sleep. Between the two are conditions in which consciousness is maintained, but the subliminal mind makes itself felt, as in light hypnosis or the kind of reverie in which the fancy, or fantasy, breaks loose, as in Robert Graves's poem about communing with a lost loved one

> . . . taken in trance, would she still deny
> That you are hers, she yours, till both shall die?

The apparent diversity ceases to be puzzling when trance is set in its evolutionary context. Animal life in general is spent in trance; but there are intimations of mind in termitaries, and in birds in flocks, which suggest the development of something more purposeful than simple natural selection could have been expected to provide. It is as if evolution had found a way to introduce a 'pull', enabling species to perform in more sophisticated ways than, examining their limitations, we would think possible.

This group mind operates telekinetically; but with the development of consciousness in man this would have caused problems, had he not been able to switch off the power, in order to make his own decisions. But consciousness had its limitations; mind continued to develop, and operate, subliminally. And when the subliminal found difficulty in putting across its messages, it resorted to hallucination.

'The conscious life of humans seems to rest on a substratum of reflex action of a hallucinatory type', the German psychologist Max Dessoir suggested a century ago; and Andrew Lang, citing him, argued that it was natural that the substratum should learn to exploit the five senses by mimicking them, to attract attention. In his remarkable second novel *The Inheritors* William Golding showed the process at work in early communities, relying for their guidance on visions – 'I have a picture' – rather than on deliberation. Julian Jaynes's theory of auditory hallucination as an aid to the development of consciousness fits this pattern, as does shamanism, and the extensive use in tribal communities and early civilizations of dreams. 'The dream hallucinates', as Freud put it. 'That is, it replaces thoughts by hallucinations.'

Dreams, however, reflect the limitations of the subliminal mind when it is divorced from a measure of conscious direction. Hallucinations are revealing of the condition of the subliminal mind; but if it is not in a healthy condition their messages, though always meaningful, are not to be relied upon. Their value depends largely on the degree of collaboration achieved between conscious and subliminal minds; when this is working well, the subliminal self can display astonishing virtuosity, and endow us with remarkable powers, whether as artists or athletes.

It is not, strictly speaking, a self. The unity appears to be composed of a number of selves, sometimes sufficiently well organized to be capable of taking over control of consciousness, as in multiple personality cases. But they can achieve harmony, and work as a single self. At best, it does not need to use hallucinations in the sense we normally think of them, except in emergency. It can break through with the cordial assent of consciousness in intuition, or inspiration, or improvisation.

Why, then, has trance so poor a standing? The short answer is scientism. We have allowed ourselves to be led by the nose by scientists who have deceived themselves and us that everything can be, and eventually will be, explained in mechanistic terms. What this has done is to replace science with, in effect, a proliferation of faiths, held often with religious fervour: positivism, materialism, reductionism, behaviourism, organicism, neo-Darwinism, structuralism and others. They have shared a common component, mistrust of mind, except as a by-product of brain. The notion of a subliminal self, with a mind of its own, has been unacceptable; and trance in its go-between role has virtually been ignored.

Scientism arose with the best of intentions. The aim was to banish superstition, submitting everything to rigorous investigation and tests. But this involved faith; faith that science was capable of coming up with all the required answers. 'The new religion had prescriptions of its own, mostly good ones, such as open-minded respect for experimental evidence, fearlessness, and the rejection of wishful thinking,' Alex Comfort has recalled in *Reality and Empathy* (1984). But '"Science" unwittingly ran the risk of doing what Christianity had done before it and pulling the wagons around a group of core teachings (causality, mechanism, stochastic-genetic evolution, the equation between mental and neural activity); in defending these one was defending not hypotheses but Science itself – re-examination was on the point of becoming "unscientific".'

On the point of? Science – or scientists, in many branches of science – *became* unscientific, refusing to accept findings which did not fit the core teachings. Worse than that, in the attempt to achieve scientific recognition the 'soft' sciences craved hard mechanistic sanction, so that psychologists abandoned Myers, James and Janet for Watson and Skinner.

'There is no piece of doctrinaire nonsense that cannot gain the support of even the best-trained philosophical mind,' the psychologist John Beloff noted sadly in *The Existence of Mind* (1962), '*provided only* it is sanctioned by current intellectual fashion.' Far from resisting, the academic philosophers themselves have indulged in their fashions; and the universities everywhere have tended to become the bastions of whatever fashions happen to prevail. The academic mind, as Harold Laski commented in a letter to Judge Oliver Wendell Holmes, 'lives profoundly in that state of resentful coma we call research.' The research has not been directed to explore anomalies, where experience or investigation has shown that the facts do not accord with the fashion; the bulk of it has been designed to confirm fashion's beliefs.

Even now that quantum physics has discredited materialism, there are few signs that the other branches of science are ready to turn their backs on mechanistic research. Biology, for example, is becoming progressively dominated by reductionism in the laboratory; and the neo-Darwinians continue to ignore the mounting evidence that their theory is tenable only by turning a blind eye to a host of anomalies. Cognitive psychology provides a bolt-hole for psychologists, but as

Neisser warned, it is only a fraction of the whole; and other parts, trance among them, are neglected.

In some ways the most serious damage scientism has done is in promoting organicism. Nobody now can seriously dispute the importance of mind in preserving and restoring health, and in treating disease. Research into hypnosis and auto-suggestion has presented a mass of evidence that they can provide a cheaper and more effective means of dealing with a range of common disorders than can drugs; but drugs remain the standard prescription, and are likely to continue to be so long as medical training is concentrated in hospitals, where organicism remains dominant.

The need for change is widely accepted. Following a conference in the summer of 1988 an international gathering of doctors produced 'The Edinburgh Declaration' calling for radical reforms in medical education, and in particular arguing that hospitals should not have so much control. But so long as the curriculum is set by hospital-based consultants who themselves do the teaching, and so long as it is the consultants who control the medical profession, who is going to take the necessary steps to convert the declaration into action? In the meantime doctors-to-be are unlikely to be taught psychosomatics, let alone instructed in the use of hypnosis, or how to help patients to use auto-suggestion.

Still less are they likely to be told that hysteria is a trance condition, capable of being exploited, as belly-laughter was by Norman Cousins, to treat organic illnesses by pitting against them the largely untapped resources of the subliminal self. Hysteria will continue to be regarded by doctors, when it is diagnosed, as unconscious malingering. So it often is. As Professor Anthony Storr notes, it has three main purposes: to allow the individual to escape from difficult situations, to enable him to punish others, and to attract attention and sympathy. But, as acute observers from Sydenham on have insisted, this does not necessarily imply weak-mindedness: on the contrary, it may be the strong-minded person's subliminal self rebelling against society's constraints.

The power of the mind over the body, demonstrated in hysteria, is itself an indication of the need to explore this type of trance, in order to learn how better to exploit it. Padre Pio's stigmata should not be dismissed as a curiosity exhibited merely to impress the gullible; they were the measure of the power of his faith. In many parts of the world where hysteria is whipped up in religious festivals, individuals and groups display the other side of that coin; they stab themselves and skewer themselves, but do not bleed. Groddeck was right: the same hysterical force that can produce symptoms can protect us from disease – or save us from its consequences; he would certainly have attributed Cousins's recovery to the power of his 'It' – his subliminal self.

Laughter is not the only form in which convulsions are linked to benefits. Often they have been associated with inspiration. When a line of a poem floated into A. E. Housman's mind his hair would stand on end, a shiver would go down his spine, and his throat would constrict. 'When you get to a new place in yourself,' Doris Lessing observed in *The Four-Gated City*, 'when you are going to break into something new, then it is sometimes presented to you like that, giggling and hysteria.' It is as if the subliminal self is chortling with pleasure at getting its message across.

This makes it easier to understand why genius is so often confused with madness. The foundations of genius lie in the subliminal mind, and the subliminal self may have massive problems with consciousness. The genius may often be a dullard, or a rogue, or deeply unpleasant, as Wagner appears to have been. The split between the two minds may lead to paranoia, as it did with Newton. Or the conscious mind may not have developed, as in the case of some child prodigies. If the subliminal's evolution has continued independently, to some extent, of the evolution of consciousness, this is not surprising. It does not mean that, say, Joan of Arc was a schizophrenic – a diagnosis which still surfaces from time to time; it means that her subliminal was using hallucination on her behalf, whereas in schizophrenia the trances represent a warning, initially, and eventually an intimation that collaboration with the conscious mind has broken down.

Contagious hysteria, too, needs to be considered in the same light, as an evolutionary device more appropriate to termites and bees but still capable of making itself felt with humans, and not necessarily in embarrassing epidemics in girls' schools and hospitals. There are other ways in which it may well be playing a part, such as in couvade and in keeping twins in communication even when they are far apart. Another possibility is just coming to be considered: that hysterical, rather than physical contagion, may be responsible for certain all too familiar epidemics.

A century ago the pathologist Charles Creighton pointed out that influenza epidemics do not travel as if person-to-person contact was responsible. The discovery of the flu viruses was taken to settle the issue, but it has come up again as a result of the findings of the Common Cold Unit at Salisbury, where it has proved extremely difficult for volunteers (of whom there has been no shortage) who go there to live and eat together, to transmit colds to each other. Taking a hint from this Sir Fred Hoyle, Professor of Astronomy at the Royal Institution, and Chandra Wickramasinghe, Professor of Astronomy at University College, Cardiff, began to plot the courses which flu takes through boarding schools; and the findings confirm that person-to-person transmission is not the explanation.

Their theory is that the micro-organisms responsible for epidemics drop down out of space, through which they have been ferried in the tails of comets. They have not, however, been able to produce confirmatory evidence. A more likely hypothesis is that the mechanism involved is the one which regulates termitaries and created the dancing mania. The viruses of colds and flu, on this assumption, are in and around us all the time but do not affect us unless our auto-immune systems allow them to. By analogy, they are not an invading army, overpowering our defences; they are the looters who emerge when law and order have broken down.

It is likely, too, that hysterical contagion plays a part in shaping public opinion on emotive issues – the herd instinct, as Trotter called it. In *Waking Up* (1986) Charles Tart emphasizes that we must not regard trance as a condition which we enter and leave; there is a sense in which we are never out of it, and this leaves us susceptible to the kind of influences which can be witnessed in any performance by a hypnotist: 'our behaviour and our internal experience are strongly controlled by others.'

This 'consensus trance', for Tart, is the second level of mental activity, sleep being the first. In the second 'we walk and talk, make and break promises, make love and war, and *imagine that we are in the third state*' – genuine self-consciousness. In its most pernicious manifestation consensus trance breeds quasi-religious cults in which the faithful accept unquestioningly the dictates of even so unscrupulous a rogue as Ron Hubbard, the founder of Scientology. They will even commit mass suicide, as in the Jonestown holocaust. But on a more everyday basis consensus trance contributes to the waves of atavism that breed football hooliganism and other forms of mob violence in which the more elementary components of trance, dating from the period when man was a predator, are unleashed without the control either of consciousness or of the later more civilized subliminal self.

Hypnosis provides the clue: if the mind switches to a channel which allows it to take its instructions from outside, it can be made to accept them and carry them out if the personality is not sufficiently in charge to rebel when they are unacceptable. The case for resuming research into hypnosis is consequently strong for the light it can throw on social, as well as medical, problems. This applies also to research into dreams; if they are better understood they can contribute helpfully in a variety of ways, notably problem-solving: pilot projects such as those conducted by William Dement at Stanford University and Morton Schatzman in London have given some promising results. Research into hallucination, too, is needed because it could provide the explanation for some biological mysteries, as the great naturalist W. H. Hudson suggested in his last book, *A Hind in Richmond Park* (1922).

Dogs, he knew, often exhibit extra-sensory perception; there are scores of well-attested reports of their ability to sense where their owners are. Was it not possible, he wondered, that when bloodhounds follow a trail they may be using a combination of smell with, in effect, 'second smell' – the equivalent of second sight? He had come across one instance of the kind with a friend who had come to stay, who complained that there were human bones in a locked cupboard in his room. It turned out that there were; they had been left by Hudson's brother, a medical student. The friend, Hudson decided, had picked up a smell too faint for him to be consciously aware of it; but his subliminal mind had picked it up and relayed it to him in the form of a hunch, rather than a smell.

As Gordon Rattray Taylor's hoax experiment in transmitting smell by television showed, hallucination may play a much more extensive part in our lives than we realize. 'I seem to have a fairly acute sense of smell, but I have learned not to rely on the information it gives me,' Professor G. C. Drew commented in his introduction to Peter McKellar's *Imagination and Thinking* (1959). As, at that time, the use of male deodorants and after-shave lotions was still uncommon, at least in academic circles, if he smelt perfume on a man he would assume it was a hallucination; 'but if it is a woman, I cannot tell whether she is wearing it.' The author and biographer Michael Harrison could on occasion 'smell' the arrival of a friend in advance. And in that remarkable book *The Man Who Mistook His Wife for a Hat*

(1985) Oliver Sacks has a tale which suggests the possibility, at least, of evolution going into reverse and providing hallucination to replace the senses which, in the past, provided its replacement.

A man Sacks knew lost his sense of smell as the result of an accident, and felt the loss keenly. One morning, he picked up a faint aroma from his coffee, and then from his pipe. Delighted, he went to report his returning sense of smell to his doctor. But further tests showed that he could not be picking up the aroma through that sense. What appeared to have happened, Sacks suggested, was 'the development of a greatly enhanced olfactory imagery, one might say a controlled hallucinosis.'

What a difference it would make, to millions of lives, if 'controlled hallucinosis' could be perfected, restoring lost or damaged senses! In the immediate future, however, the most urgent requirement is simply to establish hallucination, and trance conditions in general, as requiring research in their own right. Dual and multiple personality, in particular, need investigation which is not constrained by the assumption that they are freak pathological conditions, or the consequence of combat stress. Two recent works, both published in 1985, have surveyed the subject, showing its importance. In *Multiple Man* Adam Crabtree, a Toronto psychotherapist, has presented the historical background from Mesmer to the present day, relating it to possession, hypnosis and other forms of trance, and commenting 'the important thing is that both multiple personality and possession point to a remarkable inner versatility.' Michael Gazzaniga's *The Social Brain* harks back to Morton Prince with the idea of mind being composed of an aggregate of coconscious personalities; a possible explanation for intuition, he suggests, is that one personality provides it, but another, the 'executive', transmits it to consciousness, thereby giving the illusion of a single self.

These are not simply curiosities for psychologists to mull over, when their discipline comes to its senses and begins again to take trance seriously. It seems highly probable that dual personality provides a clue to the understanding of a symptom of one of the most pressing social problems of our time, addiction; cases when otherwise admirable individuals change character under the influence of drink and other drugs – the Jekyll/Hyde syndrome. The 'executive', in such cases, is replaced by a rival, with sometimes destructive results. Crabtree believes that there is a potential source of unity, an 'ultimate self', which can be found not by a process of fusion, but by establishing co-operation between the personalities leading to the ultimate goal of 'complete *self*-possession.'

Mediumship also deserves investigation not simply from the viewpoint of seeking to establish whether information is coming from spirit 'controls' and 'communicators', but also to bring it down to earth by learning how to use it – as 'channelling' has begun to do – to liberate intuition and inspiration. Increasingly, too, mediumship has been becoming identified with healing – as it was for the early Christians; and here, too, research has begun to make sense of what has so long been dismissed as superstition.

The experiments in the early 1960s of Bernard Grad, Associate Professor at the Armand Frappier Institute, Université du Quebec à Montréal, showed that the Christian 'laying on of hands' can be reproduced in controlled experiments with laboratory mice, with the assistance of a healer. Similar results were obtained, and have since been repeated, with plants, whose growth can be encouraged or inhibited by what appears to be a form of exteriorization, a 'fluence' emanating from the hands. Most healers, however, insist that they are merely the channel for the healing force.

'Animal magnetism is dead, killed by hypnotism', was a common verdict in the 1880s. Animal magnetism, in the sense of an as yet unexplained biological feature, has in effect been resuscitated by such experiments; and also, indirectly, by Rupert Sheldrake's theory of morphic resonance, presented in *The New Science of Life* (1981) and *The Presence of the Past* (1988), which provoked the editor of *Nature* into claiming that if books were still burned, here would be a suitable victim. The theory embraces communication of a kind that would account for ESP and much else that has remained outside orthodox science's self-imposed bounds.

There are further reasons why trance needs rehabilitation in practice, as well as in restoring it to its rightful position in science. One is for education. The prevailing view, Einstein once complained, was that its sole function is 'to open the way to thinking and knowing; the school, as the outstanding organ for the people's education, must serve that end exclusively.' He had to make that point 'starkly and nakedly', he felt, even if it was only rarely that rationalism was expressed 'in such crass form.'

The trend to making schools forcing houses of rationalism has not diminished since his death. In the United States the emphasis has been on testing the three 'R's while neglecting the three 'I's, Jan

Ehrenwald has complained – the three 'I's being Imagination, Intuition and Inspiration. On the present basis, 'Beethoven would probably have barely scored above the moronic level,' whereas any competent member of the Mensa Society 'would be certified as a card-carrying genius.'

In Britain, too, education has remained 'hopelessly biased towards the objective, logical, intellectual side', the psychologist James Hemming told a conference held in 1976 to discuss what needed to be done. 'Education of the subjective, intuitional and aesthetic aspects of the personality, in contrast, is for the most part desperately thin', the inevitable outcome being 'lop-sided curricula, low motivation and distorted personality development'. Two years later Niko Tinbergen suggested a way in which the balance might be restored – the way animals learn, by exploration. 'A return to a biologically more balanced form of education could also lead to the raising of a type of person which our society needs now,' he urged in his Croonian Lecture to the Royal Society. Where in former times competent professionalism was important for society, 'the emphasis may in future have to be rather on adjustability, open-mindedness, ability to judge, ability to plan far ahead and similar qualities.'

The aim, in other words, should be to develop intuition at the expense of consensus trance and the herd instinct. But the herd instinct is precisely what schools continue to inculcate, many of them deliberately. There is one aspect of education, however, in which the three 'I's could flourish: sport. It is not only the Peles and the Palmers who occasionally enjoy the experience of feeling possessed by a player not only more skilled, but endowed with what appear to be magical abilities. There can be few golfers, however incompetent, who have not experienced the delightful feeling of certainty that John Betjeman expressed in his poem 'Seaside Golf': the total conviction that the ball is going to follow the directions given by the 'power that is' – the possessing agent – because when this take-over occurs, it never fails to produce the right results unless something, or somebody, interrupts to break the trance. It has proved possible, up to a point, to demonstrate how this feeling can be induced, or at least how the obstacles to its emergence can be pulled down: 'inner-tennis', 'inner-ski-ing' and other forms of 'inner' have shown many people recently how to enjoy sport more thoroughly, and also given them some insight into the limitations of the rational mind.

Or perhaps it would be fairer to say, the rational*ist* mind. Through an unholy alliance with humanism, the rationalist cult in the United States has established itself as quite a powerful force in science; and in Britain it remains afloat, though it has only a tiny following, because most of us like to think of ourselves as rational, and the distinction from rationalist is not realized.

If we look upon man's whole mental life, William James pointed out in *The Varieties of Religious Experience*, 'we have to confess that the part of it of which rationalists can give an account is relatively superficial.' Rationalism enjoys the prestige; it can 'challenge you for proofs, and chop logic, and put you down with words'; but it cannot deal with intuition. 'If you have intuitions at all, they come from a deeper level of your nature than the loquacious level which rationalism inhabits.'

A personal reason for hoping that trance will be rehabilitated is that the spell put upon historians, as well as scientists, by rationalism will be broken. History has been distorted because the phenomena traditionally associated with trance have been regarded with such suspicion that accounts of them have usually been relegated to the category of myths or superstitions.

If hallucination is accepted as capable of creating forms so lifelike that they can deceive all the senses, this could explain much that has been downgraded as myth. As Peter McKellar suggested, it is not improbable 'that widespread superstitions about little people, for example the leprechauns of Ireland, had initially a halluci-natory origin' – a notion that offers a wide field for exploration, notably in connection with UFOs. But rationalists who might be tempted to accept this hypothesis find that it leads on into more dangerous territory. If fairies can be believed in as 'ideoplasts' – 'the physiological realization of an idea', as Ochorowicz put it – what about djinns, with their physical powers? Worse, what about ectoplasmic materializations, which have been photographed under conditions which rule out any possibility of faking? Is it conceivable that, as George Geley surmised from his research into materializations, that a hallucinated being may *be* 'material' – at least temporarily?

This is speculation; my contention is simply that the evidence about trance phenomena, even some of the mind-boggling kind, is sufficiently well-attested to make its rejection on rationalist grounds irrational. And what I find particularly saddening is that in order to keep rationalism afloat it is necessary for a devotee who surveys the phenomena to imply, or even specifically to assert, that some of the finest scientists, men of unblemished reputations for ability and integrity, must have been dupes or frauds or both. History will, I trust, eventually vindicate them.

ACKNOWLEDGEMENTS

My thanks to Dr Alan Gauld and to Ann Shearer, for reading and commenting on sections of the typescript; to Bernard Levin, for his proof-reading (and astringent asides); to Douglas Matthews, for the Index; and to his London Library staff, for their helpfulness.

BIBLIOGRAPHY

The works listed are those which I have referred to in the text, with the exception of a few which are peripheral to the subject, and which, along with articles, will be found among the source references. I have been faced with the problem that although trance in general has attracted little serious attention, specific trance conditions – mediumship, hypnosis, ecstasy, and dreaming, in particular – are extensively covered in books, magazines and newspapers; there is much I would have liked to include which I have reluctantly been compelled to leave out.

As I trust will be apparent, I have been primarily concerned with trance in its everyday role in the western world. Its place in the Far East, far more significant, would need to be dealt with in its own right – as, indeed, are the depressingly common psychotic aspects of trance here in Europe, and in the Americas.

The place and date of publication refer to the editions I have consulted; when it is not the first edition, its date is in brackets. In the case of books translated into English I have given only the English title.

Achterberg, Jeanne, *Imagery in Healing*, Boston, 1986.
Adare, Lord, *Experiences with D. D. Home*, London, 1869.
Allen, Gay Wilson, *William James*, London, 1967.
Angros, Robert, and George Stanciu, *The New Biology*, Boston, 1987.
Azam, E. A., *Hypnotisme – Double Conscience*, Paris, 1887.
Barrett, Sir William, *On Creative Thought*, London, 1910.
Barrett, Sir William, *Psychical Research*, London, 1911.
Barrett, Sir William, *On the Threshold of the Unseen*, London, 1918.
Barrett, Sir William, and Theodore Besterman, *The Divining Rod*, London, 1926.
Baudouin, Charles, *Suggestion and Auto-suggestion*, London, 1920.
Belo, Jane, *Trance in Bali*, New York, 1960.
Beloff, John, *The Existence of Mind*, London, 1962.
Bergson, Henri, *Creative Evolution*, London, 1964 (1911).
Bergson, Henri, *Mind-energy*, London, 1920.
Bernheim, Hippolyte, *Suggestive Therapeutics*, Westport, Connecticut, 1957 (1887).
Bertrand, A. J.-F., *Traité du Somnambulisme*, Paris, 1823.
Binet, Alfred, *Alterations of Personality*, London, 1896 (1891).

Bibliography

Binet, Alfred, *On Double Consciousness*, Chicago, 1896 (1889).
Binet, Alfred, *The Mind and the Brain*, London, 1907 (1905).
Binet, Alfred, and Charles Féré, *Animal Magnetism*, London, 1888 (1877).
Bird, Christopher, *The Divining Hand*, New York, 1979.
Black, Stephen, *Mind and Body*, London, 1969.
Blackmore, Susan J., *Beyond the Body*, London, 1882.
Bohm, David, *Wholeness and the Implicate Order*, London, 1980.
Braid, James, *Neurypnology*, London, 1843.
Braid, James, *Observations on Trance*, London, 1850.
Braid, James, *Magic, Witchcraft, Animal Magnetism, Hypnotism*, London, 1852.
Bramwell, J. Milne, *Hypnotism*, New York, 1956 (1903).
Braude, Stephen E., *The Limits of Influence*, New York, 1986.
Breuer, Josef, and Sigmund Freud, *Studies on Hysteria*, London, 1956 (1895).
Brierre de Boismont, *Des Hallucinations*, Paris, 1852.
Broad, C. D., *The Mind and its Place in Nature*, London, 1925.
Brown, Barbara, *New Mind, New Body*, Boston, 1974.
Brown, Sir Walter Langdon, *Thus We Are Men*, London, 1938.
Bucke, Richard M., *Cosmic Consciousness*, New York, 1969 (1900).
Burton, Robert, *Anatomy of Melancholy*, New York, 1948 (London, 1621).
Calmeil, L., *De la Folie*, Paris, 1845.
Carington, Whately, *Telepathy*, London, 1945.
Carpenter, William Benjamin, *Principles of Mental Physiology*, London, 1875.
Carpenter, William Benjamin, *Is Man an Automaton?*, London, 1875.
Carré de Montgeron, *La Vérité des Miracles*, Utrecht, 1737.
Carter, Robert Brudenell, *On the Pathology and Treatment of Hysteria*, London, 1853.
Castaneda, Carlos, *The Teachings of Don Juan*, London, 1970 (1968).
Clark, Ronald W., *Freud*, London, 1980.
Clarke, Edward H., *Visions*, Boston, 1878.
Cleckley, Hervey, *The Mask of Sanity*, St Louis, 1955.
Coate, Morag, *Beyond All Reason*, London, 1964.
Cobbe, Frances Power, *Darwinism in Morals and Other Essays*, London, 1872.
Cohn, Norman, *Europe's Inner Demons*, London, 1975.
Comfort, Alex, *Reality and Empathy*, New York, 1984.
Comte, Auguste, *The Positive Philosophy* (Ed. H. Martineau), London, 1853.
Coué, Emile, *Self-mastery through Auto-suggestion*, London, 1959 (1922).
Cousins, Norman, *Anatomy of an Illness*, New York, 1979.
Crabtree, Adam, *Multiple Man*, New York, 1985.
Crichton, Sir Alexander, *Inquiry into Mental Derangement*, London, 1798.
Cronin, A. J., *Adventures in Two Worlds*, London, 1952.
David-Neel, Alexandra, *Magic and Mystery in Tibet*, New York, 1965.
Davies, Paul, and J. R. Brown, *The Ghost in the Atom*, Cambridge, 1986.
Deleuze, Joseph, *A Critical History of Animal Magnetism*, London, 1816.

Deleuze, Joseph, *Practical Instruction in Animal Magnetism*, London, 1850 (1825).

Dessoir, Max, *Bibliography of Modern Hypnotism*, Berlin, 1888.

Dingwall, Eric J., *Abnormal Hypnotic Phenomena*, London, 1967.

Dixon, Norman F., *Subliminal Perception*, New York, 1971.

Dixon, Norman F., *Our Own Worst Enemy*, London, 1987.

Dodds, E. R., *The Greeks and the Irrational*, Berkeley, 1951.

Driesch, Hans, *The Crisis in Psychology*, Princeton, 1925.

Driesch, Hans, *Mind and Body*, London, 1927.

Dunbar, Flanders, *Mind and Body*, New York, 1955 (1947).

Duncan, James Foulis, *Popular Errors on the Subject of Insanity Examined and Exposed*, Dublin, 1853.

Dunne, J. W., *An Experiment with Time*, London, 1927.

Du Potet de Sennevoy, Baron, *Introduction to Animal Magnetism*, London, 1838.

Eccles, Sir John, and D. N. Robinson, *The Wonder of Being Human*, Boston, 1985.

Eisenbud, Jule, *Parapsychology and the Unconscious*, Berkeley, 1983.

Elam, Charles, *A Physician's Problems*, London, 1869.

Eliade, Mircea, *Shamanism*, Princeton, 1970 (1951).

Eliade, Mircea, *Myths, Dreams and Mysteries*, London, 1968 (1957).

Ellenberger, Henri, *The Discovery of the Unconscious*, London, 1970.

Elliotson, J., *Numerous Cases . . .*, London, 1843.

Espinas, Alfred, *Les Sociétés Animales*, Paris, 1877.

Eysenck, Hans J., *Uses and Abuses of Psychology*, London, 1953.

Eysenck, Hans J., *Sense and Nonsense in Psychology*, London, 1957.

Fabre, Jean, *The Wonders of Instinct*, London, 1918.

Feldman, David, *Nature's Gambit*, New York, 1986.

Field, Margaret J., *Search for Security*, London, 1960.

Field, Margaret J., *Angels and Ministers of Grace*, London, 1971.

Flammarion, Camille, *The Unknown*, London, 1900.

Flournoy, Theodore, *From India to the Planet Mars*, New York, 1901.

Flournoy, Theodore, *Spiritism and Psychology*, New York, 1911.

Foissac, P., *Rapports et Discussions*, Paris, 1833.

Forel, Auguste, *Hypnotism*, London, 1906 (1889).

Frazer, Sir James, *The Golden Bough*, London, 1900 (1890).

Freud, Sigmund, *The Interpretation of Dreams*, London, 1951 (1900).

Freud, Sigmund, *An Autobiographical Study*, London, 1935 (1925).

Freud, Sigmund, *New Introductory Lectures*, London, 1962.

Furst, Peter T. (ed.), *Flesh of the Gods*, London, 1972.

Galton, Sir Francis, *Inquiries into the Human Faculty*, London, 1883.

Gauld, Alan, *The Founders of Psychical Research*, London, 1968.

Gauld, Alan, *Mediumship and Survival*, London, 1983.

Gazzaniga, Michael S., *Mind Matters*, New York, 1985.

Geley, Gustave, *Clairvoyance and Materialisation*, London, 1927.

Gelfand, Michael, *Witch Doctor*, London, 1964.

Godley, John, *Tell Me the Next One*, London, 1950.

Gould, Stephen Jay, *Ever Since Darwin*, London, 1987.

Green, Elmer, and Alyce Green, *Beyond Biofeedback*, New York, 1977.

Gregory, Richard, *Mind in Science*, London, 1981.

Gregory, Richard (ed.), *The Oxford Companion to the Mind*, Oxford, 1987.

Gregory, William, *Letters on Animal Magnetism*, London, 1851.

Griesinger, Wilhelm, *Mental Pathology*, London, 1867 (1845).

Groddeck, Georg, *The Book of the It*, London, 1950 (1923).

Grossman, Carl M. and Sylvia Grossman, *The Wild Analyst: the Life and Work of Georg Groddeck*, London, 1865.

Guirdham, Arthur, *We Are One Another*, Jersey, 1974.

Guirdham, Arthur, *The Great Heresy*, Jersey, 1977.

Gurney, Edmund, Frederic Myers and Frank Podmore, *Phantasms of the Living*, London, 1886.

Hadamard, Jacques, *The Psychology of Invention in the Mathematical Field*, Princeton, 1949.

Happold, F. C., *Mysticism*, London, 1981 (1963).

Hardy, Sir Alister, *The Spiritual Nature of Man*, Oxford, 1979.

Hartmann, Eduard, *Philosophy of the Unconscious*, London, 1884 (1869).

Haygarth, John, *Of the Imagination*, Bath, 1801.

Haynes, Renée, *The Hidden Springs*, London, 1961.

Hecker, Justus F. C., *The Epidemics of the Middle Ages*, London, 1859.

Heidenhain, Rudolf, *Hypnotism or Animal Magnetism?*, London, 1888 (1880).

Heywood, Rosalind, *The Infinite Hive*, London, 1964.

Hippocrates, *Writings* (ed. G. Lloyd), London, 1978.

Home, D. D., *Incidents in My Life*, London, 1863.

Hudson, Liam, *Night Life*, London, 1985.

Hudson, W. H., *A Hind in Richmond Park*, London, 1922.

Hull, Clark L., *Hypnosis and Suggestibility*, New York, 1933.

Hume, David, *Enquiries Concerning the Human Understanding*, Oxford, 1902 (1777).

Humphrey, Nick, *Consciousness and the Physical World*, London, 1980.

Humphrey, Nick, *Consciousness Regained*, Oxford, 1983.

Hunter, Richard, and Ida MacAlpine (eds.), *Three Hundred Years of Psychiatry, 1535–1860*, Oxford, 1963.

Hurley, J. Finlay, *Sorcery*, London, 1985.

Huxley, Aldous, *The Devils of Loudun*, London, 1952.

Huxley, Aldous, *The Doors of Perception*, London, 1954.

James, William, *On Psychical Research* (eds. Gardner Murphy and Robert Ballou), London, 1960.

James, William, *Principles of Psychology*, Boston, 1890.

James, William, *The Varieties of Religious Experience*, London, 1975 (1902).

Janet, Pierre, *Automatisme Psychique*, Paris, 1889.

Janet, Pierre, *The Major Symptoms of Hysteria*, New York, 1907.

Janet, Pierre, *Principles of Psychotherapy*, London, 1925.

Jastrow, Joseph, *The Unconscious*, Boston, 1906.

Jaynes, Julian, *The Origin of Consciousness*, Boston, 1977.

Jung, Carl G., *Collected Works*, London, 1957.

Jung, Carl G., *Memories, Dreams, Reflections*, London, 1973 (1963).

Jussieu, Laurent, *Rapport de l'un des Commissaires*, Paris, 1784.

Kautz, William H., and Melanie Branon, *Channeling: the Intuitive Connection*, San Francisco, 1987.

Kissen, D. M., *Emotional Factors in Pulmonary TB*, London, 1958.

Koestler, Arthur, *The Act of Creation*, London, 1964.

Koestler, Arthur, *The Roots of Coincidence*, London, 1972.

Koestler, Arthur, *Janus*, London, 1978.

LaBerge, Stephen, *Lucid Dreaming*, Los Angeles, 1985.

Lancaster, Evelyn, and James Poling, *Strangers in My Body*, London, 1958.

Lang, Andrew, *Magic and Religion*, London, 1901.

Laski, Marghanita, *Ecstasy*, London, 1961.

Laski, Marghanita, *Everyday Ecstasy*, London, 1980.

Le Bon, G., *The Crowd*, London, 1896.

Leggett, D., *The Sacred Quest*, Norwich, 1987.

LeShan, Lawrence, *Alternate Realities*, London, 1976.

Leuba, James H., *The Psychology of Religious Mysticism*, New York, 1929.

Liébeault, A. A., *Du Sommeil et des Etats Analogues*, Paris, 1866.

Lodge, Sir Oliver, *Past Years*, London, 1931.

Lodge, Sir Oliver, *My Philosophy*, London, 1933.

Lombroso, Cesare, *The Man of Genius*, London, 1891.

Lombroso, Cesare, *After Death, What?*, London, 1909.

Luthe, W., *Autogenic Training*, New York, 1965.

McClenon, James, *Deviant Science*, Philadelphia, 1984.

McConnell, R. A., *My Search for the Unicorn*, Pittsburgh, 1987.

McDougall, William, *Body and Mind*, London, 1928 (1911).

McDougall, William, *The Group Mind*, Cambridge, 1920.

McDougall, William, *Outline of Abnormal Psychology*, London, 1926.

McDougall, William, *Modern Materialism and Emergent Evolution*, London, 1929.

McGlashan, Alan, *The Savage and Beautiful Country*, London, 1966.

McGlashan, Alan, *Gravity and Levity*, London, 1976.

McKellar, Peter, *Imagination and Thinking*, Aberdeen, 1957.

McKenzie, Andrew, *The Seen and the Unseen*, London, 1987.

McNish, Robert, *The Philosophy of Sleep*, Glasgow, 1830.

Maeterlinck, Maurice, *The Unknown Guest*, London, 1914.

Marais, Eugene, *The Soul of the White Ant*, London, 1937.

Maudsley, Henry, *Body and Mind*, London, 1870.

Maudsley, Henry, *Natural Causes v. Supernatural Seemings*, London, 1939 (1886).

Mayo, H., *Letters on the Truths Contained in Popular Superstitions*, London, 1851.

Mead, Richard, *A Treatise Concerning the Influence of the Sun and Moon on Human Bodies*, London, 1746.

Medawar, Sir Peter, *Induction and Intuition*, Philadelphia, 1969.

Medawar, Sir Peter, *The Limits of Science*, Oxford, 1984.

Mesmer, Franz, *Writings* (ed. Bloch), Los Altos, California, 1980.

Moll, Albert, *Hypnotism*, London, 1889.

Monroe, Robert A., *Journeys Out of the Body*, London, 1972.

Moody, Raymond, *Life After Life*, London, 1976.

Morin, A. S., *Du Magnétisme et des Sciences Occultes*, Paris, 1860.

Murphy, Michael, and Rhea White, *The Psychic Side of Sports*, Reading, Massachusetts, 1978.

Myers, Frederic W. H., *Human Personality and its Survival of Bodily Death*, London, 1907 (1903).

Naish, L. N., *What is Hypnosis?*, London, 1986.

Neher, Andrew, *The Psychology of Transcendence*, Englewood Cliffs, New Jersey, 1980.

Neisser, Ulric, *Cognitive Psychology*, New York, 1967.

Nisbet, J. F., *The Insanity of Genius*, London, 1891.

Noakes, Ben, *I Saw a Ghost*, London, 1987.

Oakley, David (ed.), *Brain and Mind*, London, 1985.

Ochorowicz, Julian, *Mental Suggestion*, New York, 1891 (1887).

Oesterreich, Traugott K., *Possession*, London, 1930.

Ornstein, Robert (ed.), *The Nature of Human Consciousness*, San Francisco, 1973.

Owen, I., and M. Sparrow, *Conjuring Up Philip*, Ontario, 1976.

Pearce, Joseph Chilton, *The Crack in the Cosmic Egg*, London, 1973.

Penfield, Wilder, *The Mystery of Mind*, Princeton, 1975.

Pététin, J. H. D., *Electricité Animale*, Paris, 1808.

Pickering, Sir George, *Creative Malady*, London, 1974.

Pinel, Philippe, *A Treatise on Insanity*, London, 1806.

Pinel, Philippe, *Nosographie*, Paris, 1818.

Plato, *The Last Days of Socrates*, London, 1954.

Playfair, Guy Lyon, *If This Be Magic*, London, 1985.

Podmore, F., *Apparitions and Thought-transference*, London, 1894.

Popper, Sir Karl, *The Logic of Scientific Discovery*, London, 1959.

Prince, Morton, *The Nature of Mind and Human Automatism*, Philadelphia, 1889.

Prince, Morton, *The Dissociation of a Personality*, New York, 1906.

Prince, Morton, *The Unconscious*, New York, 1914.

Prince, Walter Franklin, *The Case of Patience Worth*, Boston, 1927.

Puységur, Count Chastenet de, *Du Magnétisme Animal*, Paris, 1807.

Rhine, J. B., *The Reach of the Mind*, New York, 1947.

Richet, Charles, *Thirty Years of Psychical Research*, London, 1923.

Rivers, W. H. R., *Instinct and the Unconscious*, Cambridge, 1920.

Rivers, W. H. R., *Psychology and Politics*, London, 1923.

Rose, Steven, *The Conscious Brain*, London, 1976 (1973).

Sacks, Oliver, *The Man Who Mistook His Wife for a Hat*, London, 1986.

Salverte, Eusebe, *The Occult Sciences*, London, 1846 (1829).

Sargant, William, *Battle for the Mind*, London, 1957.

Sargant, William, *The Mind Possessed*, London, 1967.

Sargant, William, *The Unquiet Mind*, London, 1973.

Schatzman, Morton, *The Story of Ruth*, London, 1980.

Selous, Edmund, *Thought Transference or What? in Birds*, London, 1931.

Sheldrake, Rupert, *A New Science of Life*, London, 1981.

Sheldrake, Rupert, *The Presence of the Past*, London, 1988.

Sherrington, Sir Charles, *Man on his Nature*, Cambridge, 1951 (1940).

Siegel, Bernie, *Love, Medicine and Miracles*, New York, 1986.

Sigerist, Henry, *A History of Medicine*, New York, 1951.

Simeons, A. T. W., *Man's Presumptuous Brain*, London, 1960.

Skey, F. C., *Hysteria*, London, 1867.

Skinner, Burrhus F., *Verbal Behavior*, New York, 1957.

Skinner, Burrhus F., *About Behaviorism*, London, 1974.

Smith, Suzy, *The Mediumship of Mrs Leonard*, New York, 1964.

Sperry, Roger, *Science and Moral Priority*, Oxford, 1983.

Stedman, Thomas L., *Twentieth-century Practice*, London, 1897.

Stevenson, Ian, *Children Who Remember Previous Lives*, Charlottesville, Virginia, 1987.

Storr, Anthony, *The Art of Psychotherapy*, London, 1979.

Storr, Anthony, *The School of Genius*, London, 1988.

Sudre, René, *Treatise on Parapsychology*, London, 1960 (1956).

Sydenham, Thomas, *Works* (ed. Latham), London, 1850.

Szasz, Thomas, *The Myth of Mental Illness*, New York, 1961.

Taine, Hippolyte, *On Intelligence*, London, 1871.

Tart, Charles (ed.), *Altered States of Consciousness*, New York, 1969.

Tart, Charles, *Waking Up*, Boston, 1986.

Taylor, G. R., *The Natural History of the Mind*, London, 1979.

Teresa of Avila, *Autobiography*, London, 1957 (1588).

Thigpen, Corbett H., and Hervey M. Cleckley, *The Three Faces of Eve*, London, 1957.

Thomas, Lewis, *The Lives of a Cell*, London, 1980 (1974).

Thomas, Lewis, *The Medusa and the Snail*, London, 1980.

Thurston, Herbert, *The Physical Phenomena of Mysticism*, London, 1952.

Tinbergen, Niko, *Ethology and Stress Diseases*, Stockholm, 1974.

Trotter, Wilfred, *Instincts of the Herd in Peace and War*, London, 1942 (1916).

Tuke, Daniel Hack, *Illustrations of the Influence of the Mind upon the Body in Health and Disease*, London, 1872.

Tylor, Edward B., *Primitive Culture*, London, 1871.

Tyrrell, G. N. M., *Apparitions*, London, 1942.

Ullman, M., S. Krippner and A. Vaughan, *Dream Telepathy*, Baltimore, 1973.

Ullman, M., and Nan Zimmerman, *Working with Dreams*, Wellingborough, 1987 (1979).

Underhill, Evelyn, *Mysticism*, London, 1912.

Vasiliev, L. L., *Experiments in Distant Influence*, London, 1976 (1962).

Veith, Ilsa, *Hysteria*, Chicago, 1965.

Walker, Kenneth, *The Unconscious Mind*, London, 1961.

Wallace, Alfred Russel, *The Scientific Aspect of the Supernatural*, London, 1866.

Watson, John Broadus, *Behaviorism*, New York, 1928.

Watson, John Broadus, and William McDougall, *The Battle of Behaviorism*, London, 1928.

Watson, Lyall, *Lifetide*, London, 1979.

Waugh, Evelyn, *The Ordeal of Gilbert Pinfold*, London, 1957.

Wavell, Stuart, *et al.*, *Trances*, London, 1966.

Wesley, John, *Journals*, London, 1902.

Whyte, L. L., *The Unconscious Before Freud*, London, 1962.

Whytt, Robert, *Observations . . . on Hysteria*, Edinburgh, 1767.

Wilber, Ken, *Quantum Questions*, Boulder, Colorado, 1984.

Yost, Casper, *Patience Worth*, New York, 1916.

Zweig, Stefan, *Mental Healers*, New York, 1932.

SOURCE REFERENCES

In these references the words, or names, in parentheses indicate the subject on the page. The source is identified by the author, the date of the book (which will be found in the Bibliography) and the page (s). Where no pages are given, the reference is to the book as a whole or, in a few cases, to material scattered through the text which can be picked up from the book's index.

1. SETTING THE SCENE

page
7   Tart, 1969, 1–21.
8   Cobbe, 1872, 308–9.
    (Trance driving), *Times*, 28–9
      September 1988; Oakley, 1988, 65.
9   Wodehouse, *Very Good, Jeeves*, 1957, 18.
    Murphy/White, 1977.
10 (Shopper's trance), *Guardian*, 14
      March 1988.
    Hudson, 1986, 164.
    (Socrates), Elam, 1864, 416; Dodds,
      1951, 184–5.
11 Hartmann, 1882, i, 285.
12 Whyte, 1962, 163–4.
    (James v. Hartmann), Allen, 1967,
      199–204.
13 Freud, 1962, 98.
14 (Hartmann), Myers, 1907, 70–1.
15 Watson, 1928, 198.
    Gauld, 1968, 278.
16 (Subliminal), Dixon, 1971, 5–10;
      1979, 81–4; Taylor, 1979, 81–4.
17 James, 1948, 138–9; 391.
    Carpenter, 1875, 22–3.
    Cobbe, 1872, 311.
18 Hartmann, 1884, ii, 119–53.
19 Thomas, 1974, 11–15.
    Tinbergen, 1972, 386.

2. DIVINE OR DIABOLIC?

21 Eliade, 1964, xix, 8.
22 Tylor, 1871, ii, 113–14.
23 Frazer, 1890, i, 52; Lang, 1901.
    Sigerist, 1951, i, 108–15, 202–203.
24 Marais, 1937, 40–6.

25 Jaynes, 1977, 134; (Homer), 71–8;
      (possession), 339–60.
26 McDougall, 1929, 114–23; 153–6.
27 (Wallace), Jaynes, 1977, 9–10.
    Field, 1971, 55–69.
28 Eliade, 1968, 184.
    Jaynes, 1977, 295–318.
    Field, 1971; 1960, 57–8.
30 Gelfand, 1964, 81.
    Dodds, 1951, 11–14; 70–5; 152; 180–1;
      209–10.
32 Hippocrates, 1974, 237.
33 Sigerist, 1951, ii, 298–9.
    Jaynes, 1977, 318.
34 Dodds, 1951, 102.
    (St Augustine), Veith, 1969, 40–57.
35 (St Francis), Thurston, 1952, 171.
    Cohn, 1975, 259–60; (Murray),
      105–15.
37 Haynes, 1961, 155–6.
    Hecker, 1859.
38 Calmeil, 1845, 264–6.
39 (Loudun), Oesterreich, 1930, 50–4;
      Huxley, 1952.
40 (St Médard), Carré, 1737; Hume,
      1902, 124–5.
    Wesley, 1966, i, 188–91.
    Gentleman's Magazine, March, 1787.
41 (Stohr), Oesterreich, 1970, 210.
    (Harvey), Hunter/MacAlpine, 1963,
      131.
42 (Bacon), Hunter/MacAlpine, 1963,
      207.
    (Plot), Hunter/MacAlpine, 1963, 208.
    Sydenham, *Works*, 1850, ii, 231, 270.
43 Whytt, 1767, iii.
    (Gregory), Hunter/MacAlpine, 1963,
      438.

Burton, 1948, 365.
44 (Purcell), Hunter/MacAlpine, 1963,
    288–91.
    (Cheyne), Tuke, 1872, 345 and
    appendix.
    (Stories), McNish, 1830, 223–4.
45 Crichton, 1798, ii, 87.

3. THE EXPLORERS

47 (Luther), Oesterreich, 1930, 87.
    Greatraks, *A Brief Account . . . ,*
    London, 1960.
48 Mesmer, 1980; Ellenberger, 1970,
    53–68; Zweig, 1932, 1–100.
    Jussieu, 1784, 35–8.
50 Puységur, 1784; Ellenberger, 1970,
    70–6; Dingwall, 1967, 9–14.
51 Pététin, 1808; Foissac, 1833, 295–322.
52 Laplace, London, 1902, 105.
    Deleuze, 1816; Dingwall, 1967, 14–21.
53 Hippocrates, 1978, 237.
    (Monboddo), Mayo, 1851, 94–5.
54 Ellenberger, 1970, 112.
    (Archbishop), Elam, 1869, 390–1.
    Dufay, *Revue Scientifique,* December
    1885; Myers, *SPR Proceedings,* 1887,
    228–9; Binet, 1896, 21.
55 Mayo, 1851, 94–5.
56 McNish, 1830, 160; Mayo, 1951, 91.
    (Rostan), Dingwall, 1967, 40–6.
    (Commission), Foissac, 1833;
    Dingwall, 1967, 77–8.
57 (Cloquet), Dingwall, 1967, 83–4;
    Mayo, 1851, 146; Foissac, 1833,
    156–8.
    (Commission Report), Dingwall,
    1967, 77–8; Binet/Féré, 1888, 34–9.
58 (Oudet), Dingwall, 1967, 83–4.
    (Academy rejection), Moll, 1889, 11.
    (Marshall Hall), *Zoist,* 1851, ix, 88;
    Elliotson, 1843. *Lancet,* March 1851.
    (Esdaile), Bramwell, 1956, 14–21.
59 Stewart, 1827; Hunter/MacAlpine,
    1963, 640–1.
60 McNish, 1830, 101–5.
    Braid, 1843; Bramwell, 1956, 21–6.
62 Carpenter, 1875, 626–35.
64 Sandby, *Mesmerism and its Opponents,*
    London, 1844; Scoresby, *Zoistic
    Magnetism,* London, 1849.
    (Didier), Dingwall, 1967, 177–201;
    SPR Proceedings, 1898–9, xiv,
    373–81.
    Wallace, 1866, 126–8.
    Gregory, 1851, 451–8.

67 (Brewster), *Memoir of Sir D. Brewster*
    by his daughter, Margaret,
    Edinburgh, 1869, 254–5.
    (Queen Victoria), E. Longford,
    Victoria, 1964, 339.
    Faraday, *Times,* 2 July 1853; *Life* (ed.
    Bence Jones), 1870, 207–8.
68 De Gasparin, *Des Tables Tournantes,*
    Geneva, 1854.
    Thury, *Les Tables Tournantes,* Geneva,
    1855.
69 Home, 1863; E. Jenkins, *The Shadow
    and the Light,* 1982.
70 Skey, 1867, 51.
71 Paget, 'Nervous mimicry', *Lancet,* 11
    October 1873.
    (Carter), Veith, 1965, 199–212.
72 (Hysteria treatments), Veith, 1965,
    211–12.

4. TWO DECADES OF RESEARCH

74 Heidenhain, 1888.
75 (Huxley), Prince, 1885, 23.
    (Charcot), Ellenberger, 1970, 89–102.
    (James), Barrett, 1918, 19.
76 (Hahn), Leuba, 1929, 191–203.
    (Liébeault), Bernheim, 1957, 108–24;
    Bramwell, 1956, 30–1.
77 Bernheim, 1957; Ellenberger, 1970,
    85–9.
78 (Delboeuf), *SPR Proceedings,* 1892, viii,
    605; Bramwell, 1956, 116–19.
79 Bramwell, 1956, 119–39.
    (Hallucinations), Binet/Féré, 1888,
    211–303: Bernheim, 1884, 28.
    Osler, *SPR Proceedings,* 1892, viii,
    608.
80 Binet, 1888, 202.
    (Pain), Binet/Féré, 1888, 304–5.
    (Delboeuf), Playfair, 1985, 10; Moll,
    1889, 304–5.
    Tuke, 1872, 81.
    (Janet), Sudre, 1960, 294.
81 Maury, 1860, 383, 408.
    Biggs, *SPR Journal,* May 1887.
    (Jorden), Hunter/MacAlpine, 1963,
    73–5.
82 Binet, 1897, 12; Binet/Féré, 1888, 337;
    Myers, *SPR Proceedings,* 1886, iv,
    143.
83 Azam, 1887, 63–175.
    (Bourne), *SPR Proceedings,* 1892, vii,
    221–58.
84 Janet, 1889.
85 Gurney, 1884, 217–29.

Barkworth, *SPR Proceedings*, 1889–90, vi, 84–97.

86 Forel, 1906; Ellenberger, 1970, 285–6.

87 Moll, 1889, 315–19; Myers, 1907, 133.
   Bramwell, 1956, 426.
   Woods, *SPR Proceedings*, 1888–9, xiv, 109.

88 (Voisin), Myers, 1907, 381–2.
   Janet, 1907, 29–31.
   Bramwell, 1956, 91.
   Rachmaninov, *Recollections*, London, 1934, 97–112.

89 ('Unseen world'), Myers, 1907, 8.

90 (Kelvin), S. P. Thompson, *Kelvin*, London, 1910, ii, 1104.
   Galton, 1883, 167–8.

91 (Hodgson), Myers, 1907, 405–8.
   (Veridical hallucination), Gurney, 1886, i, 519–73.

92 Gauld, 1968, 153–74.
   Gurney, *SPR Proceedings*, 1894, x, 31.

93 (Census), *SPR Proceedings*, 1894, x, 14–422.
   Myers, 1906, 173.

94 (Myers/Gurney), Gurney, 1886, ii, 286; Gauld, 1968, 162.

95 (Mediumship), Myers, 1907, 274–90, 314–38.
   Cox, 1875, ii, 242.

96 James, 1960, 48.
   Flournoy, 1901; McDougall, 1926, 507.

97 James, *SPR Proceedings*, 1889–90, 658–9.

98 Hodgson, *SPR Proceedings*, 1892, viii, 1–167.
   Lodge, *SPR Proceedings*, 1889–90, vi, 436–650.
   James, 1960, 48.

99 (Palladino), Lombroso, 1909, *SPR Journal*, April 1896; Richet, 1923, 412–21; Flournoy, 1911, 244; Lodge, London, 1931, 296.

101 (Telekinesis), Myers, *SPR Proceedings*, 1894, x, 23–40.

102 (Automatic writing), Myers, *SPR Proceedings*, 1887, iv, 209–61; Moll, 1889, 247.
   (Liébeault), Myers, 1907, 422–3.

103 Barrett, *SPR Proceedings*, 1897–8, xii, 2–282; 1900–1, xv, 130–383; *SPR Journal*, December 1897; Barrett/ Besterman, 1926; Tylor, *Nature*, 17 May 1883.

104 Bennett/Barrett, *SPR Journal*, 1897, 151–8.

105 ('Elemental'), Barrett, *SPR Journal*,

December 1987, 151–5; Barrett/ Besterman, 1926, 269.
   (Liébeault), Podmore, 1894, 60.
   (Sidgwicks), Podmore, 1894, 58–81.

106 (Janet paper), Ochorowicz, 1891, 81; Ellenberger, 1970, 337–8.
   Ochorowicz, 1891.
   (Le Havre trials), *Revue Philosophique*, August, 1886; Myers, *SPR Proceedings*, 1886–7, iv, 127–38; 1892, viii, 335–404; Richet, *SPR Proceedings*, 1889, vi, 64; Ellenberger, 1970, 337–9; Sudre, 1960, 58.

108 Gibotteau, *Annales des Sciences Psychiques*, 1890, ii, 253–67, 317–37.
   Myers, *SPR Proceedings*, 1892, viii, 335.

109 (Muensterberg), Allen, 1967, 352, 367, 471.
   Jastrow, *Fact and Fable in Parapsychology*, 1901, 42–3.

110 (Hypnotism suspect), Moll, 1889, 273, 297–8, 321–3.
   Ochorowicz, 1890, 154–5, 231.

111 (Bompard), Forel, 1906, 329.
   Gurney, *SPR Proceedings*, 1884, ii, 287.
   Myers, *SPR Proceedings*, 1886, iv, 1–24; 1890–1, vii, 354.

112 Moll, 1890, 338.
   Forel, 1906, 318–52.

113 Carpenter, 1875, 606–7.
   (Physiological explanations), Moll, 1889, 267–8.
   Janet, 1907, 150–8.
   (Academy), Ellenberger, 1970, 759–60.

114 James, 1960, 28.
   (BMA), Bramwell, 1956, 36–7; Ellenberger, 1970, 755–60.

115 (Freud): (Charcot) Jones, 1953, i, 202–5; Freud, 1935, 20–25; Breuer, 1956, 21–47; (hysterical conversion), Clark, 1880, 156–7; (gives up hypnotism), 1935, 48–50.

117 Stedman, 1897, x, 840.
   Janet, 1924, 22–9.

119 James, 1960, 225–39.
   (Trance), Myers, 1907, 130, 248.

120 (Three channels), Myers, *SPR Proceedings*, 1891–2, vii, 298–355.
   (Witchcraft), Gurney, 1886, i, 172–85; Myers, 1907, 4–5.

121 (Inspiration), Myers, *SPR Proceedings*, 1892, viii, 333; 1907, 56–65.

122 (Genius), Myers, 1907, 55–92.
   (Prodigies), Myers, 1907, 64–68.

123 (Writers), Myers, 1907, 70–3.
   Maudsley, 1939, 97–102.

124 Lewes, 'Dickens in relation to criticism', *Fortnightly*, February 1872.
125 Jahn, 1891, ii, 415.
   Lombroso, 1891.
   (Four possibilities), Myers, *SPR Proceedings*, 1891–2, vii, 313.

5. MATERIALISM IN CONTROL

127 (Haeckel), Ellenberger, 1970, 810–11.
   Binet, 1905, 205, 256–61.
128 Watson, 1928, 198; 1930, 248.
129 (Bergson), Whyte, 1962, 181.
   Rivers, 1920, 222.
130 Janet, 1907.
   Sargant, p.c.
131 Cronin, 1952.
   (Freud/Groddeck), Clark, 1980, 434–6.
132 Groddeck, 1950, 16–31.
133 Jung, 1902, vi, 1–43; 1973, 125–8, 178–81.
135 Prince, 1885.
137 ('Miss Beauchamp'), *SPR Proceedings*, 1898–9, xiv, 79–97; 1906.
   (Co-consciousness), Prince, 1914, 249.
   ('Sally' healthy), Prince, 1905, 17.
   (Hallucinations), Prince, 1914, 188–228, 505.
138 Mitchell, *Medical Psychology and Psychical Research*, London, 1922, 182–8.
   McDougall, 1926, 548–9.
139 (Prince and Freud), Jones, 1953, ii, 69, 353.
   (Patience Worth), Yost, 1916; W. F. Prince, 1927.
141 (Alrutz), Barrett, *SPR Journal*, May 1925, 65.
   Hull, 1933.
   McDougall, 1926, 91–2, 115–17, 350.
142 (Coué's career), Palaiseul, *Tous les moyens de vous guérir*, Paris, 1957, i, 346–58.
143 Moll, 1889, 332; Myers, 1907, 127.
   Coué, 1959; Baudouin, 1920, 125; Palaiseul, 1957, i, 353.
144 Crookshank, *Migraine and other common neuroses*, London, 1927, 88–9; (Crookshank, 'paroxysmal lachrymation'), Dunbar, 1955, 53.
146 Langdon-Brown, 1938, 105.
147 Janet, 1907, 44–57.
   (Mitchell); Veith, 1965, 214.
   McDougall, 1926, 2–3.

148 Langdon-Brown, 1938, 62–7.
   Rivers, 1920, 2.
   (Freud and Rivers), Clark, 1980, 385–6; Langdon-Brown, 1938, 64–5.
149 ('Possum'), Rivers, 1920, 127–35; 1922, 55–63, 129–30; Langdon-Brown, 1938, 65.
150 (Duty), Rivers, 1920, 235; Sassoon, 1936, 20.
   (Fugue and trances), Rivers, 1920, 74, 114; 1922, 74–5.
151 (Sport), Rivers, 1920, 237.
   (Art), Rivers, 1920, 157–8.
152 Langdon-Brown, 1938, 66–7.
153 Le Bon, 1896, 8–11.
154 Trotter, 1942, 21–43, 105–6.
155 McDougall, 1920, 28.
   (Riley), Callaghan, P., *Tuning in to Nature*, London, 1977, 134–5.
   Selous, 1931, 42–61.
156 Wheeler, *Journal of Morphology*, 1911, xxii.
   Rivers, 1920, 236.
   Marais, 1937, 2.
157 Carington, 1945, 153–64.
158 James, 1960, 309–25.
   Smith, Suzy, 1964.
159 Feilding, *Sittings with Eusapia Palladino*, New York, 1963.
   Muensterberg, *Metropolitan Magazine*, February, 1910.
160 Lodge, 1933, 42.
161 Harts, *SPR Proceedings*, 1932–3, xli, 205–41.
   Owen, 1965, iii, 198–9.
162 Graves, 1929, 161.
   Bennett, 1939, 255–6.
163 Tyrrell, 1942, 58.
   Barrett, *SPR Proceedings*, 1920, xxx, 230–60.
   McDougall, 1926, 256–7.
165 (Eliade), *C. G. Jung Speaking*, 1980, 224–5
166 Priestley, *Man and Time*, London, 1964, 220–1.

6. THE POST-WAR SCENE

167 Sperry, 1982, 4–5.
169 Skinner, 1957; 1974, 1–24, 189.
170 Broad, 1937, 5–6.
   Eccles, 1985, 53.
171 Jaynes, 1977, 441–3.
172 Mason, *British Medical Journal*, 23 August 1952, and subsequent correspondence.

Eysenck, 1957, 25–70.
173 Barber, 'The concept of hypnosis',
       Journal of Psychology, 1958, 45,
       115–31.
174 (Wagstaff), Naish, 1986, 59–84.
175 Naish, 1986, 4.
176 Moll, 1889, 209–13, 261–2.
       Eisenbud, 1982, 145.
177 (Ewin), Playfair, 1985, 5–7.
       (Willard), Taylor, 1979, 5–6.
178 (Miller), *Guardian*, 4 November 1988.
179 Tart, 1986, 76.
       (Gill), *Independent*, 28 September 1988.
180 (Cognitive psychology), Reed,
       Graham, *The Psychology of
       Anomalous Experience*, London, 1972;
       Glicksohn, J., *Journal of Parapsychology*,
       September 1986.
       Neisser, 1967, 293–305.
181 Luthe, 1965.
182 Miller, *Science*, 1969, 163, 434–45.
       Benson, *The Relaxation Response*, New
       York, 1975.
       Greens, 1977.
       Ornstein, 1972, 220.
184 (American Psychiatric Association),
       Ziegler, F. J. *et al.*, *American Journal
       of Psychiatry*, 1960, 116, 901–10.
       Slater, *British Medical Journal*, 29 May
       1965, i, 1395–9.
185 (Amnesia), *Guardian*, 17 September
       1979.
186 Delaney, p.c.
       (Parachute death), *Guardian*, 20
       November 1987.
       (Moorgate), *Guardian*, 15 April 1975;
       Evening Standard, 8 May 1975.
187 Taylor, *World Medicine*, 21 February
       1981.
       (Pickering), *Guardian*, 27 September
       1974.
189 Zweig, 1932, 111.
       Cousins, 'Anatomy of an illness', *New
       England Journal of Medicine*, 23
       December 1976; 1979.
191 Rivers, 1920, 137.
       Adare, *Experiences with D. D. Home*,
       1969, 28.
192 Yeats, *Autobiographies*, 1980, 103–4.
       Darwin, *The Expression of the Emotions*,
       London, 1872, 201.
       Koestler, 1964, 31.
193 *Observer*, 25 January 1981.
       (Van Helmont), Hunter/MacAlpine,
       1963, 256.
194 (ECT in British hospital), *World
       Medicine*, 16 November 1977.

       Kissen, 1958; *British Journal of Medical
       Psychology*, 1963, 27–30; 1964, 203.
196 Eysenck, 1953, 215.
198 Myers, 1907, 138–41.
       Lasagna, Louis, *The Doctors' Dilemmas*,
       London, 1962, 9.
       Watts, *World Medicine*, 23 February
       1980.
       Bowsher, *General Practitioner*, 20 July
       1979.
       British Medical Journal, 4 April 1981.
199 (Murphy) Quinn, J., *Portrait of the
       Artist as a Young Girl*, 1986, 121.
       Greens, 1977, 228–30.
       Manning, p.c.
       Meares, *Medical Journal of Australia*, 23
       July 1977; *Practitioner*, January
       1979.
200 Siegel, 1986, 18–19.
201 (Eve), Thigpen/Cleckley, 1957;
       Lancaster/Poling, 1958.
       (MPDs/PTSDs), *New Scientist*, 5 May
       1982; *Science News*, 26 March 1988.
202 (Bleuler), McDougall, 1926, 209–12.
203 Kanner, 'Autistic disturbances',
       Nervous Child, 1943, ii, 217–50.
       McKellar, 1957, 4–5.
       Koestler, 'Can Psychiatrists be
       trusted?' *The Heel of Achilles*,
       London, 1964.
204 Tinbergen, 1974.
206 Pearce, 1973, 20.
       Sacks, 1985, 185–203.
207 (Psychopaths), Cleckley, 1955, 19–45,
       430–43.
208 Foulis, 1853, 125–39.
209 Gehlen, *Journal of Health and Social
       Behavior*, March 1977, xviii, 27–35.
       Roueché, *New Yorker*, 21 August 1978.
210 (Pennsylvania), *Lancet*, 19 April 1975,
       930.
211 (Planta), *British Medical Journal*, 5
       January 1964; *Medical News*, 3
       April 1964.
       Sunday Telegraph, 17 July 1977.
212 ('Royal Free Disease'), *British Medical
       Journal*, 19 October 1967, 895–904,
       927–8.
       McEvedy/Beard, *British Medical
       Journal*, 25 March 1967.
213 (Symposium), Lyle, W. H. and R. N.
       Chamberlain (eds.), 'Epidemic
       Neuromyasthenia', *Postgraduate
       Medical Journal*, November 1978,
       705–74. *British Medical Journal*, 3
       June 1978.
215 ('ME'), London newspapers, 17 July

1988; Nixon and Rosen, *Sunday Times* (letter) 14 August 1988.
(Nottinghamshire outbreak), *Guardian*, 15 July; *Sunday Times*, 20 July; Mohr, P., *World Medicine*, 23 August 1980.

216 Eden, *World Medicine*, 15 June 1977.
Colligan, *Psychology Today*, September 1978.

217 Taylor, *World Medicine*, 21 February 1981.
('Yuppie mobs'), *Evening Standard*, 9 June 1988; Newby, *Independent*, 10 June 1988.

218 Collins/Pinch, *The Social Construction of Extraordinary Science*, London, 1982.
McClenon, 1984.

219 Giesler, *American SPR Journal*, October 1984; (Lang), 291; (anthropologists) 302.
Eliade, 1968.

220 David-Neel, 1965, 227–9.

221 Sargant, 1973.

226 (Lucid dreams), LaBerge, 1985.
Ullman/Krippner/Vaughan, 1973.
Taylor, 1979, 220.

227 (OBEs), Blackmore, 1882; Monroe, 1971; Moody, 1975.
Ayer, *Spectator*, 15 October 1988.

228 Guirdham, 1974, 1977.

229 Stevenson, 1974, 1975, 1980, 1983, 1987.

230 MacKenzie, 1987.

231 Noakes, 1987.
Trelford, *Spectator*, 4 April 1987.

232 Jaynes, 1971, 84–91.
Gobbi, 1979, 88–9.

234 (Rosenhan), *Doctor*, 26 September 1974.
Garrett, *Many Voices*, New York, 1968.
(Obituaries), *SPR Journal*, March 1971.

235 Heywood, *SPR Journal*, March 1971.
LeShan, 1976, 176–8.
Beard, *Light*, winter 1984.

236 Owen/Sparrow, 1976.

237 Gauld, 1983, 28.
Beard, *Light*, summer 1988.

238 (Moore), Ghiselin, B., *The Creative Process*, University of California, 1952, 78.
(Picasso), Sabartés, J., *Picasso*, 1948, 179.
(Bacon), Rothenstein, *Bacon* (Tate Gallery series), London, 1962.
(Le Brocquy), Walker, *Le Brocquy*,

1981, 67–9: BBC Radio 3, 18 November 1988.
(Freud), Jones, 1957, iii, 447–62.

7. TWO MYSTERIES

239 Thomson, 1936, 158.
(USSR), *Psi Research*, September–December 1984.

240 Kaufman, *Parapsychology Review*, November–December 1979.
Boyle, *Philosophical Works*, 1738, i, 172–3.
Sagnier, *The Bank's World*, August 1983.

241 Vallentin, *Einstein*, 1954, 27–9.
(Einstein), Hadamard, 1949, 142–3.

242 Popper, 1959, 32.
(Planck), McKellar, 1957, 175.
Medawar, 1969, 11–12.

243 Eccles, 1935, 35–8.

244 (Sperry), Harman, 'Transcendent Experiences', Institute of Noetic Sciences, California, July 1985.
(Penfield), LeShan, *Light*, summer 1985.
(Non-locality), Davies/Brown, 1986.

246 (Iamblichus), Dodds, 1951, 122; Wallace, *Miracles and Modern Spiritualism*, 1896, 283.
Pearce, 1973, 47.
Salverte, 1846, i, 321.

247 (St Médard), Carré de Montgeron, *La Verité des Miracles*, 1745; Beloff, *Research in Parapsychology 1987*, Metuchen, New Jersey, 1988, 174–6.
Salverte, 1846, ii, 308–23.

248 Carpenter, *Mesmerism, Spiritualism, etc.*, 1877, 67.
Frazer, 1900, iii, 308.
(Hocken), Lang, *SPR Proceedings*, 1900–1, xv, 1–15.
Coe, *Psychological Record*, Wichita, October 1957.
(Epidermis), Fairlie, *The Conquest of Pain*, London, 1978, 232.
(Fire-walking), Belo, 1960, 4; Pearce, 1973, 101–3.
Feinberg, *Atlantic Monthly*, May 1959.

249 Thomson, *South Sea Yarns*, 1894, 195–207.
Stowell, *SPR Journal*, June 1928.
(Coal strolls), *New Scientist*, 6 June 1985.

(Leidenfrost), *Los Angeles Times*, 21
         April 1985; *Artifex*, spring 1985.
250   Eliade, 1970, 372.
         Adare, 1869, 66, 178.
251   *New Scientist*, 19 May 1988.
252   Hume, 1902, 109–16.
253   Mann, *Dr Faustus*.
         Myers, 1907, 338–9.
254   Happold, 1981, 45–50.
255   (St Francis), Leuba, 1929, 167–8;
         Deikman, *Psychiatry*, 1966, xxix,
         167–8, 324–38.
256   (Buddha), Leuba, 1929, 170.
         (Muslim), Leuba, 1929, 170–1.
257   (Vivekananda), James, 1975, 386.
         Laski, 1961, 187–225.
258   Koestler, 1969, 428–32.
         (Rousseau), Charpentier, *The Child of
         Nature*, 1931, 251–2.
259   Proust, *Remembrance of Things Past*,
         1951, 58.
260   Wilson, *Times*, 3 June 1974.
         Coate, 1964, 21.
261   (Hardy), Humphrey, 1983, 161–7.
         De Quincey, 1967, 179.
         (Mitchell), Taylor, 1979, 95.
262   Smythies, *SPR Journal*, October 1983.
         Huxley, 1954, 10–13.
         Rose, 1976, 332–5.
         Brierre, 1852, 267–8.
263   Hartmann, 1884, i, 345–50.
         Huxley, 1954, 10–13.
         (Plotinus), Leggett, 1987, 33.
         Smythies/Jung, *SPR Journal*, October
         1983.
264   Laski, 1980, 9–12.
         James, 1975, 411, 490–1.
265   Underhill, 1912, 3.
         Medawar, 1984.
         Rose, 1976, 335.
         (Eddington), Wilber, 1984, 198–9.

8. REASSESSMENT

268   (Dessoir), Lang, *The Making of
         Religion*, London, 1898, 35.
269   Comfort, 1984, xv.
         Beloff, 1962, 42–3.
270   (Edinburgh Declaration), *Independent*,
         13 August 1988.
         Storr, 1979, 84.
271   Housman, *The Name and Nature of
         Poetry*, Cambridge, 1933, 48–50.
         Lessing, 1972, 83.
         (Joan schizophrenic), Rose, 1976, 333.
         Creighton, *A History of Epidemics*,
         Cambridge, 1894.
272   Hoyle/Wickramasinghe, *Diseases from
         Space*, London, 1979.
         Tart, 1986, 83–106.
273   (Dement), Evans, *Landscapes of the
         Night*, 1983, 230–2.
         Schatzman, *New Scientist*, 11 August
         1983.
         Hudson, 1922, 113.
274   Sacks, 1985, 149–53.
275   Grad, *American SPR Journal*, April
         1965; October 1967.
         (Einstein), Wilber, *Quantum Questions*,
         Boulder, Colorado, 1984, 105.
         Ehrenwald, *Anatomy of Genius*, New
         York, 1974, 273.
276   (Hemming), Leggett, 1987, 219.
277   Tinbergen, *Proceedings of the Royal
         Society*, 1972, 405–6.
         James, 1975, 87–8.
         McKellar, 1957, 108.
         Geley, *Clairvoyance and Materialisation*,
         London, 1927, 180–1.

INDEX